Leonardo Balada:
A Transatlantic Gaze

Leonardo Balada:
A Transatlantic Gaze

Juan Francisco de Dios

prologues by
Leonardo Balada & Fernando Arrabal

translated by
Peter Bush

Carnegie Mellon University Press
Pittsburgh 2020

Acknowledgments

Leonardo Balada: La Mirada Oceánica was first published in Spanish by Editorial Alpuerto, S.A., Madrid in 2012.

Book design by Connie Amoroso

Library of Congress Control Number 2020943661
ISBN 978-0-88748-663-0

10 9 8 7 6 5 4 3 2 1

*To Joan and Leonardo, for all the great times we have enjoyed;
to María Ángeles, an eternal source of inspiration;
to one who's not here yet but is already making us happy,
and my whole fantastic family.*

Contents

Reflection

I feel almost surprised when I think how quickly the years have gone by, but then they go by and nothing surprises you anymore.

When you think about it, I am a composer and not a tailor almost by chance, and the fact that I stayed in the United States was also quite random. If I were a sensible person and believed in God, I would attribute everything to Him or to Providence. Conversely, it is true that nothing has come easily, or was ever given to me on a plate. For example, in my formative years when I was studying music at The Juilliard School of Music in New York, things didn't always go well. The atmosphere there was permeated by avant-garde aesthetics that derived from the twelve-tone movement in vogue, something I felt was like unripe fruit, and my stance wasn't always readily accepted in that academic world. When I had finished studying alone in New York, I felt like a sheep besieged by hungry wolves about to pounce on my "antiquated," "decadent" music. How could I be so conservative when I was the son of a father with advanced ideas, a vegetarian, atheist, and liberal who looked to an open future full of wonderful potential? I faithfully went to the contemporary music concerts that were held regularly in Columbia University's McMillin Academic Theatre, two streets from my apartment. I thought that what I heard in that showcase of international contemporary music was, at the very least, super-intellectual, incredibly boring and third rate. And I wondered: How can they waste all the new techniques on such grotesque foolishness? Couldn't these techniques be used to create something exuberant and communicative? And when I was composing, I told myself: "I will put these techniques to good use." I decided to write music that would communicate, that was at once dramatic and dynamic. And I gave my compositions rhythm, movement to something of a climax, a kind of avant-garde romanticism.

From my early childhood I took an interest in matters of the mind, influenced by my father, an exceptional man who for economic reasons was unable to continue his schooling beyond his fourteenth birthday, though in his spare time he read in the library of Barcelona's Athenaeum, rather than going to the bar on the corner of our street. Those matters of the mind inspired my work. And remembering Archimedes and his famous fulcrum I used to tell myself, "give me an orchestra and I will raise up the world" (modesty apart).

I remember how at home my parents spoke of good music—the cultured, classical kind—and bad music—the popular kind. And when my father could afford to buy tickets to the Liceu, we would go and sit with the gods—the fifth floor in that opera theater.

Nowadays one cannot talk about good and bad music. I was reminded of that by the dean at my Carnegie Mellon University, Akram Midani—a highly knowledgeable, cultured person—who argued that both kinds of music have equal merits. But when in the middle of our argument I asked what work he would prefer to hear if he could choose only one, he replied, "Verdi's *Requiem*." "So there *are* categories," I retorted. And we are still good friends. In truth, good "bad" music is superior to bad "good" music. But superior music is to be found in good "good" music. "Good" music has technical resources and knowledge available to it that the "bad" sort doesn't have or which never enters its world. A mural painted by a professional artist will always be superior to a wall painted by a professional painter and decorator. The latter will never be able to express his personality even if he imagines he is a genius because the medium with which he works is so limited. Equally, a composer of popular music doesn't have the resources of a composer of symphonies since if he did, he would cease to be "popular."

What worries me in respect of high art is the way it is now so little appreciated and broadcast on the mass media. If we think of the space devoted to classical music in daily newspapers or on television, and compare its situation to a few decades ago, we will see that every day less attention is given to what is select, to what is intelligent. On Sunday mornings in the United States the CBS broadcasts a program called *Sunday Morning*. This used to showcase various aspects of the world of culture and always included a spot for classical music. In 1989, for example, they sent a technical team from New York to Barcelona to record scenes and interview the main artists during the premiere of my opera at the Liceu. Today that part of the program has been replaced by images of, and interviews with, "pop" artists.[1]

Nonetheless, we shouldn't conclude that all is lost. What's good is good and always will be. I am convinced that, given the opportunity, the masses of fans of sport or big blasts at rock concerts would transform into enthusiastic lambs if they ever heard Beethoven's *Ninth*. And to prove my point, I will invite my gardener with his yard-length hair and tattoos of a thousand colors to accompany me to next season's performance of the *Ninth* by Beethoven, and I will let you know . . .

—Leonardo Balada

---

1   When talking to Balada about this, we commented on the presence, or absence, of music in the Spanish mass media. With the honourable exception of Spanish Radio and Television's Classical Radio wavelength, we noted that music has been relegated, thanks to legal minimums, to the invisibility of the early hours, the occasional musical column in a newspaper, usually ideologically connected to the right, or a praiseworthy, if scant, presence on Spanish state television which has a schedule that grants more than double the time to religion that it gives to musical culture. (Author's note)

Prologue

With what knowledge and know-how Juan Francisco de Dios Hernández illuminates, interprets and teases out Leonardo Balada's unique music.

Faustbal shows us how music uniquely teaches what cannot be taught and is vital to learn.

Faustbal shows us how chaos (the absurdity of the titans) and confusion (the randomness of the gods) lead in counterpoint to composition.

Faustbal shows us how rhythm hovers on the edge of the spirit, how the seagull soars on the breeze and trembles in pleasure or fear.

Faustbal shows us how splendorous glowing rays transform fugues and flights.

Faustbal shows us how marches and *cavatinas* spread the serpent's hisses in earthly Paradise.

Faustbal shows us how passionate (and in a plaster cast) Eve recreates harmony and the pavane.

Faustbal shows us how perennial perpetuity lost feels the lash of the absurd going beyond songs and chords.

Faustbal shows us how betwixt arias and nocturnes the apple is "demortalized" and thirst for Gilgamesh produced *zorongos* and *jarabes*.[1]

Faustbal shows us how listeners cling to a giraffe's neck, and fly off on a melody and the chromatic scale.

Faustbal shows us how time and space scare away concepts with chance, recitative and cacti.

Faustbal shows us how mode and tone drink deep and shower us with surprises.

Faustbal shows us how harmony harnesses happiness in the *danzón*, *trova* and *fólia*.[2]

Faustbal show us how, once reason disproves the existence of reason, polyphony takes off a while when beauty fractures.

Faustbal shows us how musical works, butterflies with death-heads and live skulls, spring from the foliage of the Golden Age.

Faustbal shows us the day will never come when swallows will be taught how to build their nests and the masters their hats.

Faustbal shows us the pharaoh-composer frolicking in starry fields in a major key and feeds on "allegretto" at the breast of the "dominant" goddess.

Faustbal shows us how, between fig trees and dogs, hopes and kites, syncopation and mange-mites, only awe-inspiring adventures can seduce him.

—Fernando Arrabal, *Treviso*, December 2008

---

1 Andalusian and Mexican folk dances, respectively
2 Mexican, Cuban and Canary Island dances

1.
Balada Without a Hat

"If I go to Andalusia and choose to wear a Cordoban hat, or a cowboy hat in Texas or no hat at all on Wall Street, I'm still recognized as 'myself' as personality stands out independent of appearance."

Comfortable shoes cushioned by dark socks, even when the sun beats down. A finely ironed trouser crease and a high waist encircled by an elegant belt. A buttoned shirt with a front pocket that's almost always tucked in when the belt buckle tightens. A dark, unassuming casual shirt, that seems quite cold for such a Mediterranean frame (a touch of America had to stick, I suppose). When it rains or hails, a buttoned-up overcoat is quite impractical, elegance says "Enough is enough" through the cracks and America wins the day with a zip. A large would-be metallic watch worn on his left wrist, although it's been there so long its monotonous raison d'être may have been forgotten. Bare, muscular hands, as befits a proper pianist as opposed to the amateur variety, gray rings under his eyes, and not like Paul Muni's Chopin who never plays a note. His shirt pocket houses a large pair of rather American reading glasses, inspired by practicality rather than aesthetics. When it's cold, he wears a warm peaked cap; when it's a heat wave, a baseball cap riddled with holes and a plastic clasp.

Leonardo Balada likes to walk a lot and quickly. His stride is long and sure after so many winters dodging black ice in subzero Pittsburgh. He usually carries a small comb he extracts from somewhere or other to tidy his hair when it's windy. He speaks intensely, with an electric charge, at times he may sound confused. He thinks in Catalan, speaks in English, writes in Spanish and feels himself to be an independent citizen in a world that is occasionally too collective. His gaze is deep, striking and even solemn behind his thick eyebrows. His eyes recount stories that can't fit within the pages of a book, though they hover in the air in leisurely conversation. Mediterranean in heart and mind, his appearance doesn't match the stereotype: bright eyes, fair hair, broad face, and no sign of the curious phantoms that possess all Hispanics and can enervate us to the point of absurdity. On dull days he seeks out luminous company and smiles as only those can who relish their time and transient happiness. He is an agnostic who believes in transcendence and posterity, in a job well done and in individuals over schools. Clear, diaphanous concepts flow from his lips, he doesn't believe in aesthetic theory, though he strives to find the manifold faces of pure beauty. A champion of lost causes, he is nostalgic for nothing and appreciates everything. His modernity is rooted in his ability to read the rivers of the past with eyes of the future, but without a hat, you and I, all or nothing. He writes music to imbue every one of us, as if each idea was directed at a single individual, so that, to our surprise, we discover we are not alone as we listen.

He gets up before dawn and sits in front of his computer screen. Like his father, he has a subscription to *La Vanguardia*, although distance means he reads the digital edition before starting to deal with the dozens of emails he receives from all over the world. While he waits for Joan to wake up and check some of the things he has dashed off in that tricky language, he smiles at the battles between Catalan and Spanish nationalists. All that seems so far away! In fact, he likes to know what's happening back home and, although he doesn't take much notice of politics, he does like to know what people are up to. He uses the early hours to cast his nets over to the other side of the ocean and to write without interruption, the mornings to learn while he teaches and the afternoons to dream of new, impressive edifices of sound. And the evenings? It is open house for his friends, although the odd stranger slips in. He always supports whatever flies the flag of culture, but can never hide a special fondness for everything that runs the risk of being forgotten, for everything that retains a little piece of ourselves and resists globalization. Thus, the right to difference merits his fervent support and applause, because culture on the grand scale is humanized by small identities, from I to we, and certainly never from they to I.

Identity? Balada is Balada, period. An individual many find prickly; his independence has always made him fly without halter, debts or godfathers. He has learned from many maestros, but much more from those just starting out. His idea of Spain can be rather simplistic and mythical, but each night his idea of America can never make him forget the sea he can contemplate from his house in Sant Just Desvern. He is no shark, but neither is he a lamb. Admired by many, envied by even more. He always thinks ambitiously, if Plácido Domingo can be Zapata or Fernando Arrabal can put words in God's mouth, why settle for second best? The degree of satisfaction felt from the ensuing high makes the extra effort worthwhile.

It always feels a tad surreal when you enter a composer's office. Some days you almost touch the ideas, quiet song and faded echoes of chords, phrases and sparks of sound that, like shooting stars extinguished thousands of years ago, have vanished into thin air before making it to paper. The creator of sounds grasps time, leaves hardly a trace of its passing. Leonardo's huge note-catching net spreads out from the dining room and looks down over his neighbors' green patios through a cinemascopic, panoramic window. Southern light doesn't have the magic of the light east of Sant Just, which joyously reimagines the sea and usually distracts the creator, is too perfect to be perfect, you might say. Carpet silences the squeaks and shoes over the wooden floor, and that's ideal for a musician, but makes it difficult to maneuver his office chair from computer to table and table to computer.

Balada was won over by technology years ago, and composes on a paradoxically mute, fleeting keyboard summoned to transform into black and white the musical ideas that flow unawares from the composer's net. The worktable he keeps for new writing is short of free space, as a profusion of scores, letters and packets almost entirely blocks out the color of the wood. Three of the four walls are lined with posters advertising a handful of the many significant concerts in the composer's career. Spanish and English names alternate in a black-and-white mosaic laden with unforgettable memories. Cupboards with doors and shutters rise up from the floor and hoard scores and more scores, copies and more copies, drafts, and folders full of motley information about music and musicians. Sometimes wonderful surprises emerge from behind those big drawers in the form of a photograph or even that score we had been looking for a couple of days ago and that, as if by magic, had slipped into that space as if it wished it were a poster and could forget it was music. Balada's record collection dominates a large part of the room: commercial and live recordings of his own work. It is scary to look into that corner and see the number of hours of musical art generated by that man. Vinyls, tapes, DVD, CD, all the formats there have been and will ever be, have battled it out to store for posterity what Leonardo Balada wanted to reveal of himself.

One cold, rainy morning Leonardo sat down in a baroque American room that was under a hundred years old to listen to John Corigliano. He was just another enthusiast, like his students who were waiting to hear what the great American composer had to say. When Corigliano's eyes met Balada's transatlantic gaze, he smiled gently, greeted him, and declared that they were in the presence of the only man who, despite adverse prevailing winds, had told him one day that his work was very personal and that he should never surrender in the fight to retain its individual character. That man is the same Balada who goes to his colleagues' concerts, while his colleagues make a point of not going to his. People . . .

There are infinite small things that define a person, but our image will always be the penultimate and perhaps later we will feel an overwhelming urge to go back to acts, words and gestures in our quest for fuller knowledge. Many of us hide behind poses, facial expressions, vitae, more or less verifiable acts, and realities that are more or less indemonstrable. All that makes us feel comfortable in our little patch of glory, it camouflages us in the morass, but we bare our teeth when someone threatens to penetrate our secret *mihrab*, our ideas or frustrations, since we are afraid that, once we sit in front of a mirror, it will show us for what we really are. That's why only someone who knows himself is able to do without a hat, can throw it to the wind and share a complicit smile.

Balada is simultaneously a citizen of nowhere and everywhere, a stateless individual of today, who feels comfortable anywhere, while he longs for what is far off. In 2006 when I launched myself on the educational adventure of a Fulbright Scholarship, I had few doubts about the person I wanted to learn from and the place where I wanted to work. It's not that Carnegie Mellon University had anything special for my research project on the repertoire for solo voices, or that Pittsburgh had a musical life that was superior to Cordoba, Salamanca or Sevilla; the real issue was that such an unusual figure, a freewheeler in a fascinating generation of composers, would give me the chance to cross an ocean without missing home. As Madrid edged its way towards summer, I asked Ramón Barce, a man I admire greatly, to put me into contact with Leonardo Balada. We were enjoying one of those luminous afternoons at Ramón Barce's home when you know you are experiencing an unforgettable moment. As happens with extraordinary human beings, the shadow cast is but the beginning of one long intellectual feast. Once I was in the United States, my admiration for the artist was transformed into gratitude towards a friend and fascination for the complex identity of that artist and human being. I worked valiantly over my first months in the city with three rivers to finish my research projects so I could start writing this biography you are now holding. A biography can barely hope to give order to a few memories that go from yellowing photos to memories vitiated by the passage of time. And that is why I don't envy you the good fortune of reading about Balada's life and work, since, on this occasion, the good fortune was mine alone. My good fortune to have been able to experience it live in voice, gesture and immediate feeling.

To write the biography of someone who is out there, who is news and rewrites himself by the day is to take a lethal leap into the void without a safety net. For the subject of the biography, it is a fair-ground mirror that more or less foreshortens him, that more or less relates to him. For the biographer, it is an attempt to extend one's admiration to others. For the reader, it is a chance to better understand this or that work, or simply an excuse to revisit what we experienced, to know what we didn't know and to understand ourselves better. One request before the curtain is raised: let's take off our hats before setting out on this journey into the soul of an artist, who is also the soul of each and every one of us.

2.
Pepito and the Adventures of Nono

A child is walking towards his new school. He is the son of a tailor, a worker who belongs to that strange middle class that exists in Catalonia and has virtually no parallel in the rest of Spain. It is the beginning of the twentieth century, though the shadow of the nineteenth still stretches out a bony hand with its burden of Spanish-style beliefs and irrationalism. Against the odds, Barcelona is an island in this world of neolithic traditions and self-interested fears. That city's social fabric *is* different and its wealthy bourgeoisie did sweep aside the land-owning nobility long ago and establish a new regime based on the capital produced by labor. That lively little fellow is Josep, or Pepito, as they call him at home or in the street. As he crosses the threshold of his new school, that describes itself as Modern and was founded in 1901 by Francesc Ferrer i Guàrdia, he enters a new world, one that is strikingly distinct, that looks askance at the past while treading firmly towards the future. His classroom has lines of benches for two pupils and Pepito will sit next to a girl. The Modern School is in favor of mixed education, girls and boys are equal in every way, thus acknowledging that the social reality in the country is absurd. In Ferrer's school, everything is questioned, argued and thought through. Sunday's classroom is heaven itself, not metaphorically, but literally speaking. Only weekday lessons were given in the usual spaces, and that was the only similarity between those schools and the official educational system. Secularism, the importance of the object of study, rationalism, an apprenticeship in learning, the distinct ethical profile of every single lesson and the individualized psychological treatment for every pupil, pinpointed the astonishing differences. There was only one indisputable guiding principle: the freedom of the individual as the bedrock of an ethical, civic, creative education. That boy, sitting next to a girl in that atypical school, will be the father of a composer and the stamp of that education will definitively shape the personality of his own family and provide key markers to help us understand that son.

Front cover of *The Adventures of Nono*, translated by anarchist Anselmo Lorenzo

In a society ruled by surplices, ancestral customs with prehistoric roots, by social hierarchies decided by birth, collective poverty and enforced illiteracy, that school with its anarchist aspirations constituted a problem, that was initially a small one, but which grew exponentially as the number of students expanded. Autonomy, that country where Nono lived,[1] a place where one could learn sensitively about justice and human happiness, was opposed to Argirocracy, where injustice, selfishness, religious fundamentalism and rules oppressed the individual, as they did in real life. Two contrary worlds—one full of hope, one frozen in time—clashed violently, bombs and shots would be exchanged and almost thirty years later, direct confrontation led to the outbreak of civil war.

On Sunday mornings, Pepito, like every other pupil, would go to school with his parents, since it was usual for there to be classes on that day of rest rooted in religion, and lessons were held in a nearby park. Classes generated culture for and by everyone, with no class distinctions or intimidation. A stroke of luck enabled Ferrer Guàrdia to initiate that anarchist educational practice. His dream of libertarian schools could be fulfilled with money provided by a French pupil of his, Madamoiselle Meunier. Every Sunday, as we said, classes were open to all-comers, fathers and daughters, mothers and sons. On one such day Dr Andrés Martínez Vargas, Professor of Child Disease at the University of Barcelona, spoke about the importance of hygiene at school for avoiding child sickness and death. Nothing obscure or technical, no moralizing commandments, simply common sense. After he finished, Dr Odón de Buen, professor from the Faculty of Science,

---

1 Juan Grave, *Las aventuras de Nono*. This was Anselmo Lorenzo's translation of *Les aventures de Nono* by Jean Grave, a leading French anarchist. It was one of the recommended reading books for children in the Modern School, with all its ideological and emotional burden. Nono, a normal child, figures as a male version of Alice, in an ideal country and constantly compares his previous life to present experience, displaying the full range of Ferrer i Guàrdia's anarchist ideas.

spoke clearly but inspirationally about the usefulness of empirical observation and the study of what was then called Natural History. The smiles of young and old alike contrasted with the contrition and shock-horror of those attending another lecture nearby, in a church. Dr de Buen had yet to finish when all the bells began to chime simultaneously, every Sunday of every week of every month. Noise pollution was so intense you could barely hear a boy tugging his father's trousers and asking for a sweet, let alone his father's reply that there would be no prizes or punishments, as he had read in the Modern School Bulletin.

"But, dad, I don't go to the Modern School."

"You soon will, my son, you soon will. . . . And clean your forehead, it's covered in ash from the confirmation."

In 1906, when Pepito was a pupil in the school, the news came: a network of thirty-six fraternal schools home to over a thousand pupils now existed. The warmth generated by that new way of understanding education meant that the idea caught on, and was adapted to meet the needs of different localities, spreading under a variety of names to Andalusia, Galicia and Valencia, and gradually to other European countries. The pedagogical key to this development lay in textbooks that were carefully written by individuals with enormous professional prestige like Santiago Ramón y Cajal or Élisée Reclus, among others, as well as in the Modern School Bulletin that periodically outlined some of their ideas. Opposition to Ferrer, accusations of anarchist indoctrination—using Mateo Morral as an excuse[2]—soon put Ferrer in the sights of educational and church authorities close to the monarchy. When he was murdered after the briefest of trials on October 13, 1909, victory for homogeneity and "God's commandments," cut short the dream of future anarchist education, although the network of modern schools changed its profile and continued up to the civil war. In his will, Ferrer wrote something that left a mark on everyone, especially on the minds of the children who had received that rationalist education and then became parents:

". . . I also want my friends to say little or nothing about me, because idols are created whenever individuals are exalted, and that does great harm to the future of humanity. Only the acts, of whoever, must be studied, exalted or derided, and praised so they

---

2   The anarchist and regicide Mateo Morral was one of the pretexts that led to accusations that Ferrer was plotting against the rule of law and exercising a pernicious influence over society.

will be imitated when they seem to foment the common good, or criticized so they won't be repeated if they are thought to be harmful to the general well-being . . ."

Born in 1898 at the time of the war in Cuba, Pepito, the tailor's son, finished his basic schooling and returned to the family workshop. However, that education impregnated his whole life in a very special way. He applied that philosophy of life to all that came his way, from professional skills to the integrity of individuals. As a utopian anarchist, he believed in work and goodness as essential for society's well-being, and that led him to clash with communists more than once. When he was a master tailor and responsible for several workers, he was even denounced and imprisoned for a few hours as a result of that ideological conflict between radical socialism, mass communism and individual anarchism. It was his fate to live in difficult, authoritarian, irrational times, but he was also able to generate a space for freedom and free thinking in his own Autonomy, though he lived within Argirocracy. Josep, Pep, Pepito Balada, was married in a civil ceremony to Llúcia, Llucieta Ibáñez, a beautiful woman, born in Sant Just Desvern, and who, despite playing with high-class toys and being a friend of many upperclass girls, was the daughter of a working-class woman who helped in those grand, turreted houses with their forbidding façades. A vegetarian, great reader and lover of music, Pepito Balada strove to find a metaphor for society itself in the difference between "good" and "bad." He learned Esperanto and even subscribed fifty years ago to the UNESCO magazine, that came to his house every month much to the postman's surprise. His main aim in life was very simple: to be different from everyone else, and consequently he applied those principles to his life and the lives of his children. His older son, whom they expected to be a tailor in the family tradition, was brought up according to all the concepts and freedoms his father learned in the Modern School. The family hoped their children would be great professionals, well-read, supporters of internationalist anarchism and generous heirs to the ideas of Ferrer and Balada himself, together with other people who could perfectly well distinguish good from evil. Fate and happenstance transformed Pepito and Llucieta's first child into a composer, and music, that metaphor for balance, goodness and the universe, both human and divine, made him an individual worthy of a biography.

3.
The Son of an Anarchist

Nardo Balada Ibáñez was born in the early hours between September 21 and 22, 1933. He was the first child of a family that was atypical for its times, since against the dictates of tradition, he was born to a couple united by a civil, not religious, act. Their decision, that was perfectly legal and normal in 1933, became something illegal and persecuted a few years later. Faithful to their distinct ethical and ideological stance, they didn't give that child a Christian name. His father was one of many anarchists who had been rendered apolitical by the convulsions in Catalan society as the monarchy died a death, and whose belief in the individual was reinforced by the confrontations between brothers in the struggles from 1936. Nardo emerged one night between two calendar days, and was thus located rather ambiguously from an astrological perspective. Esoteric and ritualistic, rather than transcendental, this detail wasn't simply anecdotal for those who believed in the powers of prophesy, like, for example, his first wife who tirelessly tried to glean the truth from that birth's stars, though always in vain. *Who cares about that?* asked his mother. *Why become stuck in that particular mire?* To add to the confusion, Nardo Ibáñez Balada was registered for reasons unknown—don't pry further, I beg—one day after his birth, which meant that on any official form he had to inscribe a date of birth that wasn't genuine, alongside his strange anarchist name. Who could rival such an initial mess and a chaotic identity? Whether or not it was written in the stars, that multifaceted infant simply had to be exceptional, either because he was an eccentric or a genius.

Balada was one of those surnames traditionally linked to a trade. Tradition and customers had made their name a guarantee of quality. Tailors over several generations, the Baladas at Ronda Universitat, 12, 2nd, 2nd, were a reference point in the neighborhood. Their tailor's shop had served a dual function for years, as it was also the family abode, where Nardo saw the light, took his first steps, hid behind rolls of cloth and played with his grandmother Elvira, who found solace in Nardo's appearance after the death

of her husband. On display in the entrance was the distinguished diploma issued, according to medieval guild custom by the Mutual Society of Master Tailors: Trust. The mark in the equivalent to Josep Balada's examination was *Outstanding with distinction*. Although he first specialized in bespoke tailoring for men, time and a desire to improve himself led Pepito to qualify as a women's tailor too. It was an era when suits and dresses were adapted to the needs of each individual, not like today when everyone must adapt the folds of their skin to ready-made material. Its position in the city center meant it was one of the most popular tailor shops and everyone was welcome, from the poorest worker to the idlest aristo. Bad payers, aristocrats were never good customers, but their pursuit of superiority made them the forebears of the guild's publicity men; although they rarely deigned to part with their cash, they acted as ambassadors for their suits. It was there that the young couple's first child learned to play and listen, surrounded by rulers, scissors and rolls of cloth.

Publicity for *Balada the Tailors*

The unusual family surname apparently comes from an idyllic hamlet on the Ebro Delta. Currently Balada has 28 inhabitants and a few streets that the sunset illuminates spectacularly every day. Given the potential geographical source of their surname, it wouldn't be surprising, if we went back to the first Baladas, and found that Jewish blood ran in their veins, which would explain the family's artistic leanings.

The case of the Ibáñez is quite different. The maternal family came from Sant Just Desvern, which, although close to Barcelona, had maintained its status as a wealthy Catalan town where large mansions had been constructed on the skirts of the mountain from the end of the nineteenth century. Sant Just was a place of privilege, sufficiently close to the big city for people to come and go and sufficiently distant to be spared its noise and irritants. The family lived in an enviable farmhouse in the high part of the town called Can Freixes, which they rented together with five or six other families. In the summer, with the maternal grandparents, they made up a new, more tranquil family in the natural setting of the farmhouse. The Baladas occupied an annex to the original building and their front door was at the back of the house.

Can Freixes, Sant Just Desvern, in the 1930s

Almost immediately after giving birth to her first child, the young mother became pregnant with her second. The constant effort undermined her already frail physique, and she became alarmingly weakened by her new experience of mothering. The absence of maternal milk and evident deterioration in the child's health led the family to send their second son, Elíseo, to a branch of the paternal family that lived in Tortosa. They hoped the child would put on weight and improve his health in an even quieter spot, but it was all in vain and the first Elíseo Balada Ibáñez died before reaching his second birthday.

When the Baladas arrived, Sant Just Desvern had some two and a half thousand inhabitants, a large population compared to the country average. Ever since the victory of the Second Republic it had been controlled politically by people on the left and in particular by Daniel Cardona, first the Esquerra Catalana (Catalan Left) mayor, and later the head of the so-called Front Nacionalista that comprised Nosaltres Sols (We Alone), among others. The days previous to the proclamation of the Catalan State within the Spanish Federal Republic coincided with the family's arrival in Can Freixes.[1] The reaction of the far right CEDA central government, with the army in tow, ensured that the family experienced a period of unstable, chaotic local politics with the closure of town halls and consequent lack of effective local government. In any case, despite the militancy of the town's citizenry, people remained relatively unaffected inside their homes, where the problems of day-to-day living were always more important than anything else.

While sea and mountain air strengthened their first child, Pepito Balada went to his tailor's shop in Barcelona, which entailed an endless work schedule that usually obliged him to stay there overnight. There was no rest for a tailor. There would be nobody, then suddenly late at night someone remembered he needed trousers and rushed to the workshop to be measured up. Besides, the journey from San Just to Barcelona was slow and onerous, even though the two places were so close. A direct successor to the old stagecoach, the bus, belonging to Autobuses La Santjustenca, juddered out of Plaza Campreciós in the early hours eventually switching from a dirt track covered in weeds and stones to the gray paving of the modernist city, before depositing its passengers in the Plaza de España. Little Nardo usually stayed at home and played with the children from the other families sharing the farmhouse, or listened attentively, eyes and ears alert, to the stories his grandmother told. But one Sunday when Pepito realized his son could handle cloth or safety pins, he immediately started him on the apprenticeship he himself had begun with his own father decades before. Nardo was now a considerable help and would soon inherit the family business, it was only a matter of time.

When there were no urgent tasks in the shop, Nardo watched his father enjoy reading whatever pamphlet or newspaper came into his hands. On special evenings the married couple donned their glad rags, put aside pins and needles, went out together and came back humming tunes they

---

1   The Catalan State was proclaimed on October 6 amid the turmoil prompted by the recent victory of the CEDA as the second government of Spain's Second Republic. Lluís Companys, the president of the Generalitat, was responsible for signing off the proclamation.

found higly entertaining. Those outings usually took them to a mysterious, imposing theater that wasn't far from home, in the middle of La Rambla, which from then on acquired a mythical aura for the young boy: El Gran Teatre del Liceu. One day, years later, his name would be posted above the entrance when he conquered that space which had given so much pleasure to his parents.

The victory of the Popular Front[2] brought the masses and havoc to the streets of Barcelona. Like all average-sized enterprises, the tailor's shop depended on a number of contracted workers whose union leadership used victory at the ballot-box to put pressure on the bosses. Socialist and communist ideologies dominated the guild and the elections had given them a majority, even though votes were spread over a range of creeds. Confrontations between anarchists and communists, that were first ideological and then physical, led some workers to take their boss to court. Mr Balada had nothing to hide, so he put on his hat and went to the police station where he was briefly questioned. Once it was proved, as was inevitable, that all his labor agreements respected the law, Josep Balada walked out pondering the uncertain times ahead. It was hard to anticipate the nature of the conflicts, but an uncontrollable lust for power might lead to fissures on the left that would favor right-wing parties that were less prone to splits. He thought about Francesc Ferrer and what he would have said if he had seen communists opposing anarchists and libertarians. The ground had just begun to shift beneath his feet.

The return to Sant Just used to be peaceful enough and most people would enjoy a siesta so as not to sleep so much at night. However, that afternoon Pepito Balada shut up shop earlier than usual and settled down to spend the night there, because public transport was less than safe, especially at night. The streets were almost deserted and a strange silence reigned over the city. Some radio stations broadcast contradictory news, while everyone impatiently awaited the response of the new government. Josep's worst fears were realized, the extremists reacted violently and he could hear gunfire on the streets. The following day the worst rumors were confirmed. A group of generals had incited the army to rise up against the lawful government. It was a coup d'état. It was civil war.

---

2 Formed in 1935, the Popular Front won the general elections on February 16, 1936.

Nardo Balada in 1942

4.
The Distant Blast of Bombs

The first months of conflict were months of tense expectation in Barcelona. News of the coup had hit the whole of Catalonia like the worst possible earthquake. The main barracks in each city, spurred on by their generals, took up arms against the elected republican government. On July 19, 1936, it was the turn of the military forces in Barcelona. The social fabric created in the city from the early twentieth century meant that the first attacks unleashed were rebuffed by the Civil Guard and citizen pickets organized by the anarchist CNT-FAI. General Goded, the general called on to lead the insurrection, was arrested and taken before a court. By the following morning anarchists controlled the city and munitions and tried to establish calm. The Committee of Anti-Fascist Militias was soon set up under the auspices of the CNT-FAI, but feelings were running high and that opened old sores. The communists weren't happy about the CNT being in control and began to agitate for a vote and a voice in the leadership of the city. When the Durruti column left for Saragossa on July 24, 1936, the anarchist areas of Barcelona were defenseless. A settling of accounts between fraternal, but rival, ideologies became increasingly frequent, given the absence of an enemy outside the city. In August, Generals Goded and Fernández were executed after the shortest of trials and the citizenry began to chorus a slogan: Barcelona will resist.

Every household lived that first year of the conflict feeling that they were being watched from afar. On May 4, 1937 a general strike was called in the city and streets were deserted. The Balada's tailor shop became the family house for a few hours, without the usual hustle and bustle. The POUM and CNT fought guns in hand against the other side of the street, where remnants of republican and communist units gathered—not the military insurgents! When peace fell over the city four days later, the wealthiest began to slip out of Barcelona in search of a safer haven. The city was gradually armed, weapons fell into the hands of the most militant rather than the most disciplined groups. Support for the communists from abroad reinforced their bid for control, and their greater degree of organization and military firepower made them a more feasible force than the CNT's idealists and agitators. Both engaged in direct confrontations that often endangered the lives of passersby. One side wanted to be in charge of training the

The church in Sant Just on fire, June 1936

new troops to go to the front, the other wanted no orders from above, particularly when they believed they were on the threshold of a freedom that exalted the individual against the collectivity.

Meanwhile the territory of the Republic diminished by the day, and now that the Ebro front had stabilized, Madrid seemed to be the priority target for the insurgents. The government, headed by Negrín, decided to move to Barcelona on October 28, 1937. That was a signal. Tensions were rising. Radios broadcast the news that the Germans were making incursions through the Pyrenees and that the Italians were also intent on cracking open Barcelona. Simultaneously, the leadership of the military rebels gradually sorted itself out. The deaths of some generals who had led the coup opened the way for one name to begin to dominate the headlines: Francisco Franco.

Money minted by the Sant Just Desvern Town Hall during the civil war

On December 8, 1937, the first bombing raids on the Catalan capital could be clearly heard from Sant Just. At the beginning of the war, the town church had burnt down and that became the focus of the drama of war. The lack of control was such that the Balada family saw the first—and last—banknotes minted by the town hall. They were one peseta and fifty cent notes that bore the name of the municipality. This tactic had been encouraged to attempt to deal with the monetary crisis across the republican zone. Any town hall that wanted to issue money for local use could do so by previously depositing an equivalent amount at the Bank of Spain.

Though they had been reinstalled in Sant Just for some time, the family still looked to Barcelona as its home. But the night of October 8, 1938, was the most tragic of the war in Sant Just. A squadron of Italian planes bombed Sants Station ten minutes before midnight. As the archives bears witness, a child and his mother died on Calle París in Barcelona.[1] On their way back to base, the same planes dropped bombs on the main road into Sant Just and a few seconds later, five shells hit the town center. As the then mayor Alfred Arís relates, two didn't explode, while the others left six injured, three houses destroyed and two badly damaged. The peace of the Balada family had been violently disturbed by a reality that promised to become even more nerve-racking.

Nardo traveled less and less to Barcelona, because he was still very young and the journey had become increasingly dangerous. Pepito stayed in the paternal home, which made his family extremely on edge since the area of the Ronda Universitat was the

Nardo Balada and his mother on La Rambla in Barcelona, September 1936

---

1 The Historical Archive in Sant Just Desvern (Barcelona) and sources in the General Archive of the Spanish Civil War in Salamanca

one the bombers punished most. When air raid sirens wailed, adults and children went to the shelters as quickly as they could. If that happened in Barcelona, the Metro was the lifesaver; if it was in Sant Just, a shelter dug out of the rock at the back of the old Can Freixes farmhouse was where the tenant families spent many sleepless, panic-stricken hours. A feeling of defenselessness forced the Balada family to hold an emergency meeting, decide to pack necessary items and return to Barcelona where safety measures for the civilian population were much more effective. Since the move didn't just involve the nuclear family of father, mother and son, but also other relatives in the town, the tailor's shop was too small. The final destination chosen was Sarrià and, specifically, one of those mansions which, in those gloomy times, rented out rooms. Fortunately, they managed to find a room for themselves and others for the grandparents and rest of the family.

While the enemy bombed night and day, a show-trial was organized in Barcelona against members of the POUM that ended with the imprisonment of many young republicans on October 29. On the other side of the table, republicans preferred to defeat former allies rather than resist the common enemy. Divisions were so great that Barcelona offered no resistance when on January 26, 1939, Generals Yagüe and Solchaga took the city. The work of fifth columnists had meant there was no determined

Family photo on the beach in 1939; Balada seated first on right

defense. Although the legally elected government was still in Figueres, Franco was already preparing his victory parade through the streets of Barcelona. At the last moment, huge concentrations of people took to the roads leading out of the city, or boarded trains and boats: any route that seemed practical. A new era was beginning.

In the mind of young Nardo, that first scenario began to meld with the memories of his grandmother who later recounted details of that general drama that had fortunately escaped his young eyes and ears. Nonetheless, a few scraps of memory, some perhaps acquired later, left an indelible impression of the last days of the war. One morning Moorish troops rode their horses through the Tibidabo tunnel, turbans blowing in the wind. They were like beings from another epoch, ones that could only be found in the books his father used to read to him every night. Those once fearful hordes brought by Franco from Africa now began to distribute food and sing the praises of the New Spain. One approached Nardo, who was barely five at the time, and offered him a magical fruit he had never seen before, let alone tasted. It was a banana . . . his first banana.

When the war was over, the Baladas were keen to return to everyday normal life. After the early days when there was an abundance of food and promises of better times to come, things started to change. Penury and shortages forced the family to abandon Barcelona yet again and return to the small town, where food was easier to find. One of Nardo's aunts

The Balada family

worked for a butcher, so they were lucky never to experience the plight of the defeated and their wretched mixture of hunger, disillusion and terror in respect of the future.

Sant Just was a traditional base of Esquerra Republicana and a drastic purge was carried out at the end of the war. Over thirty individuals who opted to stay in the town were accused and taken to concentration camps and forced labor battalions. In spite of Pepito Balada's well-known anarchist leanings, his lack of political involvement and stable work situation meant he could go back to his shop without major restrictions. In the eyes of the new Francoist Spain, Josep Balada was a petty bourgeois and, consequently, a *respectable* citizen. But there was still a range of factors that wouldn't allow him to sleep peacefully for some time. It wasn't just a matter of ideas or ideals, but realities that were only too close to home. He was the father of a non-Christian family, with a wife blessed by a civil rite, and a son who hadn't been baptized and they now lived in a fascist state with Catholic-nationalist roots. None of that would pass unnoticed by the town's new powers that be. The Baladas had to live with all due caution.

5.
The School for Girls

The sound of the footsteps of refugees fleeing along muddy roads towards France could still be heard when victory lodged in the heart of Spain in the form of a new Catholic, nationalist regime with a single ruler. That new scenario was especially hard for a city like Barcelona. Streets fell silent now that their words and language were surely banned. Those who headed to France hoping to find freedom on the other side of the frontier began to trickle back. They spoke of concentration camps on the shores of the Mediterranean, of subhuman conditions and their endless nostalgia. If they raised their grief-stricken eyes from those cold, filthy beaches they could almost see the Costa Brava. After the first few months most saw that exile was a luxury for a minority, and that the rest must survive as best they could, which was always easier close to home. A much harsher, even crueler chapter now began for most, and was more terrifying than the recent war: the era began of averted gazes, fear of betrayal, inner exile, and the inability to be what you really were. The path to take was evident enough: don't attract attention and let time pass by. If you had voted for the left or didn't go to Mass . . . you'd be better off moving out of town. The legal system became a sharpened knife wielded by rancorous victors thirsting for revenge. Some regretted smiling when the Popular Front had won, or even accepting an invitation to go to the bar on the corner when the Bourbon king left the country. If someone denounced you as a red, freethinker or atheist, you faced hard times. The fact that informers were rewarded only increased the sense of panic. This is the only way to understand the terror of those first few months of the *Victory* as it was lived by people like Josep Balada, the anarchist tailor. But Catalonia wasn't Castile or Andalusia, there the difference was part of the DNA, and the anomalies were such that there was no choice but to wipe the slate clean. The situation in Sant Just was quite similar to the big cities. The left-wing, nationalist tradition of the community created a state of tense calm where everybody seemed to have something to hide.

Explanations and admissions of guilt for past actions were voiced in conversations in the warm fug of cafés and in front of police in the police station. But when it came to talking politics, everyone looked down and news of the Second World War was whispered in hushed tones from a few inches above the table. One day when Nardo was playing on the pavement in the square with his friends, the town priest, *Mossèn* Antonino Tenas,[1] who had expanded morally and physically since the end of the war, walked by the boys and shouted angrily at the boy who hadn't been baptized: "Clear off, *bordegàs!*"[2]

It was common knowledge that the Balada couple hadn't been blessed by the church, which was even more dangerous, because their situation could very well be illegal. Civil marriages were repudiated after the war and couples had to remarry according to God's mandate. The law of March 12, 1938 repealed the 1932 Civil Marriage Law and declared that civil marriages were illegal and nonexistent with retroactive effect. In those first post-war months, appearances and commonsense obliged the young boy to go to Mass, until all that was forgotten and everything returned to its normal lay state. The Baladas didn't have enemies in Sant Just and nobody much worried about anyone's ideology after the persecution of those early days. People removed from the scene were usually those who had held important positions in the town hall. The only one who might be dangerous in terms of possible betrayal was *Mossèn* Antonino. In the maternal grandmother's final days, the priest had appeared unexpectedly, with his black rictus and presence, and proceeded to administer the last rites. After making sure that she was conscious, he started to declare at the top of his voice that she was to blame for every blemish on her conscience, and that, even though he would administer those sacraments, he couldn't guarantee she would go to heaven. She had clearly sinned, she had allowed her daughter to marry in a cold, atheistic town hall and not in a sacred

---

1   This parish priest had presided over the church in Sant Just from 1917 and continued to do so until his death in 1954, and that meant he had detailed knowledge of all the ins and outs of town life; he was a decisive, influential figure in the town.

2   According to Catalan dictionaries, the term *bordegàs/bordegassos* simply refers to a boy, though in some places it is used pejoratively—"bastard." That is the sense of what Balada himself remembers of that encounter with the priest and his scornful expression.

space as the divine law ordained to which she was now appealing on the last stretch of life's path. That was such a serious sin it would irrevocably drag her soul into purgatory. The priest's vengeful, violent attitude towards a poor dying woman made the family fear a betrayal that never in fact materialized. All those dismal theatrics became landmarks in the young boy's mind and distinctly shaped the way he saw life and society. It was the first close family death; his brother had died long ago when he was too young to remember. It was a harsh farewell. Nardo remembered how his grandmother had told him all those things he couldn't remember about his early years and played a special role in shaping his sensibility.

But that wasn't their first conflict with the church or the workings of the new state, that at the time were almost one and the same. Before the age of compulsory schooling, Josep Balada had taken his son to the Núria Parish School, one of those religious educational spaces that had the advantage that it functioned normally during the war years. That premature foray that took Nardo to those classes in the middle of the war brought many a tear. When the war ended, Pepito realized that the control of education by a church that was more national-Catholic than ever, with the connivance of the state, would be a serious obstacle to his son's early education, and took him out of that hallowed sphere of power, much to Nardo's relief. In 1939, the end of the war meant that daily life for the civilian population regained a semblance of normality and each family faced an important choice. A decision had to be taken that implied the legal end of infancy and the beginning of institutionalized education. Nardo had to attend a normal school. He was six, and though his knowledge was clearly more advanced than any local child of his age, the laws of education were clear, he had to be sent to a school immediately.

The town had had three schools during the Republic, but afterwards only two functioned. On the one hand, there were the National Schools, on Carrer de la Creu, where, following the new legislation on education, boys were separated from girls

The National Schools on Carrer de la Creu—the Street of the Cross—in 1925

in different huts. On the other, the Athenaeum School, that was more elitist and would soon disappear, attached as it was to the town's only cultural center. Finally, there was the inevitable religious school established in the Núria Parish Schools on calle Bonavista that had left Nardo with such bad memories. His father knew that Nardo's schooling had been a problem he had solved with the passage of time, that his brief stint in a religiously dogmatic school was counterbalanced by the education his family gave him, and had had little impact on the boy's mind. But they couldn't

Carmen Pérez Verdú, Balada's school teacher in 1937

delay things any further. One day they went to the state school, where they knew one of the teachers, Carmen Pérez Verdú. They told her how they were frightened by the kind of state school envisaged by the new regime. The teacher shifted uneasily on her chair and asked them to bring their son at the end of the school day and she would see what could be done. This teacher was an example of the cohort of teachers trained by departments established by the first Republican government, people who were committed to education based on values closer to the ethos of the Modern School than the one offered by religious schools, although they had been terribly affected by the collapse of the Republic. Like the Baladas, the teacher's family had been able to stay in the town despite the change in regime, and hadn't suffered any betrayals or sudden shocks, or at least not at a personal level. Her husband, Josep Maria Bas Roselló, had been punished at the end of the war and could never resume his public teaching career. Nonetheless, his figure was to be very important in the immediate future both of Nardo and the town. In any case, Doña Carmen would become the school's headmistress and her diligence was always highly praised by the townspeople. Something very special was happening there.

That afternoon Nardo and his father arrived at the school's front door when the footprints of the pupils were still fresh in the sand. They entered the classroom and the schoolmistress asked them to sit behind desks made shabby by wear and tear. It was the second time that Nardo's eager eyes had observed such a place and it was nothing like the first. The teacher told his father that she was going to test his son's ability and level of knowledge in order to be able to decide what was best for him. Nardo was left alone for a moment. When the teacher returned, he calmly concentrated on memorizing everything she said and giving her prompt replies. After a while, Nardo ran out of the classroom to tell his father that it was all very easy, she had made him read and he had done so fluently, without making a single mistake.

The teacher soon came out and asked his father to go in while Nardo inspected the playground and kicked mounds of sand the youngest pupils had made hours ago. The teacher informed Nardo's father that his level was clearly above average and that he should be placed in the right year otherwise he might get frustrated in his studies. The real problem was that, given that church schools had been ruled out, a state school wouldn't be the solution, or at least not straightforwardly so. The boys' section in the school was very behind and Nardo would soon get bored. The teacher's proposal was bizarre; she suggested a highly unusual path.

"I want to propose something that you must consider very carefully. You are aware that the new educational regulations insist on children being divided up according to their sex. Well, I would like you to consider the possibility that your son join the girls' section . . . I know that sounds odd, but I promise you it won't affect his natural socialization and it will allow me personally to work with him and ensure his studies find their right level."

Father and son had a first serious conversation on the way home. The next morning, someone unexpected appeared in the girls' school—a boy. The girls stopped whispering when Doña Carmen introduced the new pupil who would stay with them for the next few years. Reasonably enough, there were no problems, except for those generated in the playground when the girls lifted their skirts when they were playing, and Nardo hid his embarrassment as best he could. It is well-known that the problem is never with the children, but with those who have forgotten that they were children once. He was the only boy in the class for the whole of his compulsory schooling and almost certainly one of very few cases of the flouting of the law that decreed the separation of sexes in school.

It was a time when Nardo made lots of discoveries, some good, some bad, and all destined to shape his personality. In 1939 the schools still maintained the norms for compulsory education inherited from the civil war, for those aged between six and nine, but from 1940-41 the norm was raised to eleven-twelve, depending on the level attained in studies, and finally to fourteen, and that was the system that defined Nardo Bala-

The Girls' School in Sant Just in 1942; Balada is second in the row on the right and the only boy.

da's education. Although his teacher was brilliant, and no doubt espoused republican rather than Francoist ideas, Spanish education was ruled by the Catholic Church, which injected great doses of terror, religion and iron control even in state schools. Every subject Nardo studied was subject to the regime's patriarchal control, although he had been spared one of the most basic, the separation of sexes into different classrooms. Nardo was a strange exception and it must have made life uncomfortable when a routine visit by inspectors was on the horizon. Even so, there are photos of excursions from over several years and Nardo is there among the girls, usually looking grumpy and standing out like a visitor from Mars at the winter sales. Apart from Carmen Pérez Verdú, he was occasionally taught by other teachers, as is evident in the photos; they must have been temporary replacements. Doña Carmen was clearly his first point of reference outside the family. She was a highly educated, principled woman who made a great difference to the childhoods of many children of the war in Sant Just Desvern. However, although school provided a learning experience for everyone, Nardo enjoyed the cosmopolitan advantage of a house and a father who worked in the capital. On some afternoons and holidays, Nardo would go to the tailor's without fail, as he had been helping for some time and lending a hand in a business he would surely inherit or not.

His adventures with music began quite naturally, when Nardo began

School group, 1942; Balada is third from the left in the second row.

to show an insatiable thirst for knowledge. Now he had embarked on his compulsory education, the next step was what were called complementary activities, ones with a certain social resonance, apart from the extraordinary formative role they might have. A music teacher lived by the corner of Carrer de la Creu with Bonavista and she was the person charged with introducing Nardo to that strange, beautiful language that was a source of fascination from the very beginning. María Oliveras, his first teacher, was the one responsible for creating the first fantasies of musical sound for a child who would become a composer within a few years.

His growing knowledge was making him ever more useful both at home and in his father's workshop, but one afternoon in 1941, shortly after Nardo's eighth birthday, his father, dressed with all due elegance, told his son to put his hat and jacket on because they were off to the Liceu. The boy was delighted. When his father had a little spare money, he spent it on invitations to cross the threshold of what was certainly the only temple he recognized as such. Meandering along carpeted corridors, enjoying the luxury of those sumptuous rooms, glass chandeliers and elegant people, was a pleasure forbidden to most inhabitants of Barcelona. He would have so many things to tell his friends in the morning! Most hadn't even been to Barcelona, so he was clearly privileged to have the parents he had. When father and son were walking down La Rambla, Nardo asked his father what opera they were going to see. His father replied that they weren't going to the Liceu, but to its Conservatory of Music.

That was like a school where you only studied music with other children and teachers, and was his unsuspected initiation into a life devoted to the art of music. But who would think of such things then? With its light and shadow, its successes and frustrations, the mysterious, unique, universal language of music couldn't rival the canaries chirping cheerfully on both sides of La Rambla. It is hard to grasp why Pepito Balada decided his son should extend his musical training in an official conservatory. One thing seemed obvious, in the Liceu's Conservatory of Music, his son would learn about proportion, elegance, precision and beauty, essential qualities every good tailor should have at his fingertips, which is what Nardo would be . . . or would he?

In any case, in under a year the boy was studying piano and music theory, a sinister concept which encompassed Sol-fa, theory as such, notions of harmony, counterpoint and the odd venture into composition that would become his driving passion as years went by. A young pianist was among Nardo's classmates: he was slightly older and was also to emerge as one of the most important voices on the Spanish musical landscape: Joan Guinjoan. His experiences at school and the conservatory filled the young boy's mind with an urgent desire to learn, experiment, communicate, transgress the boundaries of what is human and accede to a pure world that was remote from everything that was official life in that downtrodden society. Only an intellectual could sidestep the impermeable frontiers of class and predestination.

The Baladas had to take further decisions about Nardo's future at the end of his compulsory education. He had made excellent progress at the Conservatory and at school and it seemed a shame for this twelve-year-old to be buried under kilos and kilos of cloth to cut, scissors and invoices that were never honored. The world was just coming into being for Nardo, and his parents decided there was only one way to go: straight ahead.

But as challenges tend to surface when least expected, the direst kind made its appearance in January 1944. The New Year dawned with the worst nightmare that could haunt a family of tailors and turned their dreams into ash in a second. They had only just locked up the tailor's shop when a shout was heard that there was a fire in the building's basement and ground floor. These were the premises of Papelería Industrial Bolsera, that, as its name suggests, was in the business of manufacturing bags and other materials related to paper. Like a biblical plague, the paper in the basement transformed the entire building into a flaming torch within minutes. The Baladas' stocks of cloth were consumed by those uncontrollable flames. It was such a dramatic spectacle that the Ronda de la Universitat became an improvised cinema visited by all manner of bystanders. Alberto Alcocer, the mayor of Madrid, happened to be visiting Barcelona and with Miquel Mateu, the local city mayor, he came to see the show. It was a catastrophe for the families whose lives depended on the building and it also ruined the insurance companies. A lot was said about the lack of a proper institutional response and the interests hiding behind the company. It was truly a wretched beginning to the year for the Balada family. All their work materials and tools were gone and the building was declared out-of-use for a long time, but a worse fear had yet to be confirmed. As the years went by, and there was never a fire, the family had stopped renewing the fire insurance they were paying: what was supposed to be a great financial saving became a source of drama, ruination and brought shrill exchanges of "I told you so," "it was bound to happen" etc. With their shop reduced to ashes and no possible recourse to insurance, the family decided to leave the Ronda de la Universitat and make great economic sacrifices in order to move to a smaller flat and workshop in the nearby calle Pelayo.

What was once the Balada family abode, with a large room that served as a shop and was home to a fine table for displaying cloths and sewing materials, and an adjacent workshop, was replaced by such a small space it proved difficult to accommodate everything they required. The worst was that those hard knocks were accompanied by other blows. Franco's policy of economic self-sufficiency ravaged the country in the 1940s and sorely hit every family's pocket. In the eternal tug-of-war between customers, workers and entrepreneurs, "the everyman-for-himself" ethos and basic struggle for survival led small business like the tailor's to face recurring crises. While customers only added to a roll call of debtors, Balada had no money to pay for the textiles from the Sabadell manufacturers, who had their own lists, in large cycles of negative accounting, that must certainly have led to the doorsteps of the wealthiest pillars of the regime.

That situation of penury dramatically sharpened people's thinking. Unable to afford various technological innovations, Pepito Balada was forced by necessity to mount an operation worthy of the country's finest picaresque traditions. One of the tailor's neighbors had a telephone line but didn't have money to pay for his suits. Barter looked like the best option. In a few seconds they installed two cables where there was one, and bought a second telephone that used the same open line. Evidently family alarms went off when someone not from either side picked up the phone, but at the end of the day those weren't times to waste money, but to take decisive choices.

Once they were over their frights and battles with insurance companies, the Baladas became only too aware that a tailor's shop was perishable goods, and that the family patrimony could quickly end up in flames. It was there for the moment, but could disappear in a flash. All that influenced the future marked out for Nardo, who from then on was given carte blanche to continue his studies. The old problem of unsuitable schools resurfaced even more critically when it came to choosing a high school. As the range of high schools was minimal compared to the compulsory sector, choice led to a bottleneck from which it was difficult to escape without bumping into the church. However, given this wasn't an obligatory branch of education, the state was more prepared to tolerate alternative routes to the official schools. That loophole, generated by the precarious nature of the state system, meant that Nardo began to study for his school certificate in the private sector. It wasn't that the Baladas had suddenly become moneyed folk able to send their son abroad or to an elite institution. It was much simpler. Thanks again to the generosity of Carmen Pérez and the appearance on the scene of her husband, Josep Maria Bas, Nardo could go to his teacher's home every afternoon and, alongside four other students, prepare each year of high school over seven long years. The entrance examination to the school certificate, sat at the end of compulsory schooling, was the first big recognition of Nardo's academic abilities. His high marks confirmed it made more sense to choose books over scissors, at least for the time being.

Warmed by the brazier under the round table in a small, welcoming sitting room, the youngsters keenly studied at a high level way above the country average. Doña Carmen taught Latin, history and literature while her husband, Josep Maria Bas, was a first-rate mathematician and was responsible for the sciences. Between lessons, he challenged his pupils to the occasional game of chess, a sport at which he excelled and had won important national prizes. It wasn't unusual for Nardo to come to his daily class and find Señor Blas opposite the board with the pieces arranged according to the last game he had played in the championships of Catalonia. Nardo took such a liking to chess he even won a competition in 1949, though his teacher kept reminding him he would have to practice a lot if he wanted to triumph in that sport.

On the other hand, one leaden-gray afternoon when he was taking a break and glancing at the books in his teachers' library, he discovered that those shelves hid two big surprises. He became convinced that his teachers had communist leanings, which in Spain at the time was a clandestine, dangerous business. But his other find proved even more influential. Although the youngster had been to the opera and occasional enjoyable concert, and played the piano more than well, he had never knowingly listened to recorded music. And there, among those unattractive book spines, he discovered wonderful shellac records where live music in the form of sound waves preserved the miracle of the muses forever. The mystery of the language of musical sound was revealed to everyone by that fragile surface.

And Señor Bas, carefully, almost reverentially, extracted one of those records from its resting place, took it out of its sleeve and placed it on the gramophone. The needle came down and life began to change to the tunes from the regular revolutions of that turntable. *Tannhäuser* filled the young boy's astonished ears and aroused his longing for the infinity of music. It was then that he fantasized how one day he would own a similar treasure, a record, but not just any record, one with his own music. Over time he would remember those *folies de grandeur* when the first vinyl came into his hands and he read "Composed by Leonardo Balada" on the label around the center. As he walked home, Nardo Balada thought for the first time, half anxiously, half thoughtfully, how what had resonated around that room was the product of the human imagination, of someone like himself, a person who had dreamt up the music and been able to create a micro-world with a beginning and end that was etched on the dark matter of that record and in the bright open spaces of people's souls. After recounting that mystical experience to his parents, he was clear he had found a dream worth fighting for.

According to the high school curriculum under Franco, as well as Catholic doctrine—that was avoided or kept to a minimum in those private classes—it was necessary to secure the go-ahead of a member of the Falange, the single party in that one-party state, who taught a subject that was inevitable in a totalitarian regime and that rejoiced in the pompous name of "Formation of the National Spirit." A local well-known Blackshirt came to impart that fount of knowledge. It was a matter of seconds before that individual's inflammatory outbursts needled the patience and ideas of the most radical there. However, that was simply the way to comply with legal necessities and that Carlist hothead left the house convinced of his immaculate truths, preening and proud because he had been born to experience such exciting times.

The first great challenge came at the end of the fourth year of high school. Every young student had to sit a public test and give evidence of the levels of knowledge they had acquired. The much-feared final school examination was held in what was then the Verdaguer High School, in the Ciutadella Park, named after the distinguished Catalan man of letters, Jacint Verdaguer. Nobody relished the prospect of confronting those professors with waxed mustaches and sly, irritable expressions, with cars full of odds and ends, wives, children, parasols, watermelons and mothers-in-law, waiting to go on their summer holidays, while they now looked daggers at those adolescents, impatient to hear the end of the nonsense they were spouting and begin a well-earned summer break.

After passing his final exam, Nardo had access to a much greater level of intellectual and ethical knowledge than he could ever have imagined. Classes were taught in Catalan, a language that was officially banned and nonexistent in the Francoist educational system, and that gave a sharp clandestine edge to his liberal education. Occasionally individuals would visit the teachers' houses at night and begin to speak about the political situation in the country. Those meetings charted an unambiguous ideological map in the young student's mind. People entered the house one at a time, at ten-minute intervals, so as not to attract attention, given that any kind of meeting was illegal. Once inside, a dissident individual would employ words erased from dictionaries in those years: class struggle, freedom, dictatorship or democracy. Inspired by their rhetoric, on their way home after clandestine meetings, Nardo and his friends played out their own individual resistance to the regime via acts of street vandalism. Nardo plucked up courage and wrote *Visca Catalunya Lliure* on the side of the house of Sant Just's mayor. When the father heard about those encounters, he tried to warn his son of the danger of entering the loop of clandestine politics and began to wonder about the attraction exercised by those communists and the conflict it implied in terms of his own anarchist, internationalist ideas. The wounds from "friendly" communist fire on the anarchists in the Rambla during the war were still too fresh to be forgotten.

But Nardo was too young to grasp the import of those ideologies, so that, apart from those youthful flights, he was, reasonably enough, more concerned about the day after than the years to come. It was cobbler to your last and student get ready for your final exam, the so-called State Examination, that was enough to make any adolescent grit his teeth. On that occasion, the feared examination was held in the university, on the square of that name, where all the students who had passed the first round had to come and take the final test in order to get their diplomas and access to higher education. Rumor had it that there was only a one-out-of-three pass-rate and there were veterans who returned every year to fail yet again while their beards kept growing. The examiners' frowning visages seemed increasingly terrifying as your turn approached.

"Geography. Tell me the names of the most important rivers in Korea."

He recoiled in horror. How could he know the rivers in Korea if he couldn't remember where Korea was?

"The Jonshi, the Chonly and the Chuanchuan."

"Next one . . ."

Nardo walked up to that table that was more like a guillotine than a workspace.

"As you must be a habitual reader of *La Vanguardia* . . ." a stare over reading glasses deep into his eyes, "your question will be related to what this newspaper wrote last week about the economic situation . . ."

Panic was personified in the face and person of that individual from a nineteenth-century painting. *La Vanguardia*, once prescribed reading in any Catalan home that deserved the name, was then, as it is now, young students' usual reading matter, but in recent days he had barely glanced at it. The art of improvisation began to gather energy and Nardo Balada was awarded his final school diploma, the first in the family to get one. He would be the first tailor with a diploma.

Inertia set in after the joy brought by the diploma, and Carmen Pérez tried to persuade Nardo's father to let him continue his studies at university. More inspired by the sciences than the humanities, the universe of music and the mathematics of the family trade helped him reach a firm decision. He wanted to study engineering . . . the civil variety. University study for someone from a small town near Barcelona, and from a modest social background of honest toilers was beset by many hurdles: entry to elitist degree courses only involved entrance tests if one wasn't the son of Señor X. And that was why Nardo switched from the sitting room of his Sant Just teachers to an expensive, highly specialized academy that prepared people for civil engineering degrees. It was madness from the very first: a frenzied race to remember useless data that had to be spouted at the right moment and in the right slot. With every day that passed, Nardo arrived earlier at the tailor's: all that was a waste of time, and fate loomed inexorably. His father suggested he study anatomy, not to become a doctor but to be a good tailor, since you needed precise knowledge of the human body to design and cut cloth correctly. But music was what continued to obsess him, his lessons at the Conservatory, *Tannhäuser* echoing around his head, his dream of a life in music seemed the most beautiful challenge possible. Conversely, all that stuff about civil engineering and anatomy . . .

He was pondering such conundrums when a new bombshell hit. It came with cap and gun, high boots and marches, flags and hymns. And was delivered in a letter that bore the shield and letterhead of a barracks. It was time to go into the armed forces.

6.
Baptism Under Arms

It was the last act of blind obedience to the fatherland that a Spaniard was forced to endure in life. The first had been to go to compulsory school and ingest a big dose of dogma and creed; then one pearl remained that was fit only for the male side in every household—military conscription. Before anyone embarked on military drills, those peculiar notions of patriotic fervor and obligatory public service assumed the form of a small ball in a giant drum that was called on to draw out the fates of so many young Spaniards with a lottery ticket mind-set. The letter they received had led to several sleepless nights in the Balada household. The idea of serving the fatherland seemed like a joke in rank bad taste to a convinced anarchist. And the fact was, to rub it in, the "boy" had been eagerly attending clandestine communist meetings and scrawling slogans against the fatherland and the jackboot. Who knows, any day now he might end up in jail in Madrid's Carabanchel for a few years.

As the drum turned, Nardo discovered he had been born under a lucky star. All the postings had been covered, even those to Africa, and some balls stayed in the other drum. It meant that much to their regret some youths were surplus to requirements. It might seem incredible, but that military state was incapable of offering a military spot to every member of a generation. Nonetheless, the real meaning of that "surplus to requirements" was a mystery to all those abandoned outside the gates opened by that prize or punishment. With such a fate one might imagine being herded into a sinister truck on its way to the desert or being forced to dismantle one of the concentration camps dotted across the peninsula, or even worse, quarry stone in the Valley of the Fallen. Luckily, that phrase "surplus to requirements" hid nothing so grim. On the contrary, it was an excellent outcome from every point of view; it meant there were more soldiers than postings, and that Nardo wouldn't have to do full military service. That torture which had so tormented the Baladas morally and physically now amounted to little more than a few months of basic military training. At the end of that period those with postings would go to them and become fine, upstanding men, and those who were surplus would stay at home and become evildoers working on tasks that would undoubtedly be detrimental to the general good.

The family breathed a sigh of relief. Nardo wouldn't do military service, or at least wouldn't have to go to remote parts wearing khaki and behaving like a temporary soldier. Obviously he wouldn't be spared military indoctrination during his four months, but at least he wouldn't be a full-on conscript. He received this basic instruction in the highest, coldest place in the Seu d'Urgell, in the impenetrable depths of the Catalan Pyrenees, which meant his teeth would chatter. He went up to that spectacular, if inhospitable, terrain in the freezing January of 1954. No doubt some twenty-year-olds might greet such an experience as a challenge or adventure, but disgust at the senselessness taking him away from what he really wanted to be doing was stronger than anything else. He reached that place of natural beauty with an unusual queasiness in his stomach that provoked total collapse when he saw how those officers, so proud of their recent victorious crusade, treated everybody like lumps of walking shit. Still in civilian gear they had to stand to attention, listen to the roll call and have their first taste of military discipline. That roll call remained engraved in Balada's unconscious as a simple act in which a man bawled out a series of names and those names, reified at every second by the term of "soldier," would respond with a barely articulated grunt that was surely a rough approximation to "Present." Then came the great moment of his fictitious baptism.

"Balada, Nardo."

"Present."

"What fucking kind of name is that? Who is this individual?"

"That's me, sir."

"Don't damn well sir me! Captain!"

"Yes . . . captain."

"Come on then. Tell me what kind of name that is. Nardo. That's a mistake, isn't it? No Spaniard in this Catholic country of ours can possibly be called that. Don't you mean Leonardo?"

And understanding that was a very delicate moment that could shape the months ahead among those crags, he bit his lip and replied.

"That's right, sir, I mean, captain. Leonardo."

"That's more like it. No Nardo, no spikenard. . . . Let's try again!"

"Balada, Leonardo."

That was how Nardo Balada was renamed Leonardo Balada on both his military and subsequent national identity card. It was during that act, carried out in a ceremony in a military encampment in Seu d'Urgell, that the name in the title of this book made its first official appearance. He would continue to be Nardo or Nard to his family and childhood friends, and Leonardo or Leonard to the rest of the world. It was true enough that his strange, flowery name had already caused problems, out of lack of recognition more than anything else, even among his neighbors, so Leonardo didn't sound all that unusual to his ear, and that baptism under arms presented him with what seemed more like an artistic name.

One icy morning, a few weeks later, a different reveille rang out. They lined up outside their huts with their bedrolls and set off to climb those fearsome mountains in search of an encampment where they would bivouac and undertake various survival tests. As they stumbled up steep escarpments, they uttered every kind of curse, especially the city soldiers who couldn't imagine what the point of all that would be in the middle of the Castilian meseta or the Spanish Sahara. In one of those unfortunate sallies, Leonardo didn't manage to keep dry and caught a severe bout of pneumonia that kept him in bed for several weeks. That nasty illness led him to "enjoy" a longer stay in that place and the lung condition lingered on for months.

The military training sessions were marked out, as ever, by their extreme pointlessness and a violence that were meaningless for anyone of average intelligence and reasonably well read. The training camp was sordid, cold and poorly equipped, even for goats. Years later, when he had become a composer of international repute, Leonardo returned to that spot with his wife Joan, who described it as one of the most awful places she had ever visited. The grub was of such poor quality that the budding soldiers went hungry until the longed-for Sunday arrived, a free day when each and every one, using their own money, could eat wherever and however much they fancied. Those Sundays highlighted each individual's economic status. The best off went home, if they lived nearby, but the worst off waited for their families to appear in that fastness with tasty food, medicine, and news of home, friends and fiancées. As the journey to Sant Just was difficult, Leonardo spent the money he had on a good meal in a local restaurant to build his strength and not feel so famished during the week.

As if his start, baptism included, hadn't been eventful enough, he now received a summons to the final examinations at the Conservatory. They marked the end of a cycle of musical education that had brought Nardo considerable knowledge of the piano, a course in notation and theory with a final examination in order to receive a diploma, and an extensive introduction to harmony and counterpoint. All that knowledge had begun to forge his creative appetite, prompting his first forays in a career as a composer that began there, between dead time and musical imaginings. His final studies at the Conservatoire inspired him to compose the occasional piano piece in Haydn mode with a hint of Mozart. Those first works, now only the fruit of memory, satisfied the deep need to create that was growing within Balada. His style might be closer to Beethoven or Haydn than to Wagner or Liszt, but at any rate it was a door open to communication. Some restless nights caught him sketching a movement for a sonata that stirred his soul for a while. That summons to the final tests at the Liceu made him pluck up the courage to ask for special permission to take leave of absence from the camp and bring those studies to a proper conclusion. Of course, his exchange with the captain was a happening in itself, since it wasn't usual for a conscript to ask for leave in the middle of training to face a series of examinations at a musical conservatory.

In any case, bright young Leonardo Balada returned to his beloved Barcelona, hair cropped and hopes intact. The Conservatory bid him farewell with the diplomas bestowed by those examinations, after infecting that youngster who was or wasn't to be a tailor with the benign virus of music. And as everything must come to an end, Leonardo had been confirmed surplus to military requirements and could complete his musical studies for a time while he did his duty in respect of the fatherland. A lot had happened in the course of those months. He had been given a new name in Seu d'Urgell, and his brother had been born;[1] he had qualified as a musician and been spared full-blooded conscription. But there was a dark side to his encampment in the mountains: it left him with a health problem that almost killed off his dreams soon after, when the opportunity of a lifetime dropped by the tailor's shop on Carrer Pelai to have a suit made.

1   Elíseo Balada Ibáñez was born September 25, 1953, sometime before Leonardo had to go to do his military duty.

Nardo Balada at the end of the 1940s

7.
From Happenstance to Happening

There is no doubt that life can take us along strange paths, sometimes slippery ones that may confront us with reality and enable us to change the "inevitable" course of events. This happened one morning when an elegant, eloquent gentleman with a fat wallet walked into the brand-new Balada tailor's establishment. It was a musician who had come to the calle Pelayo shop on the express recommendation of a regular customer also connected to the art of music, Arturo Menéndez Alexyandre.[1] The latter was a critic who wrote for *Ritmo* magazine and *La Vanguardia* among others, with the byline of those two curious surnames. The person he had recommended went by the name of Jean Redd, a man who soon became a main player in a great leap forward in the young musician's career. As he was there to order a bespoke suit, the pianist followed the shop's usual routine: measurements were taken, cloth was chosen, a style was defined. It was a brief period of time usually filled with exchanges that were banal, if not plain stupid. It's so hot, isn't it. . . . In my day it used to snow a lot more. . . . Barça is playing incredibly badly this year. However, on that occasion the conversation took a different, unexpected turn. The pianist saw Leonardo completing his tasks in the tailor's and asked what he was studying. Although into his twenties by now, Balada still looked like a youngster fresh out of high school. His replies kept coming until their exchanges focused on the subject of his piano playing. And that was when *the* big question was asked: "So what kind of work would you like to do?"

---

1   Arturo Menéndez Aleyxandre gave his byline to several reviews of Balada's work. A case in point was one published March 7, 1967 by *La Vanguardia* on the occasion of the European premiere of the *Sonata for Violin and Piano* (1960) launched with the title of *Sonata in Four Parts* and performed by Xavier Turull and Ángel Soler in the *Art i Cultura* program of concerts held in the Balmes School in Barcelona. The review was full of praise.

That question which Leonardo had asked himself so often when he was engrossed in his own thoughts struck him like a bolt out of the blue. Looking at his father out of the corner of an eye and knowing full well that once he finished his degree course and musical studies his future was tied to rolls of cloth and scissors, he replied, "I would like to be a composer."

His response wasn't laughed out of court as a young man's fantasy but met his father's eternal smile and the musician's thoughtful silence. Apparently, Jean Redd was a cousin of Menéndez Aleyxandre and taught piano in New York, and consequently the possibility existed that Balada might be able to apply for a scholarship that would allow him to study there and not be short of cash. It was left to the critic and regular customer at the tailor's, Menéndez Aleyxandre, to negotiate a possible scholarship from Spain.

That chance encounter now obsessed young Nardo, who stoically rode out his natural panic at the unknown and began to organize a dream that had become real, so his dreams could take off as soon as possible. Thanks to two of his father's customers, happenstance had led to a new reality, a reality that would change the way he lived, saw and felt. Up to that point his flirtations with staves had been vague: rough starts to a sonata he was working on, that owed too much to his environment or the last work he had listened to, but that might be the start to his life as an artist and the end of a cycle to which he had been sentenced by chance, or it might not. . . .

The bureaucracy quickly got to work. It was crucial to have an invitation that came directly from the United States, and that was hardly a problem given the family connections between music critic and pianist. Secondly, he needed a grant that would give the budding composer some income and make it easier for him to leave the country: that detail clouded everything considerably. The prospect of students leaving Spain in the early fifties, when the country was stuck in an economic situation worse than under the Republic, was as unlikely as fishing tuna out of a river. The key to the door came from the Foundation for Foreign Students that gave him access to a fixed study grant. That American institution, a feature of the United States' self-interested relationship with Spain, appeared at the right time, in the right place, for the right person. The last hurdle seemed the simplest, a positive medical report that would allow him to depart to the city of skyscrapers.

When everything for the trip was all set, a jug of cold water was thrown in his face. The medical report noted that Leonardo was still suffering from a respiratory illness that might prevent him from getting that certificate of good health. The wretched pneumonia from Seu d'Urgell had effected his pleura and needed lengthy treatment, a radically different diagnosis to the one given in that encampment where it had been dubbed a common cold. He was incredibly disappointed. He would have to wait a

The Orfeó Enric Morera, Sant Just, 1952

year until he was completely cured and then make a fresh start on all the preparations that would make a composer of him.

It was a strange period. There were days when his dream seemed remote and quite out of reach, while on others euphoria made him want to walk into the street and shout with joy. They were gray, leaden days, that drifted by, marked out on the calendar with a single date in his mind and an end in sight on the horizon, the day he would climb into an airplane and be transformed into what he wanted to be: a composer. Despite everything, that wait was important for Leonardo's intellectual development. In Barcelona and Sant Just, he began to make his first tentative steps as a composer and became involved in the most select alternative artistic circles. He and several friends joined the only choir in the town, the Orfeó Enric Morera,[2] where he had his first contact with Catalan folklore in Morera's versions, as well as the usual predictable repertoire. Leonardo alternated the roles of second tenor and pianist in the group's performances. That opportunity to use his voice sowed a very important seed that grew over time and which today makes him one of the few contemporary composers who really understand and write with a deep knowledge of the human voice.

As well as participating in cultural life in Sant Just, Balada started to rub shoulders with individuals active in Barcelona's cultural scene. He frequently participated in café discussions, went to exhibitions, concerts and lectures where some of Leonardo's finest friendships took root. In the course of those café conversations, he met Alfonso Mier,[3] a painter with a

2   The Orfeó Enric Morera was established in 1951 and was funded by the Athenaeum in Sant Just. Leonardo was one of the first members to be part of the group conducted by Pere Mañé.
3   Much older than Balada, Alfonso Mier, born in Barcelona in 1912, began to paint in a Mediterra-

very individual style within the diffuse boundaries of Catalan informalism in the middle of the 20th century; Mier had participated in the famous Vienna Biennale and the International Exhibition in Pittsburgh, in the early fifties, and soon became a very close friend. His visually striking work, with its primitivist tendencies, showed him to be an intense, lively, genuine artist. Some books on the aesthetics of painting portray him as one of the fathers of three-dimensional art, though in the end the country's moral and physical poverty hampered him to such an extent he had to work as a full-time artisan and be a painter in his spare time. The Baladas own two exceptional Mier paintings that he gave them as wedding presents. Little remains of Mier, except for the admiration of those who knew him as an individual and an artist, and a handful of articles, one of which is high-lighted, written by Juan Eduardo Cirlot[4] in *Papeles de Son Armadans* that introduces a figure who was to be very important on the artistic journey undertaken by Balada: Camilo José Cela, the journal's editor.

The charming Paco Rebés[5] also moved in these circles, sweet-talking and cracking jokes, a personal friend of many great Spanish painters and whose prestige, gave him carte blanche to travel the world exhibiting and discovering stars. It wouldn't be strange for Rebés to talk in those meetings of his friendships with Pablo Picasso or Salvador Dalí. He was someone with an extraordinary artistic culture, and although he tended to be swept away by dreams and eternal projects that often came to nothing, Rebés was one of those intellectual activists who was always cordial and well-man-nered. In Mier's house he also met Josep Cercós,[6] a renowned composer in Barcelona in the early fifties, who invited him to attend concerts at the Círculo Manuel de Falla,[7] that had been encouraging contemporary music in the city from 1947. In that small room in Plaza Cataluña, Balada also

nean impressionist style, but from 1953—the years when they started to interact—he embarked on a period of greater abstraction that, as Lourdes Cirlot notes in her book, *La pintura informal en Cataluña 1951-1970*, led him to show ". . . a special interest in emphasising the impact of thick layers of paint . . ." Then from 1957 he made a big aesthetic leap, practically abandoning figurative painting and dramatically reducing his chromatic range.

4   Cirlot, Juan Eduardo, "Evolución de Alfonso Mier," *Papeles de Son Armadans*, XXVII, p. 349.
5   Francisco Rebés discovered La Chungla and La Singla, among others, and was very knowledge-able and active in the worlds of music, film and advertising.
6   Josep Cercós i Fransí (1925-1989), is a composer difficult to locate aesthetically, as he cultivated both traditional and avant-garde tendencies. He was very important in Barcelona in the 1960s as a composer and researcher.
7   A musical response to the aesthetic awakening experienced in Barcelona towards the end of the forties, the Círculo Manuel de Falla was founded in 1947 with the help of the Institut Français by Albert Blancafort, Juan Eduardo Cirlot, Ángel Cerdà and Joan Comellas who were soon joined by other important composers, musicologists and musicians. There is a crucial book that describes the

met Xavier Montsalvatge,[8] Manuel Valls[9] and Ángel Cerdà among others. This period was very important for the shaping of the young composer's aesthetics. Every night added to his creative perceptions, as he discarded some tendencies and embraced others.

Balada eagerly grabbed the medical report confirming his good health, as you do when you have been forced to wait. On March 3, 1956 Leonardo Balada arrived at the airport with one trunk full of clothes suitable for all occasions—as to be expected coming from where he did—and a lighter one, packed with high hopes and euphoria. Even so, that rush of adrenalin didn't make him underestimate a step that was going to change his life completely. Leaving behind his home which offered him a comfortable, if gray, future, New York, seen from Sant Just, was clearly only a short trip from Mars and was one vertiginous leap. He would now be launched into a society where individual freedoms were valued above collective freedoms, where a new language was spoken and different values were accorded to things. On the days

Llúcia Ibáñez and Josep Balada, in the 1950s

before he embarked on his great journey into the unknown, father and son talked about the society he could expect to find. An individualist society dominated by fierce liberalism where almost nobody thought about anyone else but themselves. The sentiments taught in Ferrer's Modern School indicated that a human being was all the better, the more he or she

---

impact of this pioneering avant-garde music group in Barcelona: Miquel Alsina, *Cercle de Manuel de Falla de Barcelona: L'obra musical i el seu context*. Institut d'Estudis Ilerdencs, Lleida. 2007.

8   Balada always had a close, respectful relationship with Xavier Montsalvatge (1912-2002) based on healthy mutual admiration. When Montsalvatge retired from his post as a teacher of composition at the Barcelona Municipal Conservatory, Balada was on the point of returning to Spain for good to replace the deceased composer.

9   Manuel Valls i Gorina brought a humanist background to the incipient aesthetic adventures of those years and is a figure of great interest for any study of that moment of cultural renaissance.

Nardo, his grandmother and
brother Elíseo in 1955

could project themselves on others and apply a natural sense of ethics. Be distinct, flee from the obvious, and be different to everyone else.

It was as if two trains careering at a dizzy speed were on course to crash. He was going to make the leap from a city where time passed slowly to one where lack of space meant that people lived and worked always on high. Those ethical conflicts intensified as the abyss between both societies became more and more patent. The anarchist patina, sense of social justice and the common good remained intact and permanently flowed into his creative projects and his reading of society when facing the realities of North American society. This is no mere anecdotal detail because it has meant that Balada is considered to be a European composer in the United States, not so much because of his sound or aesthetic aims as for the inspiration behind his musical thinking. That huge leap assumed a big effort, a revolution promising blood and fire that could as easily destroy him as make him invincible. That random train was only going to pass once through the station of his life, and he would have to appear in the media and create work that would be a source of pride for all those who had put their trust in him. When he started walking up the stairs to the airplane, he could hardly imagine he wouldn't be back for four years: he could only think about returning as a fully fledged composer.

A large number of friends came to the airport to do the honors for their distinguished colleague who was departing to the great beyond on an astonishing adventure. The four-engine plane took off with all manner of creaks and squeaks, while Leonardo daydreamed and adapted to that cubicle which was to be his home for twenty hours of purring engines and turbulence. The plane touched down in Lisbon, hours later, in the Azores and then in Canada before entering the United States via Boston, finally reaching New York's International Airport shrouded in mist. When he stepped on land, it was March 4 and it had taken twenty-three hours to come from home, a place that already seemed remote although its smell still lingered on his clothes. It was a new beginning, the beginning of a new life. Leonardo Balada, like a modern-day Christopher Columbus, now stepped out on American soil. He only had one mission in that life, to succeed, whatever it took.

8.
Working in the Dark

The first English word Leonardo understood and felt fully in his flesh was "jet lag." Like the walking dead, he gathered up his belongings in Idlewild International Airport[1] and thought of the name of the teacher who had enabled him to realize his dreams, to come that far without really knowing him: Jean Redd. His house was on the West Side of Manhattan, close to Columbia University, though he taught piano at the Manhattan School of Music. The distinguished teacher welcomed Leonardo with all kinds of presents. A friendly face is always a boon for someone arriving in a strange place. Redd's large house was divided into small apartments that he rented out to other students who thus enjoyed the privacy of a private abode within a space that was similar to a residence. Leonardo's stay there was covered by the grant from the foundation, that also supplied a dollar a day for living expenses. When they had done their sums in Sant Just, he and his family had concluded that he could live fairly comfortably on that amount. He was surprised when he stepped into the street and saw that New York prices weren't Spanish prices. Everything was four times more expensive than any shop back home, so that dollar was practically symbolic and only enough to eat meagerly once a day.

Jean Redd was an extrovert, and evidently not short of money or love for Spain. He went to Europe every summer and wouldn't return until mid-October. He met his fiancée and later wife, Margarita, a native of Elche, on one of those trips. That partly explained his generosity towards Leonardo who must have brought back memories of the Mediterranean. After recovering the hours of sleep he had lost on his long flight, Leonardo's next step was to sort out his status as a student. He first went to

---

1   Completed in 1949, that airport is now the JFK International Airport.

the Manhattan School of Music, that was then located on the East Side and considered to be a highly prestigious academic center. That space for learning, so unlike dusty, shabby, Spanish classrooms, allowed him to take his first steps in the complex, idiosyncratic world of American universities.

The first point of tension was Leonardo's *de facto* inability to communicate. His knowledge of English had been gleaned from a handful of classes during his last years at school and some poorly managed attempts to learn in the months before he set out to conquer America. Things soon changed with immersion. He progressed from laborious, ungrammatical sentences he worked out in his head to an everyday, supple use of the language, distinguished by his accent and bass tone of voice, which initiated the young student into a period when he was virtually working in the dark.

His first day at the university was full of expectation. After waiting so long, he now walked into the composition class at Manhattan School with high hopes. It was mid–March 1956, the final half of the academic year and, for him, the beginning. Sitting at one of those desks, that seemed so alien, as he hadn't been inside a conventional classroom since leaving the girls' school in Sant Just, he began by adopting that famous maxim from his military training days: go unnoticed. He didn't look like a typical foreigner, let alone a typical Spaniard. He didn't wear a bullfighter's cap and had left his wide-brimmed Cordoban hat on his donkey next to his musket and water pitcher. He was carrying his first compositions, that he had managed to find and pack into a folder he had carefully secured. Nardo thought they would be his best introduction and would open many doors; not for nothing had he come from old Europe, the land of Monteverdi, Mozart, Beethoven, Chopin and Ravel, the continent of music as an aesthetic art. He dressed elegantly, as was the style then, in a made-to-measure suit and a simply knotted tie he accompanied with a smile. He didn't stand out from the rest of the students. Slim, with his white complexion, bright eyes and gleaming teeth, he belied his foreign extraction, and the other students assumed he must be a latecomer with a good reason to be arriving near the end of the course.

The class began. Nicolas Flagello (1928-1994), a well-known composer and teacher stood in front of the lined blackboard and started speaking at a devilish rate, mixing musical terms with resonant onomatopoeias and clichés. It was a group composition class! Leonardo barely understood a dozen words in those first fifty minutes of class, and didn't even get the *tiara-tiara*, or the *ninonani-ninonana*. How could you learn composition in a group class? Was it possible to impart general notions about how to compose without worrying about each individual's thought patterns and sensibility?

He waited a week for the individual class when he could introduce himself to Flagello or Vittorio Giannini (1903-1966), who was the other departmental teacher who wandered down the corridors in a daze. But it never happened. If he could learn to speak and understand the English language over the next few months, he would be more than happy. The end of the year came and he was still at sea. It was the middle of May and he was just starting to get the hang of life in that hall of learning. Regrettably, in two months he had produced nothing, which meant the Manhattan School refused to let him come back the next year. Surprisingly, that was one of the best pieces of news he could have hoped for. He was released from the nightmare of those group composition classes and it was time to look for something more in line with his idea of what a composition class should be like. Around that time, Redd filled his lobby with suitcases, said he was off to Europe and asked Leonardo to look after the house and collect the rent from his tenants. Suddenly, he had slightly more cash in his pocket, almost a whole house to himself and a bad attack of nostalgia. Some people were so lucky!

Letters to and from his family traveled cheerfully from both sides of the Atlantic. As one flew home, another crossed its path and more then flowed from the pens of Nardo and his father. There was so much to recount and to learn on each street corner, that the pangs of nostalgia lasted only a few moments every night before fading into the sweet sleep brought on by exhaustion. Nardo had a whole summer to plan his next year of study and gave himself one target: to find a prestigious university with renowned teachers and an individual-centered pedagogy that would enable him to mine all that music that was still bubbling in a mineral state in his mind and only waiting for the right encounters to be cut and polished. That summer he drew on the companionship of the painter Josep Benet, a classically focused artist, who was convinced of the excellence of representational art, and a serious professional. They saw each other a lot in the humid heat that was so reminiscent of Barcelona.

After taking the pulse of all manner of institution, he found what he wanted in the New York College of Music. It was a well-known center that prided itself on its distinguished teachers and fine reputation in the city's musical circles. The presence of foreign students brought prestige to the institution, so Leonardo met no hurdles when he crossed its threshold.

What promised to be an exciting year of study finally began in August. He spent the rest of the summer sending out those letters of recommendation from Barcelona that would open the doors of Spanish households in New York. Most of them bore fruit immediately and Leonardo recovered a sense of homeliness and intellectual engagement that had been sidelined during that period when he had been working in the dark. He began to forge a series of close friendships that filled his afternoons and evenings with conversations, meals and partying.

In any case, despite all the external support, Balada's real passion was focused on learning from everything and everybody, and starting at the New York College of Music was much more than a simple challenge.

Balada in New York, 1958

It was the end of August 1956, and the humid heat in Manhattan was still sticky, making you want to live on ice creams and cold drinks, but the academic year was about to begin, and Erich Katz fired the starting pistol.[2] Leonardo felt at ease in those new corridors, both well treated and able to become involved. Classes were individual, which was much better for his now fluent English, but above all for what he understood as musical creativity. Katz was a serious, hardworking, demanding teacher, who laid the formal and stylistic foundations essential for any would-be composer. Anything that Leonardo didn't understand, he worked on and fathomed out enthusiastically, wrestling with it tirelessly. When it wasn't yet time to harvest fruit, but still to sow on fertile ground, his grant of a dollar a day came to an end. He had forgotten that his stipend only covered a year. He had been so busy tackling those new challenges that

---

2 Erich Katz (1900-1973) was one of many musicians who, in flight from Nazi terror, left the Germany of their birth; he first went to the United Kingdom (1939) before landing in New York in 1943. A doctor in Musicology and a music and organ teacher, he taught at the New York College of Music from 1944 to 1959.

66

On the campus of Columbia
University, summer of 1956

he hadn't noticed he had been in
the United States for over three
hundred days. The Founda-
tion grant had run out and that
meant he would have to pack his
bags and return home.

He really wanted to hug
his parents and little brother
Elíseo, who by then must have
been running happily around
the yard, but before he started
on the torture of packing everything back in his trunks, he
was invited to a party held in
the house of another of New
York's exiled painters. Josep
Bartolí was a man with very
well-defined ideas, that had
clashed with the political, social
and cultural ethos of post-war
Spain. His expressionist work
explored paths that would
hardly be accommodated within
that system, so he had settled down comfortably in New York.[3] When
Leonardo entered his house, Jaume Miravitlles, Carles Fontserè or José
de Creeft[4] would already be there, among others, whom he had met only
recently as a result of his letters of recommendation or one of the monthly

3 Josep Bartolí (1910-1955), painter, set designer and cartoonist, left Barcelona and went into exile
in France in 1939; he spent time in several concentration camps, including Dachau which he survived
by jumping from the train transporting him to be exterminated. He traveled across a good stretch
of the Americas, settled down in Mexico, before finally moving to New York in 1947, though he
didn't receive U.S. citizenship until 1962. His professional activity encompassed cartoons (Holyday)
and a relationship with members of the painting group, the 10th or the New York School, formed by
Franz Kline and Jackson Pollock among others. He was awarded the Mark Rothko Foundation Prize
in 1973. He returned to Barcelona in 1977 and continued to appear on the occasion of a number of
exhibitions. He died in New York at the age of 85.
4 José de Creeft (1884-1982), a sculptor born in Guadalajara (Spain), was a self-taught man and
began his artistic career paying his way by making figures for Christmas cribs. His friendship with
Rodin brought him to France to learn his art. He settled in the U.S.A. for good in 1929, and only
applied for U.S. citizenship after the Spanish civil war in 1940. He is the creator of the famous group
of sculptures devoted to Alice in Wonderland in Central Park, New York.

interviews he had done for a Spanish magazine to bring in a little money. However, what impressed him most in that meeting of friends wasn't the pleasure at being able to speak his own language, or even enjoying the stories told by Miravitlles or Dalí's witticisms, but his conversation with Bartolí's wife, a beautiful, very young American, and a painter to boot, who reignited Leonardo's hopes. Michelle Stuart was[5] the one responsible for the fact that Balada applied to renew his

Working with José de Creeft on the *Temas* magazine

grant the next day, something that was ratified shortly after. Her conversation with Balada that night was providential and it was with gratitude to her that Balada was able to face the challenge of a second year in New York with some financial support.

He studied that year (1957-1958) with the Jewish German composer Siegfried Landau,[6] who, as well as being a thoughtful composer, had founded the Brooklyn Philharmonic Orchestra[7] around that time. Both Katz and Landau taught him to work in a very precise, detailed fashion, and pay careful attention to sound and structure; they always emphasized the need to control the quality of everything that you did, whether it was on

---

5   Michelle Stuart (1938) is one of the most important living American painters. She married Josep Bartolí in 1953 and collaborated with him in the explosion of material art and abstract expressionism. A pioneer of organic art, she has also been a leading activist on behalf of the female artistic presence in the world. Her relationship with Bartolí ended in his own words "in order to be able to fly and let the other fly . . ." Michelle Stuart and Leonardo Balada are still friends.

6   Siegfried Landau was born in 1921 in Berlin where his father was a rabbi. His family emigrated to England in 1939 and the young musician moved to New York the following year. He became a teacher at the New York College of Music in 1943. He also taught Jewish theology and was musical director at one of New York's most important synagogues, the Shearith Israel. He also conducted the Westchester Symphony Orchestra. He died in 2007 when his house in northern New York State was burned down.

7   It was actually called the Brooklyn Philharmonia when it was founded and Landau was its conductor until 1971 when Lukas Foss took over. The orchestra was made up of various musicians living in the New York area and from the start specialized in contemporary repertoires or music that was little played, which gave it a complex, distinct character in a city like New York.

the grand scale or a small exercise in harmony. It was a particularly sensitive approach and had an extraordinary impact on his future way of working.

Like all energetic souls, Landau also led a choir that complemented the musical offerings in the neighborhood, in addition to teaching his classes and conducting his orchestra. One morning Landau suggested to Balada that he could accompany the choir in rehearsal. Leonardo's teacher was familiar with his student's high level of performance on the piano, and assured him that that work would help him to learn one of the most important acts that every resourceful composer must feel he can express in his style: the rhythm of human breathing. It was customary, even more so in those times that were aesthetically marked by the now moribund neoclassicism à la Stravinsky, for compositions for instrumental groups to be dominated by long, complicated melodic developments, and that concealed a major problem: the absence of musical breath. It was essential to apply the tempo of human breathing to every kind of composition, independently of whether performance was conceived for violin, piano, flute, or voice. If audiences were able to feel the breath of the music within their own, it would ensure a degree of emotional and physical involvement with the new work that would guarantee intelligibility, whatever the language used. And that lesson could be learned, according to Professor Landau, by accompanying choirs and solo singers and taking heed of their tempi and breathing. Although the intellectual benefits looked promising, that occupation, if not employment, was seriously exhausting because of the long rehearsal sessions and there was no financial gain, even if he soon learned his lesson well. That was when one of the most significant elements in Balada's musical style was born: he is one of the few contemporary composers who has been able to apply human breathing to every one of his works, for voice but, most of all, for orchestra. Today he is undoubtedly a reference point as a maestro in the enigma of establishing a bond with audiences. But one evening Leonardo finally threw his jacket over his shoulder and came out with the classic cry of "Enough is enough." He was aware late in 1958 that the end of his participation in the choir was equally the end of his endeavors in that university.

That summer was another time for quick, vital decisions. He was two years away from finishing his degree, but could feel the desire to return home beating stronger by the day. Partly guided by his teachers and partly pulled by his natural attraction to excellence, he opted to finish his degree studies in the most prestigious musical institution in the world, The Juilliard School of Music. Once he had matriculated, without a grant as yet but retaining his status as a foreign student in the country, he began to bolster his precarious finances with written and musical collaborations in various performance spaces and institutions, and all that left him with something to send home every so often, which gained fourfold in value by virtue of the exchange rate. Times weren't good for the Baladas in Sant Just. The regime was deeply entrenched and thanks to U.S. help the economy was bearing up despite the reek of corruption. The family wasn't exactly flush and Leonardo's dispatches of dollars expanded exponentially back home. Realizing that the well-being of his parents and brother might depend on his success, Leonardo went after perfection and the prestige of an educational space like Juilliard. His fingertips now touched the heavenly cusp of world music in its former site on Claremont Avenue.

The list of names at Juilliard took your breath away. The names of the best teachers in every area dotted the doors along those long corridors and most were foreigners who had found refuge from the Second World War in the United States and had stayed on. Balada's composition teacher in his first year at Juilliard was Bernard Wagenaar (1894-1971), an elderly Dutchman, whose father, Johan Wagenaar, had also been a distinguished composer. It was a long, stimulating year, though Wagenaar was much less demanding than Katz or Landau in his composition classes. But everything has its pros and cons and the Juilliard system introduced a distinct element: musical analysis. That was a window wide open on to a new world that was unknown to Leonardo. Delving into the structural techniques of the most important composers who had ever lived, was a way to learn how to compose in every style and era from the inside, as if you were accompanying every creator in their creations. He finished his final year with one of the school's most brilliant stars and one of the finest teachers of musical composition in the twentieth century, Vincent Persichetti (1915-1987). The aesthetic orbit of Juilliard was relatively conservative, as a result of the average age of its staff. Late-Romantic style predominated with a few neo-classical forays, but the presence of twelve-tone techniques had gradually become more visible and, though the renowned professors saw Schönberg almost as their contemporary, the serial approach was gaining ground by leaps and bounds every year in the composition curriculum. These were years of transition for Juilliard as an elderly distinguished professorate gave way to a younger, more modern generation. And by the sixties they would become years with a single aesthetic way of thought as the mathematical serial system

Aaron Copland, a photo dedicated to Balada, 1959

triumphed in the classrooms, with its scientific codifying that was much easier to explain than the previous more humanistic style. Balada still drank from the wellsprings of intuitive creativity and their spirit remained in his style forever, even though over time his own nature led him into the camp of the extreme avant-garde.

However, Leonardo didn't simply leave Juilliard with a diploma in composition under his arm. He simultaneously attended courses in Tanglewood, where he met and learned from Aaron Copland (1900-1990) among others. He attended the maestro's classes there as a private, non-paying, student, that soon after continued in Copland's house. As things were tight, Balada accepted a job as a monitor in a summer camp near the festival. When it was his day off, Balada hitchhiked to Copland's classes.

JUILLIARD SCHOOL OF MUSIC

THIS IS TO CERTIFY THAT

Leonardo Balada

HAS COMPLETED THE GRADUATION REQUIREMENTS FOR THE DIPLOMA COURSE IN

COMPOSITION

IN WITNESS WHEREOF, WE HAVE CAUSED THIS DIPLOMA TO BE SIGNED BY THE PRESIDENT OF JUILLIARD SCHOOL OF MUSIC AND OUR CORPORATE SEAL TO BE HEREUNTO AFFIXED AND ATTESTED BY THE SECRETARY IN THE CITY OF NEW YORK, ON THE TWENTY-SEVENTH DAY OF MAY, IN THE YEAR OF OUR LORD ONE THOUSAND NINE HUNDRED AND SIXTY.

ATTEST

SECRETARY

DEAN

PRESIDENT

Juilliard Diploma in Composition, 1960

Leonardo Balada had succeeded in fulfilling his dreams and had overcome all the hurdles of a fate that had once pointed to a different kind of toil.

By the end of spring 1960, Balada was a composer with solid foundations. His first works could be heard in concert halls and he felt he had realized his longings. He wasn't going to be a tailor. On May 27, 1960, Leonardo Balada was awarded his university diploma in composition from The Juilliard School of Music; his education had been crowned with success and now came the most complicated part—applying all that knowledge to effective creations. Contrary to what one might imagine, Balada's catalogue had already begun to grow at Juilliard with works that had a striking individuality. He was about to reach his twenty-seventh birthday, and his path through life had brought him a series of elements that few of his graduate peers could rival. The son of an anarchist, fated to be a tailor, he had now qualified as a composer.

9.
Elective Affinities

When he first arrived in New York, Nardo Balada carried an additional burden from Barcelona. Many friendships had been fractured by war and exile and it was hardly surprising if each journey by an acquaintance or relative, be it to France, England or America, stirred old memories in individuals looking for a contact to take news to friends and family. That was why Balada left for New York with a bundle of letters of recommendation that promised to open doors to the homes of some of the most distinguished exiles living in the Big Apple. All those who have traveled to foreign parts because of life's demands rather than tourist reasons have experienced that dark sense of emptiness entering the pores of the skin when we find ourselves alone on those first nights. That deep sense of bereftness is the first great incentive to make the effort to achieving one's aims. Clearly, Balada didn't let himself be daunted by those first moments of absolute vulnerability and soon began to seek out what Goethe called "elective affinities" among the crowds and skyscrapers, that group of individuals who humanly and intellectually become family and close support in any heaven or hell. What is called "real friends" is an ambiguous concept that is difficult to break down when speaking

The Spanish Center in New York.
Photo by Carlos Fontserè

of places that are alien to one's own culture, and thus it is quite normal for the process of a search for compatriots to be generated in any emigrant community.

The Spanish community in New York was clearly marked by the war. Almost all those who had left the frontiers of the extinct Spanish republic had stopped over in Mexico, then left definitively for the streets of New York where they settled down and waited to complete their anabasis and return home. Mid-fifties New York wasn't the melting pot of races and languages that it is today. The percentage of Asians and European didn't pass 3 percent in what was an overwhelmingly white population. The Spanish presence in New York dated from the middle of the nineteenth century when merchant ships anchored in the Hudson River and their occupants ended up in the streets mostly to the southwest of Manhattan. The small Spanish colony developed between 12th and 14th Streets and reached its zenith in the fifties. It included a concentration of shops selling Spanish products, restaurants, the famous Casa Moneo,[1] La Sociedad Española la Nacional and the Iglesia de Nuestra Señora de Guadalupe,[2] that also had Spanish priests who were exiles to boot. As for the Catalan presence, that was more distinctive than other Spanish nationalities in the city, it had its own base, the Centre Català, located on 19th Street.

One of the first letters Leonardo decided to deliver was addressed to a renowned politician from the Second Republic who for obvious reasons had had to go into exile making all the usual detours in order to escape Francoist repression. He reached the United States in the middle of 1940 and always retained his function as a point of contact with the government of the Second Republic. He was rather more than a myth, despite having been a leading left-wing Catalan nationalist and member of Esquerra Republicana de Catalunya from 1934. He had been a key player in anarchist activity as a result of his ideological position: witness his participation in the 1925 attempt on the life of Alfonso XIII and later, in an invasion of Catalonia. Jaume Miravitlles, Met to his friends,[3] was undoubtedly one of

---

1   The Casa Moneo was founded in 1929 in what was known as "little Spain" by Carmen Barañano and her husband, Jesús Moneo. It was a small grocery store, the only place to find all manner of Spanish products. It was a meeting point for Basque residents in New York.
2   The Iglesia de Nuestra Señora de Guadalupe is situated between 229 West and 14th. It was built in 1902 and its baroque façade is the religious center for all Spanish and Hispanic Catholics in Manhattan.
3   Jaume Miravitlles i Navarra (1906-1988) was imprisoned during the dictatorship of Miguel Primo de Rivera. Subsequently, exiled in Paris, he began his creative work as a writer and sporadically as an actor in *Un perro andaluz* (1929)—where he appeared next to Dalí alongside that piano that's

From left to right, Carles Fontserè, Maruja Pintado, Jaume Miravitlles and Sofía Alberti, in the 1950s

those individuals who put their mark on an era and always wrote positively about them. André Malraux christened him "the smile of the Republic." The Generalitat de Catalunya's Public Relations chief, Miravitlles was the way of entry into the best there was in New York.

He had an office at 11 Broadway, on Wall Street, in the hub of the city's business world. He wrote from there for the *Spanish Information Bulletin* published by the republican government exiled in Mexico. He was handsome, always energetic and cheerful, with a character that could be overwhelming. He was married to Maruja Pintado, from Salamanca, famed for her extraordinary beauty, and that was quite paradoxical for such a Catalan nationalist. Met wrote for various newspapers and magazines that showed him to be a first-rate writer. Right from the start Leonardo didn't hesitate to ask him for help in correcting and fine-tuning some of the articles he was writing to earn money. Apart from writing, Miravitlles devoted his office hours to a rather peculiar occupation with a dubious legal status: he exchanged money. Some years previously he had established Interchange Corporation, a front to allow Spanish workers to change the dollars they earned on the black market into pesetas that they sent to

Carles Fontserè and Jaume Miravitlles

being dragged along. He was the Generalitat's Commissar for Propaganda during the civil war. He then went into exile in Paris and Mexico before heading for New York, where he stayed until 1963, the year in which he returned to Spain. He wrote more than a dozen books, most of which are political in character. He was awarded the Josep Pla Prize in 1981 for *Gent que he conegut* (*People I Have Known*) published in 1981.

their families in Spain. That business activity led Met Miravitlles to abandon his brand-new office at 1475 Broadway for the one much more to the south.

Miravitlles was a close, lifelong friend to Balada. Being able to speak Catalan among those skyscrapers was a victory over the cultural castration exercised by Spanish nationalists. Years later Miravitlles was a witness at Balada's wedding and, later, an individual who was unusually influential on the course of his life. Jaume Miravitlles returned to Spain in 1963, much to the surprise of his close republican friends. Once there, the gentleman's agreement he signed meant he had to avoid expressing any opinions about the Spanish civil war, which can't have been easy. Miravitlles must have had a good reason to act like that, since, as Balada remembers him, Met was a great conversationalist who would speak about politics and Catalan traditions as gleefully as about a young woman who happened to walk down the street. In the book of essays, *La revolució de bon gust. Jaume Miravitlles i el Comissariat de Propaganda de la Generalitat de Catalunya (1936-1939)*, there is speculation about the possibility that Miravitlles might have signed an unofficial agreement with Francoist Minister, Manuel Fraga, the terms of which meant that the Catalan could return home provided he didn't enter politics, even at the level of talk. Miravitlles wrote two books of memoirs that focused on the people he had known, the first of which was awarded the Josep Pla Prize. Regrettably, neither mentions Balada, though in subsequent conversations Miravitlles told the composer he was writing a third volume where he would.

Miravitlles and a letter of recommendation from a cousin who was a journalist on *La Vanguardia* concluded the magic trio of Barcelonan elective affinities in New York with a stop on Fifth Avenue. The last link was Carles Fontserè.[4] Photographer, poster designer, décor expert and comics illustrator to keep hunger at bay, Fontserè is undoubtedly Leonardo Balada's alter ego. Despite an age difference of seventeen years, they were close friends from the start. Thanks to his connections with Miravitlles, Fontserè had been active drawing posters for the CNT-FAI during the civil war,

---

4 Carles Fontserè's importance in Balada's life will become clear over the next few pages, but we will note a few facts about him here. He was born in Barcelona in 1916 and his first artistic ventures were linked to anarchist posters issued during the Second Republic. He followed a similar path to most exiles, France, Mexico and the United States. He worked designing cinema posters, as a magazine photographer and a comics illustrator. He returned to Spain in 1973 and settled in Girona. He died in January 2017. He became known over recent years for his activism in the campaign to get the so-called *Papeles de Salamanca* returned to Catalonia, as he himself had lost the originals for his own posters to the Archive of the Civil War in Salamanca.

Fontserè with Cantinflas and Gelman

which influenced him ideologically and meant he was
forced into exile. Francesc
Fontserè, his brother, had
been active in the defense of
Barcelona and years later he
too became a close friend of
Leonardo Balada's from his
post as a university lecturer
also in New York. Carles had
first gone into exile in Paris,
where he worked on numer-
ous fronts as an activist keeping Catalan culture alive
in exile. His contact with
republicans and dynamic
activism meant that from
the very beginning he was
one of the most energetic
defenders of the memory of
the Second Republic. Days before the Nazis took Paris, Miravitlles left for
Mexico, leaving Fontserè in Paris. When the war was over, he worked as
a painter in the production of a musical, *Bonjour Buenos Aires*, with other
Spaniards. The project was unusually successful and put him in contact
with people working in the cinema and theater. Mario Moreno, "Cantinflas," the most famous Spanish-speaking actor in the world, showed up
one day. With Cantinflas as his patron, Fontserè became the director of a
big project, *Bonjour Mexico*, that took him to Mexico City. He developed
a special friendship with Mario Moreno and they became extraordinarily
close. After the Mexican premiere, the economic future looked bright and
Fontserè came to New York in 1949 as if he were a tourist on a pleasure trip.

It was supposed to be a fortnight stay but he left fifteen years later, with
a wife. He initially worked as a comics illustrator and after a brief round
trip to Paris with a view to settling in the French capital, he returned to
editing magazines, directing theaters, working as a photographer, etc. He
liked to salvage the poetic from those white, black and gray streets. Fontserè
was Balada's true guide to New York for over a decade. The composer
remembers a handsome, well-built man and a beautiful wife. His slicked

A civil war poster by Carles Fontserè

down hair and neat Hollywood star's goatee were but a front for a full-blown anarchist and faithful representative of all that was most progressive and alternative in Catalan culture throughout the world.

Balada's first encounter with Fontserè was very direct and far removed from the etiquette of polite Americans. Leonardo had managed to get hold of the number of Fontserè's house, and though he didn't know him personally and didn't ring in advance—there was no money for such niceties—he simply turned up on their doorstep. The daughter of Catalan emigrants and now the photographer's wife, Terry opened the door and was blown away by the courtesy of the young man who opened his arms and started speaking Catalan. That friendship was vital for Balada's survival and would remain intact for years, after Fontserè returned to Spain, grew old and continued to bless the world with his vision of things. The era of Hispanic partying in the Big Apple was nigh

New York skyline at the end of the 1950s

and the photographer persuaded the composer to start writing for some of the many burgeoning magazines that maintained the pulse of Spanish against Anglo-Saxon. We shouldn't underestimate how important these collaborations were for Balada's social and intellectual life in those years.

The two of them also showed up at the Centre Català, a secluded space with a piano and small stage, where patriotic events were held like the *Jocs Florals* where Catalan songs were sung and *sardanas* danced. It was there that he met Agustí Borgunyó[5] seated at the piano, a composer renowned for his *sardanas*, who had also successfully composed for all kinds of genres, especially advertising jingles. His output meant that a whole generation was able to recreate their nostalgia for the Catalan countryside amid New York's skyscrapers. Of the cultural activities emanating from the Centre Català, *L'hora catalana*, its radio program, had a huge following and its factotum was Borgunyó. Balada's friendship with Borgunyó was also close and Leonardo visited him in his house in Queens. But the way the Catalans behaved meant, in the words of Fontserè, "that there were few of them and they were very ill-matched." The taxes that ravaged the Manhattan middle classes—that included a good number of Spaniards—emptied the island and only left the very rich, the very poor, and that strange species of human being known by the rest of the world as intellectuals. Unfortunately, Carles Fontserè's memoirs, published in three volumes, don't go beyond 1951, five years before Balada appeared on the scene. Fontserè told him he was writing a fourth part in which he would be one of the main players, but it seems it was never published.

Both friends gave him crucial help at a human and professional level, that allowed Leonardo to earn his living in the city in years which were financially precarious, and later their presence was important at other key moments in Balada's creative life. Elective affinities no doubt mark out the horizons for one's life and, whether chosen or fortuitous, these encounters forever leave their stamp on one's eyes or ears.

---

5   Agustí Borgunyó i Garriga (1894-1967) was born in Sabadell. The son of a textile worker, he studied at the city's Municipal School of Music: piano, violin, clarinet, saxophone and composition. In 1915, he went to the U.S. to avoid military service and the war in Morocco, although he ended up in that country's army at the end of the First World War. He met Xavier Cugat, another musical immigrant, and they made up a piano and violin duo during the Roaring Twenties. He took U.S. citizenship and began to play with swing orchestras until Alfred Wallenstein gave him the opportunity to work for the WOR channel as an orchestra leader and composer. The strictures of the agreement meant his aesthetic contribution had to be typically Spanish. He also worked for the NBC Firestone series of great singers and even composed music for the publicity spots. He returned to Spain in 1963 where he continued his creative endeavors. Although his catalogue includes a large number of *sardanas* and works for the *cobla*, he was also a prolific composer of ballet, operetta, chamber and symphonic music.

10.
Of Friendship and Other Surprises in Writing

Fontserè and Miravitlles acted as Leonardo's hosts in New York from the beginning. Such an immediate immersion in the city's cultural to-and-fro meant that Leonardo always had someone to go to in an emergency. In any case, he always managed to find a proper balance between leisure, time for learning and personal expression. At the time Leonardo was a sponge soaking up everything, from everybody. It was also true that his friendship with Alfonso Mier led him to be particularly sensitive to influences from fine art, rather than anything else, even music, though that may sound strange.

Consequently, it was hardly surprising that one of the first friends to welcome and intrigue Balada was Josep Benet the painter.[1] As already mentioned, the painter from Tortosa was crucial to the composer's life in New York. He arrived in the city a year before Balada in 1955, and was a very important humanistic point of reference in the period when the composer was finding his feet.

Once Leonardo had settled down in mid-Manhattan, with his studies on course and a group of interesting friends in step with the local scene, he decided to try out the other letters of recommendation he had accumulated. Most of the surnames hidden on the back of each letter corresponded to a civil war exile. There were political exiles, and economic exiles, driven by

---

1 Josep Benet Espuny was born in Tortosa in 1920, a town where Balada had family roots. He was called to the ranks before his eighteenth birthday and fought with the Líster Batallion in the battle of the Ebro. He wasn't able to finish his studies in Fine Arts until 1980, but from childhood dedicated himself body and soul to painting. He traveled throughout Europe, met Picasso, and thanks to a grant from the Pensión Conde de Cartagena, came to New York in 1955. He exhibited work in the Barzansky Gallery thanks to the Spanish Embassy and in a collective exhibition at the Waldorf Astoria. He left New York for Venezuela in 1957 and returned in Spain in 1971. He was considered one of the most important landscape artists of his generation. He died in November 2010

need or work—a collective comprising professional performers or artists who passed through New York on their tours—or by murkier interests. All of them, even the temporary visitors, felt an understandable desire to meet their compatriots, and recreate a friendly, homely environment where they could slake their sadness like sailors back on terra firma. The list of friends grew exponentially, weaving a thick weft of family that brought them frequently together. Initially, they included Josep Bartolí, Andrés Segovia, Salvador Dalí, José de Creeft, Joan Josep Tharrats (the painter from Girona),[2] Fernando Valentí,[3] the publisher José María Thomasa-Sánchez[4] and an endless flow of people who stopped off in New York for professional or personal reasons. Given his contacts and background, it's not surprising that Balada wrote regularly for all the Spanish-language magazines that were established in New York between 1957 and 1960, of which there were many, often short lived. Leonardo began to earn money writing articles

From left to right, Balada, Andrés Segovia, Joaquín Rodrigo,
Fernando Valentí and Carles Fontserè, from *Temas*

2　Joan Josep Tharrats (1918-2001) was the clearest exponent of artistic informalism and one of the founders in 1948 of the *Dau al Set* Group, the associated magazine and their concept of the book-object. He fused in his painting various aspects of other arts and his work figures in the catalogues of the most important museums in the world.

3　Fernando Valentí (1926-1990) was a musician, harpsichordist, and pupil of José Iturbi and Ralph Kirkpatrick, who put Leonardo into contact with other colleagues. Although he was a New Yorker, his family came from Majorca, where it owned a house. Today he is remembered for his great performances of J.S. Bach and D. Scarlatti.

4　Data about José María Thomasa-Sánchez is rather hard to come by, though the encyclopedias he wrote in the sixties on childcare and women and pregnancy are well known.

on artistic or more mundane subjects, from interviews to society gossip. Everything that sprang from this night-time work was positive for the young composer. The list of contents of these magazines was conditioned by the tastes of their potential readership. Even though the Hispanic colony at that time comprised a most diverse array of individuals, the majority were intellectuals. People exiled for their ideologies, businessmen from the most buoyant economies of Latin America or students of varied branches of learning were evidence of a demand for cultural magazines. The magazines that saw the light of day depended on various sources of finance, but many were either financed or directed by Catalans.

The signature of Leonardo or Leonard Balada (the byline for some articles) appeared in dozens of the most diverse, intriguing pages. Balada's style was elegant with powerful unifying ideas and appropriate stylistic flourishes. He reached Barcelona in this journalistic vein in musical chronicles for *La Vanguardia*,[5] and, as we mentioned, for *Ritmo* magazine, as well as the occasional contribution to *Destino*.

Getting paid for those articles was another matter. Naturally, Spanish publications brought next to nothing to Leonardo's wallet—how were they going to pay somebody for something they could get others to write for nothing!—while payment in New York went from a miserable pittance to the thirty-five dollars he was paid by *Temas* for interviewing Salvador Dalí or the sensational fifty dollars he earned for a surrealistic article for the Cuban magazine *Bohemia Libre*.[6] The most prestigious of these magazines was certainly *Temas*. Balada had a monthly column with an interview

Balada with María Rosa, *Temas*

5   These articles—usually in the form of chronicles—were mostly written after he made his first return to the United States in 1961.

6   *Bohemia Libre* was a Cuban exiles' magazine. It was first published under the name of *Bohemia* in 1908 as a news weekly. It suffered from censorship in all the dictatorships of the first half of the twentieth century. After the victory of Castro's revolution, it began to be published in New York as *Bohemia Libre*. Balada wrote sporadically for it. Balada's article on page 29 carried the title: "John Cran, the abstemious millionaire who lives among drunkards." It wasn't artistic or intellectual but simply a news item about social life. *Bohemia* has been published as a fortnightly magazine from 1991.

that always carried the same heading, "Con . . . en Nueva York," and that enabled him to meet the most important figures in the Hispanic world of music, theater, dance or cinema. Those interviews put him across the table from Joaquín Rodrigo and Victoria Kahmi,[7] the famous flamenco dancer, María Rosa[8] and even Ricardo Zamora, the renowned goalkeeper.[9]

When one reads Balada's articles today, they leave an aftertaste of Hollywood films from the fifties set in a black-and-white New York with an infinite range of grays that as readily appeared covered in snow as full of De Luxe color. The most political magazine he wrote for was *Hablemos*, but *Temas* was more important and led to greater things. Carles Fontserè was its artistic director and he imposed his striking personality on the printed page. Now and then Leonardo slipped into a press conference to interview a Philippine or Puerto Rican actress in vogue, a dancer who had triumphed recently in a New York season; he even saw fit to interview a Japanese company performing an opera in the Big Apple. He interviewed dancer and choreographer, Alicia Alonso, José de Creeft (introduced as "the most important North American sculptor in Spanish"), Salvador Dalí, Andrés Segovia, Federico Moreno Torroba, Joaquín Rodrigo, actress Marta Romero, Joan Josep Tharrats, and the great soprano at the Met, Graciella Rivera, for the publications *Bohemia Libre*, *Destino*,[10] *Amigos*,[11] *Hablemos*, *Gran Vía*, *Distinción*, or *Europa*. As well as meeting those celebrities, he would be invited to all the parties thrown by the glamorous New York Hispanic set on Broadway, even though it was never enough to blot out his father's wise words about the real qualities of individuals. That string of interviews prompted a number of incidents, some of which had repercussions later. One of the strangest stemmed from Leonardo's interview of

---

7   "Con Joaquín Rodrigo en Nueva York," August 1958.

8   "Con María Rosa en Nueva York," June 1958. María Rosa Orad Aragón was an important figure on the Spanish musical scene. She was born in Jaén in 1937 and belonged to dance troupes that accompanied the most important Spanish artists around the world until she herself became a star in her own right in the sixties.

9   "Con Ricardo Zamora en Nueva York," June 1958. In this article Balada tells a really extraordinary sporting story, recounting in detail the behind-the-scenes tale of a match between a Czech team and R.C.D. Español, from which he salvages the homage to the then ex-goalkeeper Ricardo Zamora, "*El divino*." By the way, El Español lost the game.

10   *Destino* was a leading Spanish magazine published in Barcelona and the young Balada was its Trojan horse in America.

11   A magazine published by a Catalan with Colombian financial backing that barely lasted for one issue but which carried a juicy interview with Dalí and a sequence of photographs in which the genius from Figueres watches as a sudden intruder clipped one end of his arty mustache. They promised to reveal more about that set-to in later issues.

Andrés Segovia[12] for *Temas* in 1957. To have an idea of his influence, we must bear in mind that Segovia was synonymous with the guitar in the United States and had been a guide in New York to no less a figure than Federico García Lorca. He was idolized and considered almost a wonderful relic, a magnificent representative of a bygone era. He was as renowned as any film star and his concerts and recordings were followed passionately in America. They agreed to meet to eat in Segovia's house on the East Side, but the meal was delayed while they waited for Federico Moreno Torroba who was to join the lunch party. Minutes and quarters of an hour passed by, then an hour. Segovia was furious and said, "These Spaniards. . . . When you invite them to eat, they always come late, and bring somebody else you never invited."

Meanwhile they filled the time talking about music and musicians.

Balada, with his interest in contemporary music in Spain, and Segovia, clinging to the music of a glorious past and its great names, soon started to disagree. That was when the composer, in the spirit of youthful daring, said he wasn't particularly interested by de Falla because he was a follower of French impressionism. Shock-horror! Segovia's face darkened and the rest of their conversation was reduced to a series of succinct Yesses and Noes, while the guitarist looked at his watch and hoped that someone would strike down that anti-

Interview for *Temas*

---

12   Segovia is one of the most famous Spaniards of the twentieth century. He is the musician who most promoted the guitar in the last century. Born in Linares in 1893, he was trained in Granada which he left as a professional guitarist who toured the world until he was incredibly old. A friend of Unamuno, de Falla and García Lorca, his friendship with the composer from Granada led to a misunderstanding with Balada. Suffice it to say, Segovia was a musician who had been trained within the nineteenth-century musical tradition and his tastes didn't fit well alongside the aesthetics of the second half of the twentieth. He died in 1987.

de Falla fellow. Leonardo didn't know that in his youth Andrés Segovia had been a close friend of Manuel de Falla and even traveled with him on a long, eventful trip from Paris to Venice that sealed their mutual admiration and friendship forever. He had obviously put his foot well and truly in it. Moreno Torroba never turned up.

Three years later Balada and Segovia met in Santiago de Compostela and the Andalusian was so furious with Balada that he left the room where the composer was presenting his music. They met up again as the result of an invitation from the Spanish Embassy in Washington in 1977. When Leonardo heard that Segovia would be there, he equipped himself with a special helmet in case the guitarist threw something at his head. When he went into the room, Leonardo spotted Segovia and walked over to him, half-fearing he would walk away once again. When their gazes met, Segovia smiled broadly and said in that sharp, nasal twang of his, "Balada, Balada! It's been so long! I have an idea. I am looking for new repertoire and would like you to compose something for me for the guitar."

"But, maestro, you know I write contemporary music. I don't compose in the manner of the old masters."

"Yes, I know . . . I've listened to some of your more recent pieces. I know you're something of a modernist," he replied, rocking back and forth in a friendly manner. "Do you have anything I can listen to?"

"Of course, I do, maestro, tomorrow morning I'll send you a recording."

"The moment you return to Spain, call me in Madrid and we'll meet there."

He sent Segovia a record of *María Sabina*, with its avant-garde or modernist tone, as Segovia put it, plus its harsh, violent subject. On his return to Spain Leonardo called Segovia and they agreed to see each other over the next few days. As he hadn't managed to speak to Segovia in person, Balada appeared on his doorstep once again equipped with helmet and double-bladed sword, really not knowing what to expect. Apparently Segovia had been delighted, not upset, by the work and was extremely interested in commissioning a piece.

"You know, my dear Balada, I would like a work with themes from popular Catalan music," said the maestro, hitting him hard, because he was commissioning a work and setting conditions at the same time.

"That's fine . . . and is there a melody you particularly like?"

"I leave that to you to choose. You know what there is. I look forward to them with great interest."

The piece was given the logical enough title of *Four Catalan Melodies*, and they were finished the next year, 1978. Back in Spain for the summer, they met again, and Segovia told Leonardo he liked two of them a lot, but needed more time to digest the others. That was the last he heard. Segovia died soon afterwards and the work was never played as it had been conceived.

To return to his journalism, the content of other articles brought surprises, like the one that came when the classy, glossy *Distinción* magazine, published in Barcelona, hit the streets and Balada filed several articles as their New York correspondent. When Leonardo returned to Barcelona in 1960, several friends asked him, "Some people are so lucky, Nardo. What she's like? Did she sing for you?"

"Who on earth are you talking about?"

"Who do you think? Come on, don't act the innocent, we've been friends since childhood. . . ."

"Who then?"

"La Callas."

"I don't know Maria Callas."

"Come off it! Look at this. . . . I carry the cutting in my pocket, so I can feel important."

Apparently *Distinción*'s gloss was mere veneer because the caption under the photo in which Alicia Alonso appeared to the left of Leonardo alleged that Maria Callas was the person being interviewed. That all seemed so remote now. . . .

With Alicia Alonso, *Distinción*

In terms of music properly speaking, those magazines treated him as a critic and, consequently, he merited a journalist's card that gave free access to all manner of concerts, operas and plays. One attractive side to this meant he could feel the pulse of the latest musical offerings, and also take a guest. Though money was in short supply, even to buy food, he could allow himself the luxury of inviting one girl or another to a top-rate concert, and that gave him real cachet. But Leonardo's articles weren't only about music or exploring the life of someone famous; he also tried his hand at theater

Interviewing Marta Romero, *Temas*

criticism. He wrote a very critical review of Arthur Miller's latest work in the *Europa* magazine and even felt able to pen praise in the memory of dancer, Doris Humphrey. Hunger spawned attendance at many openings and every opportunity had to be grasped if you didn't want to wake up to a nasty surprise in the morning.

One night Leonardo Balada, the composer and journalist, turned up on a willow chair in a *tablao flamenco*, clapping his hands like the best gypsies from the caves of El Albaicín. And it was no dream, it was for real. Or at least as real as a flamenco show can be on Broadway. Artists appearing in New York would often turn up at Spanish parties. It was June 1958 when the dancer José Barrera[13] and some of his troupe did just that. That party with painters, musicians and the odd writer soon became a flamenco fiesta with the fiery Barrera and everyone shouting *Olé!* Barrera was looking for a pianist and musical director for his show and Balada was eager to try out live music and the stage. The poster was plastered on the Newark Opera House on June 13, 1985. Leonardo Balada, pianist, composer and conductor, figured there as part of José Barrera's flamenco company. The program contained a bit of Spain in each click of the heels. The show started with *palos jondos*, *seguiriyas*, *alegrías* and *tientos* followed by Albéniz, de Falla, Turina and Granados. After the interval, there was a burst of pure flamenco before the grand finale of *The Three-Cornered Hat*. It was a huge success and Barrera was approached by Broadway agents. Leonardo told

---

13   José Barrera was born in Ulldecona (Tarragona). Barrera came to New York as a member of Vicente Escudero's company and tried to introduce the innovations wrought by José Limón and Martha Graham into Spanish dancing.

Balada at the center of José Barreras's Ballet, New York, 1958

Barrera his father was the best tailor in Barcelona and that when he returned to Spain he should make sure he went to his tailor shop if he wanted suits made for a new show. And Mahomet went to the mountains. For a few weeks Leonardo felt like a real flamenco artist.

His journalist's pass allowed him to show off the suits made by his father and court the opposite sex in style. One of his special friends from Juilliard gave him the opportunity to meet Wanda Landowska.[14] After a conversation in a corridor, Leonardo was suddenly in a car with a leading pianist on his way to Connecticut. They stopped outside a large house and knocked at the door. A frail old lady appeared who carried on her shoulders all that living breath from the past, all those memories and experience still near the surface of consciousness. The great harpsichordist talked about de Falla and that concerto he wrote for her which she hadn't really liked. That cacophony jarred against her nineteenth-century taste. On the way back,

---

14   Wanda Landowska (1879-1959) was perhaps the most important harpsichordist of the twentieth century. Polish by birth, her technique playing an instrument that had been sidelined during the nineteenth century inspired some of the great composers of the twentieth to write for her and rediscover the instrument.

LEONARDO BALADA
Pianist - Composer - Conductor

SARAH REED
Dancer

TICA QUETZALA
Dancer

BARBARA WITRIOL
Dancer

ISABEL MORELL
Dancer

ANITA SHEER
Concert and Flamenco Guitarist

Program

1 - **Cuadro Flamenco**

   a - Seguiriyas   .   . Tica Quetzala
   b - Alegrias .   .   . Sarah Reed, Barbara Witriol
   c - Tientos .   .   . Isabel Morell
   d - Romeras   .   . JOSE BARRERA
   e - Soleares .   .   . JOSE BARRERA and Company

2 - **Classical Dances**

   a - Triana   .   . JOSE BARRERA and Company   Albeniz
   b - Danza 1st Vida Breve. Sarah Reed, Tica Quetzala,
                          Barbara Witriol, Isabel Morell   Falla
   c - Sacromonte   .   . JOSE BARRERA   Turina
   d - Danza 2nd Vida Breve. Sarah Reed, Tica Quetzala
                          Barbara Witriol, Isabel Morell   Falla
   e - Homenaje al Viejo Reloj de Mi Casa . JOSE BARRERA   Popular
       (Homage to the Old Clock in My House)
   f - Rondalla Aragonesa. JOSE BARRERA and Company   Granados

INTERMISSION

3 - **Fandango de Candil** (Candlelight)

   a - Panaderos de la Flamenca   JOSE BARRERA and Company... Popular
   b - Malaguenas   .   . Sarah Reed, Barbara Witriol
   c - Ole' de la Curra.   . Tica Quetzala, Isabel Morell
   d - Bolero Liso.   .   . JOSE BARRERA
   e - Seguidillas Manchegas . JOSE BARRERA and Company

4 - **Adaptation of El Sombrero de Tres Picos**   Falla

   El Molinero   JOSE BARRERA
   La Molinera   Tica Quetzala
   El Corregidor   JOSE BARRERA
   El Conquistador   Sarah Reed
   Las Conquistadoras Barbara Witriol, Isabel Morell
   La Pregonadora   Isabel Morell
   El Cieguito   Anita Sheer
   El Perrito   Lindo

LAUTER PIANO USED EXCLUSIVELY

Entire production choreographed and directed by JOSE BARRERA

Costumes: Jean Clower, Pat Collins, Sarah Reed

José Barrera Ballet program

Leonardo smiled contentedly; he had met Landowska and enjoyed a day with a most beautiful woman. And why shouldn't one make the most of one's youth?

Carlos Suriñach[15] was another illustrious Spaniard in New York. Leonardo was quite horrified by the speed at which the Catalan filled scores without rubbing or crossing out a thing, directly onto paper and ready to be published. There seemed to be no thought or development, only action and payback. But, naturally, his Spanish ballets á la Stravinsky were a great success.

The springboard of Juilliard also provided a number of big names from American music who could read Balada's music and make the odd useful comment. Sometimes the opportunity appeared down a corridor, as was the case with Norman Dello Joio;[16] others meant traveling a few kilometers to spend an intense afternoon with Aaron Copland, whom he had met at the courses in Tanglewood. Leonardo's double life was a fact and he was perfectly integrated into both worlds. They all brought benefits that sowed their seed in his creative and social consciousness. At the end of one year, Jean Redd sat Leonardo down in his kitchen and said he was leaving for good. His wife was encouraging him to return to the old continent and he was tired of fighting the asphalt in New York. Leonardo took charge of Redd's house and the profits that came from the rents. The seasons of penury were gone; he could devote himself to his creativity.

Photo with dedication from Norman Dello Joio

---

15   Suriñach was born in Barcelona in 1915 and had been a pupil of Enric Morera there. He later went to Germany and was taught by Richard Strauss. In 1951 he decided to leave for the United States, and became a U.S. citizen in 1959. He was very popular there thanks to his work with Martha Graham and her dance company. He died in the U.S. in 1997.

16   From an Italian, background Dello Joio was born to a family of musicians in 1913. He studied at Juilliard with Wagenaar and won the Pulitzer in 1957. He taught at the Mannes School, where Balada worked with him, and was one of the reasons why Balada could apply to matriculate so he could engineer a student visa and join that institution. He was one of the most important composers of contemporary music in the U.S.A. He died July 24, 2008.

Despite the long list of distinguished individuals with whom he conversed and who taught him so much, the most significant of all came his way through his other life. It happened one afternoon when Fontserè told him to put on his best suit and come downstairs at once, because he had to interview an illustrious compatriot. They quickly reached the Saint Regis Hotel and sat in the lobby to wait for the individual in question. That was when the elevator door opened, out walked Salvador Dalí . . . and everything changed.

11.
Feeling Like a Composer

The years Balada had spent at Juilliard had given him confidence enough to project his music in public. When you study the genesis of a creation, whatever the art, you often sense the titanic labor, the creator struggling within himself to order and pour out in the best way possible the flow of rich magma he needs to communicate. And there is no doubt that a musician's creative process is particularly complex. What drives a composer to create? Can you spot talent in first works? Or, on the contrary, is it necessary to possess a sufficient backlog of experience to be able to feel the need to express that inner life? To what extent can the absence of historical resources influence that need to communicate? Philosophers, aesthetes and artists have written endless essays on the subject, and they all voice something that is fascinating and universal. A layer of transcendence exists, a strange film, visible to the eyes of the artist, that transmits a halo, a strange but energizing electricity that you also recognize in outstanding individuals after they have emerged from wrestling with themselves. As if each beat expressed creative ability and claimed the gift of communication.

When confronting blank staves on the page, Balada hoped to show, at the top of his voice if necessary, that his decision not to be a tailor had been the right one. The connections were obvious: a sense of proportion, satisfaction at, and the beauty of, the final product shared something in common, even in their public dimension—both music and suits were subject to public display and criticism of all kinds—but a musical work didn't have to fit a preestablished schema, or at least the music he wanted to make didn't. This is one of the elements essential to an understanding of Balada's music: the flight from any preestablished system that would endow his music with a brand and predictable homogeneity. And here once again we encounter the great lesson he learned from his father: aspire to be different.

Times weren't good for intuitive creation, for volcanic outbursts that surged and filled souls eager for art. The avant-gardes that cried out from Darmstadt had reached the United States late and had been negated by their own excesses. It was no surprise that in a country like America, that had deeply rooted concepts of ownership and pride in its youthfulness, the extreme avant-gardes, when called upon to shift the axes that supported such a system of values, only resonated with intellectual minorities. They didn't find the following they had in Europe, but their scientific nature meant their stances attracted a younger generation, who liked the intellectual challenge. Musicians had abandoned the role of bit players a long time ago and had entered the artistic Olympus of the chosen few. Even so, the shadow of amateurism still hovered in the air—so essential if we are to grasp the nature of musical life in the United States even at the present— and they were still gripped by vague Romantic longings they aspired to create via sudden inspiration, subject to classical norms. The systematic, the numerical and the concise found it difficult to loosen the tight hold of the sonorous pull of the infinite.

Thanks to the post-avant-garde, for the first time, creation could be established at a purely scientific level and that swelled the chests of many opportunists who tried their hand at composition though they had little to say and were driven by pure speculation. All in all, the new scientism was very attractive. Why didn't Balada assume these tendencies from the start? There is a reasonable, though far from simple, explanation. His aesthetic thinking couldn't easily be detached from his sociopolitical feelings. His fate at the tailor's and his country's politics had etched a creative spirit subject to norms that acted as buffer in the face of the unknown. From such a perspective, one can see that in the composer's eyes, creation was an act of freedom, an act of free communication which eschewed subterfuge, evasion or prohibition. Why shut yourself up inside a system? Did he need a school where he could lodge his thoughts as in a nest? Wouldn't it be better to give free rein to his feelings or rather to the need to express his longings? This didn't mean that Balada conceived of music as an exercise in historicist nostalgia, but that he preferred to apply the freedom he found fascinating in contemporary art to the crucible of creativity simmering in his mind. In the years when he was perfecting his skills at university, Balada's project was to fill that incandescent lava with structural content, so his first works tried to maintain a difficult formal balance, wore neoclassical clothing that, like a tailor's pattern, allowed him to cross frontiers from the inside, though they never lost their Spanish sources in their genesis. The breaking of those lines of constraint came later after a process of deep, conflictual thought.

When does a composer decide his work is sufficiently personal to open his catalogue? There are two well-defined parameters. The first is aesthetic conviction, satisfaction at attaining a moderate level of perfection in terms of the threshold of the demands of the time. But, conversely, there is a subterranean flow that, though not totally persuasive, sustains faith in works that remain in a semiconscious state. Of course, one key factor in considering whether a piece is worthy of a catalogue is public reception, whether via premieres or media comment, or commercial publication. Both possibilities relate to external criteria. So why bother to hold on to work that hasn't been premiered or published commercially? What emotional or aesthetic factors lead a composer not to jettison them in one of those unexpected clear-outs before a house move? There have been a good number of those in the life of Leonardo Balada, though not all have been as radical as the first. Why does a series of works exist that haven't been sacrificed on a bonfire or in a trash can, yet aren't in his catalogue and consequently aren't available for public performance? Naturally, sooner or later those subterranean rivers surface in the light of day and flow freely, though they may require someone to dig a hole and look for fresh water.

On a summer's afternoon in Pittsburgh, while we conversed and drank water from tall blue-tinted glasses filled to the brim, Balada struggled to recall some works that were poking out from his desk, flattened under the weight of scores, copies and proofs. All of a sudden, he placed a large brown folder on the table that was open down one side, the ancient kind closed by a stud. When that gave, huge sheets began to emerge that looked much the worse for wear after being hidden for so long. They all had a similar manuscript format. The yellow paper had been a real battleground and was now turning brown around the folded edges. The front page bore a title written in clear, straight but elaborate lettering above the name of Leonardo Balada. These were his first musical dreams, worthy of surviving over time, even though they were in an out-of-the-way corner under a pile of now well-known works that had been recorded and performed in half the world. One could only imagine that they *must* possess something that warranted their continued existence. There were early works, but surprisingly later works too, given that there was no order to them, even from the most hallowed era of Balada's repertoire, that must surely have been filed away after rigorous revision. It was like a tailor's chest full of remnants, half-sewn buttons and other much lamented relics. Bringing those secrets to the surface made you tingle like an archaeologist stumbling across a hidden wall or unexpected capital. Oldest of all was *Tema i set variacions*, (*Subject and Seven Variations*) composed for piano and orchestra in 1958. There was a notable dedication "*to Amparo Iturbi*," the sister of José Iturbi,[1] who had such a high profile in the media in the forties and fifties. The score was complete and written in pencil in large, clear hand. It began with the air of the great concerto pieces from subsequent years. An impressive orchestral introduction eased the path for the piano's jarring entry—as was to be expected given it was written for such a distinguished soloist—with all the musical grandeur you would anticipate in a concerto of that kind. This average-length piece shows a debt to Neoclassicism at its height, formally offset by quasi-brass outbursts worthy of late Stravinsky. In terms of the later Balada, it shimmers rhythmically and bears his trademark freshness.

That exciting adventure pursued by an overmodest Balada was followed chronologically by a title that can only be described as both significant and a discreet tribute to Mompou, *Música Tranquila*. It was 1959, for string orchestra, and dedicated to Jean and Margarita Redd, who had so warmly welcomed him into their home when everything was looking so difficult. This work starts off on what is already a truly Baladan note: a slow tempo and sumptuous cluster breaking the silence to unleash the clash of emotions simmering within. The work was one of his first premieres and took place in December 1959. It was the first of many. *Música tranquila* became Balada's letter of recommendation to many venues and was even selected by the Spanish section of the International Society for Contemporary Music as its choice for the festival held in London in the summer of 1962.[2]

However, that afternoon's big surprise was found on the back of the final

---

1 Amparo Iturbi (1898-1969) was the little sister of José Iturbi (1895-1980) and was also a pianist. She began her career at the age of 15 in Barcelona and it launched off spectacularly. She made her debut in America in 1937. She was the pioneer who introduced the Spanish repertoire for piano in the U.S.A. and was succeeded by Alicia de Larrocha. She performed in several films in the forties helped by her brother's success. Balada wrote that first work for Amparo Iturbi off his own volition; there was no commission.

2 The Spanish delegation's selection also included *Sucesiones* by Xavier Benguerel; *Formantes*, mobile for two pianos by Cristóbal Halffter; *Metamorfosis III* by Enrique Raxac and *Introducción, doble canon y pasacalles* by Josep Soler.

96

Beginning of the original manuscript of *City*

page of *Música tranquila*: a score that had been reworked, torn and restitched, showing it must have been important in its day. It was *City*, the first English title in that group of scores, and dated 1959, the year when Balada launched into the merry-go-round of *City*, a one-scene ballet and fruit of an exercise in excellence at Juilliard. When he was in his last year, Persichetti and others organized a competition—a reading of a ballet composition aimed at final-year students. Three were selected and they included Balada and Peter Dickerson, who would later give up composing and become a music critic for the English magazine *Gramophone*. The mysterious side to the project was that all the works had to be based on a single scene suggested beforehand by choreographer William Hug. In fact, it involved a trio of works in a single scene that was divided in turn into three sections (quick—slow—quick). No live music was needed for the final staging, only a recording that would help the dancers in their movements, since when it came to premieres of contemporary work, they were too difficult for students at a conservatoire. To record the music, the composer had to find the right instrumental grouping, write the parts for each instrument and proceed to record the work on a strange sort of vinyl that was neither a single nor an LP. Leonardo composed the first two movements that were immediately recorded by Jorge Mester, but there was a long wait for the third to round off the work. In the last stage of the competition, Leonardo was struck down by a bad bout of influenza and could hardly get out of bed. Time passed, and he didn't get any better, and the delay in submitting the material was further extended. The jury comprised Persichetti, Wagenaar, Gianini and William Bergsma.[3] The latter, one of the school's composition teachers, was annoyed by Leonardo's late delivery and his anger was such it lasted at least fifteen years to when they came face-to-face again. Balada was by then a prestigious composer, at once controversial and feted in half the world, and he had made a bid to the National Endowment for the Arts to find time to devote to an orchestral work. Bergsma was on the panel taking the decisions. Balada's bid was surprisingly rejected, or perhaps not so surprisingly. Another member of the committee, Ezra Laderman, a good friend of Balada, told him in confidence that the illustrious but sly Bergsma had announced that Balada was a composer who couldn't be trusted as he didn't meet deadlines and took ages to finish anything. He then assured the others that if he were given the grant, it was very likely he would never finish the work and the money would have been wasted. A year later, in the absence of Bergsma, the grant was given and the work, as was almost always the case with Balada, was composed long before the deadline expired. Bergsma, a rather conservative composer, had harbored the memory of the unfortunate delay in respect of the prize and recording of *City*.

The score already reveals a personality and clear-sightedness in respect of Balada's later style that one can only describe as extraordinary. The work

---

3   William Laurence Bergsma (1921-1994), an American composer, started working at Juilliard in 1946 where he stayed until 1963. He composed two symphonies, six string quartets and two operas, an output marked by deep post-Romantic conservatism.

Published score of *Suite no. 1* for Guitar

begins to develop from a broad, heterogeneous chamber ensemble with orchestral aspirations, but sustains a small group's precise beat and definition of timbre. Its twelve minutes develop intense, harmonic textures marked by open, lingering dissonances, that give the work an unusually beautiful character. *City* possesses all the virtues of ballet music, since it has a striking rhythm without being repetitious and at the same time its well-defined melodic strains never drift into vapid melodies. The texture is colorful and works perfectly without a stage thanks to stellar percussion backed by a piano. Here are found some clues to the later Balada, so that *City* is much more than a creative prologue. The work is divided into three sections defined by their titles: *I – On the Street*, *II – Idyll* and *III – Party*. The work was premiered in Europe a few years later at the biennial Contemporary Music Festival in Paris in 1963, in addition to the recording that was the indispensable requisite for the competition for which it was written.[4]

Balada's catalogue officially opens with a piano work, *Música en cuatro tiempos* (1959), that was also his first published work. Balada was still a

---

4   Nevertheless, the work was kept out of the catalogue until it was revised in 2011. If we take into account the fact the work is so impressive, we can venture a reason for that absence. Everything seems to indicate that Balada wasn't very aware of the work. After the catalogue was revised, the work would soon be professionally recorded for the Naxos label.

student at Juilliard when he wrote this work which is remarkable for its inner dynamics. Premiered in New York by Jonathan Sack, *Música en cuatro tiempos* evolves from a much more neoclassical structure than *City* and is full of mostly polytonal elements with sequences of complex sound. The work was so well received that a bold, well-heeled publisher approached Balada and gave him the opportunity to publish the score. The company was General Music and the publisher Paul Kapp,[5] who wasn't worried by the profitability of these scores, as he published according to the criterion of quality. He was the young composer's first mentor. Kapp's editions were published with care and good taste, and had front covers with attractive modern engravings. Over time those editions became profitable and led to recordings of the same works that were of equal high quality and merit. The work originally had another title, *Música en cinco movimientos*, which was changed to the title that now appears in the catalogue for marketing reasons. The purely financial side to publication meant that a series of guidelines had to be followed, and first and foremost, it involved not frightening off potential buyers with titles that seemed overly grandiose.

The next two titles in the catalogue, composed on the eve of an eagerly awaited return home, followed a similar path. The *Sonata for Violin and Piano* (1960) premiered by Ariana Brone and Masha Cheransky was a great success underlining artistic gains in a distinct neomodernist style with very Catalan features. Its original title was *Sonata Allegro in Four Movements*, that Kapp changed to the simpler *Sonata*. Years after General Music published a special edition of this work, with a front cover with Leonardo Balada's name and the work's title handwritten, while further down an illustration with smudgy black and red squares was truly modern in its aesthetic. Both works, for piano and the sonata, were premiered in Europe at the Biennial Paris Contemporary Music Festival in 1965.

A composer's life tends to suffer from a large number of projects that remain relegated to the limbo of impossible dreams. One of the biggest from that period was triggered by Central American choreographer, Roberto Iglesias. The U.S. impresario Sol Hurok was the agent for Iglesias's company on Broadway and was then regarded as the leader in the

---

5   Paul Kapp (1908-1984) was one of the main promoters of Balada's work in those first years. He set up General Music Publishing at the beginning of the fifties with a special interest in contemporary music and recording young composers. People said he had made lots of money publishing songs from Hollywood films and used the income from new editions to invest in the madness that was live music. Among Kapp's successes "I Left My Heart in San Francisco" is always associated with Tony Bennett.

field.[6] He represented among others: Rubinstein, Victoria de los Ángeles, Marian Anderson, Feodor Chaliapin, Van Cliburn, Sviatoslav Richter, Anna Pavlova, Andrés Segovia and Mistlav Rostropovich. Hurok was planning to put Roberto Iglesias's name in flashy neon letters on New York theater's golden mile. A project was being touted for a contemporary ballet based on *Blood Wedding* by Federico García Lorca and it would be able to draw on the largest funds imaginable. In preparatory meetings Iglesias suggested that the music should be written by a Spanish composer with firsthand knowledge of the emotional intensity of Lorca's world. They were quick to choose Leonardo Balada as the best suited: a young, highly educated, restless composer, who knew the New York milieu as well as the Spanish scene in Catalonia, which was something else in his favor, since the company was set up with Catalan financial backing and a number of the dancers were also Catalan. Many names were mentioned who might adapt the text, since it was an ambitious project requiring actors as well as dancers, and, as it was Broadway, big names were essential to lure big investors. Tennessee Williams would be responsible for the text and then the bar was set extremely high for the sets. There was no shortage of names! Picasso and Dalí were in the hat . . . could you reach any higher? However, the last hurdle was the worst. The rights to the text were in the hands of Federico's brother, Francisco García Lorca, who taught at Columbia University.[7] Balada was responsible for making contact with him via a letter of recommendation from Dr Norman Lloyd, a teacher of music theory and composer at Juilliard, who had established a degree of friendship with Francisco García Lorca after composing a ballet based on the *Lament for Ignacio Sánchez Mejía*. Balada invited García Lorca to one of the shows being performed by Iglesias's company on Broadway. At the end of the show, they all agreed to meet in García Lorca's apartment on the West Side the next day in order to exchange views and work out an agreement. As they left the show, nothing indicated that García Lorca wouldn't give the green light as regards his brother's work, but despite all the big names in the mix, Lorca's brother was quite adamant: he didn't find Iglesias's proposal at all interesting and he wouldn't give the go-ahead. The project was revamped, the choreography would go to Jerome Rob-

---

6   Sol Hurok (1888-1974) was really Solomon Izrailevich Gurkov and was born in the Ukraine into a Jewish family. Fleeing from the pogroms in Tsarist Russia, Sol Hurok came to the U.S.A. in 1906. He was one of the key twentieth-century agent for artists.

7   Francisco García Lorca (1902-1976) was Federico's younger brother. Exiled after the civil war, he was a literary critic and taught at Columbia from 1955.

bins, who had been given awards for his work on *West Side Story*, but even then the project didn't kick off. It remained a work out of catalogue that was Leonardo's creative response to the idea. Today the *Jota* is only a pale reflection of what might have confirmed Balada's international reputation as a composer, but that had to be deferred. The project had failed and it was time to move on to something else.

That something else was Hurok's last maneuver to find a space for those he represented. The music wouldn't be original—there was a natural fear at the idea of such a risky enterprise—and a Spanish ballet that sought success should have a more nationalistic brand of music. However, the musical company did need a musical director. Balada put himself forward, confident his recent attempt at collaborating with Hurok would help. Faced by one of the great manager's retinue, he was asked about his gifts as musical director, and Leonardo responded positively: he had attended classes on conducting an orchestra. The following question seemed inevitable: "But have you ever conducted a ballet?"

Dry tumbleweed blew silently from one side of the street to the other, as in a Wild West movie. Perhaps that job was too much for the moment. Besides, he would be jumping on a plane in a few days to return home after four years. The heavens could wait. They chose Antoni Ros Marbà.

That wasn't the end of Balada's collaborations with Iglesias. Years later, in 1965, he wrote the original music for four much more modest ballets than the first, but only two reached fruition. They were performed off Broadway on the alternative theater network, and Balada was involved both as composer and performer of his own music at the piano.[8] The scenes were under ten minutes and the composer still has his original pencil version.

All those early attempts had left a good number of bars by the wayside and, above all, represented a steep learning curve that had placed him between the devil and the deep blue sea, or what amounted to much the same, between a blank page of staves and a head full of music. All of which made him feel he was a composer.

---

8   Although Balada hasn't included these works in his catalogue for years, they were undoubtedly influential in his development as a composer. Tomás Marco, in his *Historia de la Música Española*, (the twentieth-century volume) mentions these formative pieces, even though they were incidental exercises for the piano: *La casa* and *Triángulo*. These works are also mentioned in the entry on Balada's music for the stage in the *Diccionario de la Música Española e Hispanoamericana*, 10 vols, Madrid, 2002, Emilio Casares (ed.), "Leonardo Balada," by Marta Cureses.

12.
Organs and Their Pedals

His experience with the Brooklyn choir and the lessons he learned from friends and teachers were an important apprenticeship for Balada the composer, but they had an equal influence on his personality. Friends, the status of artist, his ability to communicate, and the choir convinced him that by performing he could earn enough money to say goodbye forever to economic insecurity and its attendant woes. The sums of money he earned as a journalist were sporadic at best, whereas regular payments were the ideal, so once he had recovered the practical use of his fingers, he pledged to find a more stable form of income. That was how he came to a Catholic church in Brooklyn intent on honestly selling himself as a qualified organist. Leonardo stepped inside a temple once again, though this time it was through the sacristy and to make music. When he handed his vita to the priest, the latter was impressed that a student from Juilliard had visited his neck of the woods to seek a position traditionally taken by a conventional middle-aged lady from a middling family. It was a good first impression. The priest felt he was lucky being able to count on a good musician who had apparently fallen from heaven and, what's more, from Catholic Spain, but there had to be a drawback. In this case it was the sensitive area of fees. The church paid nothing for playing at Sunday Mass.

When he saw Leonard already donning his hat to make his exit from that incense-filled room, the priest, who had now tested whether the youngster had any artistic dignity, hastened to add in a piping voice, as if in a mystic trance: "But on the other hand . . ."

Balada swung round on his heels, eager to hear what would follow such a promising "but."

"On the other hand, you get a fee for every wedding and although it's not a set fee, that might appeal, because we hold a lot of weddings in this church."

"Could I see the organ?"

"Of course, come with me."

And they began the eternally wearisome ascent to the choir. When they reached the top of the stairs, the path stretched out over kilos of dust that had accumulated over years. Leonardo felt he was treading on the sand of a virgin beach, though it was much colder there. He spotted a small organ, almost a toy, a far cry from the huge instruments you find in big churches. When he sat down, the miracle turned to sound from his fingers and the priest rubbed his hands because music brought distinction to Eucharists in search of new souls. They shook hands and the following day the young composer was appointed the church's official organist.

It was springtime and one day when he was walking towards the sacristy, as he often did, someone told him to start loosening his fingers because there would be ten weddings that day at the rate of half an hour per couple. The cash register rang out cheerfully and compensated for the ordinary Sundays he did gratis. That worked, thanks be to God, and there was no better way to put it. Clearly that deal had been a good idea. Improvisations were the norm because they enabled Leonardo to practice harmonic progressions for his own compositions as he made those shabby vaults vibrate. In any case nobody noticed a thing. But the good times came and went and the birds started to emigrate in their v-shaped formations and weddings declined as

Balada in the early 1960s

the first heat of summer struck, so now he had more free days than paid. It seemed like a good time to stay at home; nobody got married for several weeks, as if it was too hot for wedding outfits. His wallet was empty, there were no savings to send to Sant Just and the freezer was bare. It was better to return home than earn the occasional dollar, so he flung his jacket over his shoulder and walked out, hoping anew.

Time went by and Leonardo wrote new, meaty chapters in his life story, but the tale of his interactions with churches and their organs shouldn't be abandoned. The next chapter was written in 1961. Balada was outside an employment office looking for a good job to put food on his table. His experience as an organist encouraged him to apply for a new position as maestro in a modern chapel. A new opportunity soon appeared to allow him to replay his idyll with the saints in a New Jersey Protestant Church.

Leonardo took the train to the other shore of Manhattan hoping to earn a supplementary wage now he was no longer a student with a dollar-a-day grant, but a postgraduate student of Dello Joio at Mannes College. The pastor had been warned that an experienced Spanish organist was coming who had a diploma from Juilliard. It was all very polite and prospects looked even better: a weekly wage and well-remunerated services. Leonardo made another ascent to a new choir, though on this occasion everything seemed cleaner and shinier. As he looked up, he registered the towering shadow that loomed implacably overhead. Leonardo's muscles tensed; that wasn't so promising. When he was up on high, the huge organ, compared to the Brooklyn harmonium, tried the young musician's nerves. All the better, it will sound louder, thought Leonardo. "I'm not going to be worried by such detail, after all, I sang in Enric Morera's choir!" The organist sat opposite the console while the pastor switched on the booming monster. There was a score on the stand that looked like a Bach chorale, and it was black with a mass of notes, all full on, and various. He started playing the music and it sounded shoddy, if generally acceptable, in Leonardo's mind. That organ was pretentious, but that huge bulk wasn't as good as it looked and sounded weak and faltering. He had entered an eternal spiral of music when he felt cold fingers grip his left shoulder. Leonardo stopped playing, looked at the priest who said: "Why don't you use the pedals?"

"What pedals?"

The next thing Leonardo remembered was rushing down those stairs three at a time and out into the blinding New Jersey sun. He had learned an important lesson—those Protestants wanted notes from the manual keyboard but also wanted someone who could use the dozen pedals lurking under the console. People in New Jersey were so capricious. He went back to the employment office that same afternoon. From behind his desk and files, the bureaucrat looked at him askance over the top of his spectacles as if to say, "I know you from somewhere," while he waited for Leonardo to sit down.

"I'm looking for work as an organist."

"But weren't you here this morning?"

"That's right, but the place wasn't suitable. Don't you have anything nearer?"

"Well, my friend, you were sacked in record time!"

The bureaucrat started shuffling his files, took one out and handed it to him with a smile. His luck was in. The next morning he turned up at the second address. The church seemed less ancient and the vibrations felt better. He spoke to the minister and began the ascent to another choir. Halfway up Leonardo asked if the church was Protestant. Surprised by the question, the pastor replied that it was. When they reached the top, Leonardo caught sight of the pedals, felt a last-minute indisposition, apologized and left before those blessed pedals threw him downstairs. An hour later he was back at the employment office. The bureaucrat, who hadn't moved an inch since his last visit, kept looking at Leonardo and then tried to hide.

"What's wrong with this guy?" wondered the august functionary.

"Hello . . . again. Look . . . the fact is I do need a job as an organist, but preferably in a Catholic church."

"Oh, I see, you must be a true believer, I guess?"

"You've got no idea."

Leonardo bit his lip and controlled his laugh with a pedal extremity. The new card handed to him by that gentleman employment magician, bore the address 96th Street East. It was an imposing church by the name of Saint Francis de Sales, a Roman Catholic, Apostolic Church. When he walked in, he immediately glanced at the organ from the central aisle. It too was huge. New beads of sweat pearled on his forehead, but he plucked up courage and told himself it probably wasn't necessary to use his feet. He introduced himself to the priest, and, without any need to display his expertise, he was contracted with a soft-hearted "it's a deal!" For a time there were only funerals in that church but they were paid at the rate of fifteen dollars per Mass and into the bargain, he could improvise. Now and then the odd wedding fell from the sky, and that was no hardship since he boosted his

The organ in the Chuch of St Francis de Sales

improvisations with louder chords and everyone was happy. Things went well right away, and occasionally he even augmented dominant and tonic with the pedal, as if to cock a snoop at those capricious Protestant pastors. The truth is that nobody in a contemporary Catholic church was the least concerned about what was being played or how it sounded, provided there was some noise along the aisles. In conversation one afternoon he discovered that one of his cinema idols, James Cagney, was born in the neighborhood and was a well-known member of the congregation.[1] By the time Leonardo came to the church, Cagney wasn't the mythical star he once was, but it is more than likely he may have heard him play at a high Mass. It was an illustrious place for that reason alone. As it went swimmingly well, the team of priests suggested he took charge of the children's choir that he could include in special Masses. He was now given a fixed wage, since those duties meant regular rehearsals and more dedicated efforts, to the tune of one hundred

Josep Balada building Andrómeda Cottage in Sant Just Desvern

---

1 James Cagney's relationship with the church started with his own baptism and at his end the actor also preferred to be buried within those walls where he had taken his first steps as a Christian.

and fifty dollars a month. He sent all that money home towards the construction of the family house his father was building stone by stone in Sant Just, slightly higher up behind the original farmhouse. Staying true to his desire to be different, the house was given a quite novel—and English—name: Andrómeda Cottage. Leonardo's adventures with the organ and those blessed pedals ended in 1965. By now, Leonardo was a composer of repute, had a wife, a small child and a steady job.

Balada conducting in the 1960s

13.
Spain in a Plane

Four years and one month. Four years had passed since a young man from Barcelona, summoned by other horizons, took his first steps in a city that was then the center of the world. In those four years he had acquired as much knowledge as in the previous twenty-six. His address book of friends and acquaintances literally encompassed a whole world and all kinds of occupations, ambitions, nationalities, races and social classes. But how much had that intense experience changed Nardo Balada from Ronda de la Universitat, 12? On his way to board the plane that would fly him home, Leonardo, the composer, and Leonardo, the individual, were quite clear they would return to New York. That wasn't an issue. There was no turning back in that sense. It didn't mean he thought his homecoming was a step backwards; it was rather a sensation that he was on his way back to a country sunk in a long dictatorship with no end in sight to what from the outside looked gray, stagnant and boring. It would be to reenter a musical universe where everything he mined from his head would come with the eternal refrain that he did so of his own volition, never with the support of a culturally mature society, and always in a climate of latent rancor.

On the other hand, once he was no longer working in the dark, Leonardo had melded in New York, had breathed in a bit of his own country from each of his friends, at home, in his life and forged a new country for himself that was free, luminous and exciting and he enjoyed every moment. He had created an individual world in which Madrid or Barcelona had stopped in time. He was sure it wouldn't be difficult to convince himself and his family that returning to Spain wasn't part of his plans for the future. Nevertheless, to secure a return to New York, even though he now had his certificate from Juilliard, Balada needed an educational or professional pretext to guarantee a new visa that would allow him to travel back. He had tried to cling to the thread of further study by maintaining his matriculation at the Mannes School of Music, and that would permit him to fly back if things didn't go well in Spain, or if a real opportunity didn't chance to come his way. A visa was a utopian dream for a Spaniard who didn't have a work contract in the United States and his friends there had recommended he should keep his student status, as that kind of visa was much easier to obtain. For some time Leonardo had been gathering materials to support his professional return to the United States. He looked to every important figure in the world of the arts he had befriended or had dealings with to be a possible guarantor of his work as composer with the aim of securing the residence permit he so craved. The list still sends a shiver down the spine: Victoria de los Ángeles, Andrés Segovia, Salvador Dalí, José Iturbi, Aaron Copland or Alexandre Tansman, among others, endorsed Balada in his quest to remain in the country.

Four years and one month later, a physically different Leonardo Balada had experienced other more important changes, changes relative to his vision of life and politics, the need for a culture and society that distanced him daily from all he had abandoned on his way to the American dream. Many of those experiences were grounded in the bereft sadness of a sailor in a remote port, plus lots of nostalgia and happy memories. His vision of Spain, Catalonia, Barcelona and Sant Just Desvern wasn't the same and the expanse of the ocean's abyss was immense. Now everything looked very different from the other shore. He now understood better the internationalism his father had practiced every day of his life and the changes he noted on the faces of those who returned. One couldn't put up

Letter of recommendation from Aaron Copland

barriers from a distance. He remembered the *Visca Catalunya Lliure* he had painted on a wall, and smiled, realizing that that free Catalonia was free, but free of hypocrisy, of dictatorship, of sectarianism, without stronger nationalist impulses that would mean pulling the shutters down, closing doors and reproducing gray times far from freedom with a capital F. He was moved by good flamenco dancing, a negro spiritual, the songs of American Indians, by reading García Lorca or Josep Pla or standing in front of a Picasso painting. He relished every word he heard from Met Miravitlles and Carles Fontserè in that Catalan he so adored, but also enjoyed reading Cervantes in that Castilian the Spanish nationalists distorted by imposing a version that lacked the magnificence Cervantes had given it, extinguishing all other potential. The truth was identities couldn't be imposed, could only be felt, period.

When he boarded the airplane, he could already feel in some way that breath of homey fresh air, the lightheartedness of the games he played as a kid, the sea and friendship. It was difficult to curb his euphoria. There was so much to tell, so much to hear and so much still to live that emotions throbbed in his throat and he struggled to preserve the demeanor of a would-be experienced traveler. As he sat back in his seat and smiled, his soul stirred, he sensed that Spain was inside that airplane, not only in spirit, but also in a solid, liquid, gaseous state. A few minutes later, Leonardo watched as the airplane filled up with dark faces and ringlets. Creating a cheerful commotion, a group of animated, elegantly dressed gypsies had just walked in and behind them the familiar face of Paco Rebés. In the following hours, in that journey into the sun, he had all the time in the world to rehearse with Rebés all he would then recount left, right and center. The passengers included someone who was introduced as an artist of world standing, one of the emerging, international stars of Spanish art. After he had heard that praise, a beautiful gypsy girl appeared who dispensed wit

Balada in the 1960s

and art with her every gesture. Leonardo barely had time to give her two kisses when Rebés made the necessary introductions. The most charming woman to have stepped on stages in the U.S.A. since art was art, was now returning from Hollywood after seducing all the film and theater moguls in America. A muse of painters and sculptors, her return to Spain was a mere technical stop before initiating a new conquest of South America. She was La Chunga.[1]

As they sat down together, Paco Rebés and Nardo Balada began to recount what they had done with their lives since they had last seen each other years ago. They revisited their pasts and suddenly Rebés began to dream of the future. They were returning to Madrid to begin a project to revamp the glories of Diaghilev's great Russian ballets but in a Spanish key. They would recreate an immortal drama to follow on from the success of *West Side Story* in the shape of a masterpiece of Spanish ballet that would propel La Chunga to international stardom and make the art of flamenco everyone's cultural heritage. A proposal wasn't long in coming. The work's text would be the responsibility of Alfredo Mañas[2] and they were still looking for a composer. What they were seeking was obvious enough, a young, active, brilliant musician, who was international and modern, above all, modern, but at the same time someone imbued with the mother country, as it would be a work produced from Spain for the whole world.

That was when he looked at Leonardo, sat back slightly and told him: "You are that composer." The first notes immediately struck up in his head as he caught glimpses of the narrative structure of a ballet where nothing would be left to chance. No. It would be pure music, dance and song, a different kind of ballet. It already had a title and, of course, a plot. *Los Tarantos*. It would tell the eternal story of Romeo and Juliet *a la española*. Two feuding families and a star-crossed love. La Chunga's powers of expression and the music would be up in neon lights across half the world. Perhaps Leonardo Balada would be the one to create the right rhythms to square that impossible circle.

Rebés was the kind of artist who would own several Pacific islands if

1   Micaela Flores Amaya, La Chunga, was born by chance in Marseille in 1938. She was discovered by Rebés in Montjuic and was soon transformed into a flamenco dance star. She first went to the U.S.A. with Pastora Imperio's company and, thanks to her friendship with Ava Gardner, she acted and made an impact in Hollywood. After that success she went to New York and appeared on a number of TV programs. She was muse to some of the great artists of the time like Alberti, Dalí, Picasso or Léon Felipe who were captivated by her sparkle and *duende*. She is now a painter.
2   Alfredo Mañas (1924-2001) signed off eleven screenplays, and worked as an actor and director. His first screenplay was shot in 1963, *Los Tarantos*.

they could be paid for with all the ideas he had tried to sell, which was a real virtue if the mission was to persuade capitalists to invest their money. The project seemed well set up and even in preproduction phase, according to Rebés. Mañas was on board and waiting in Madrid to get to work immediately. They agreed that Rebés would keep in touch as regards progress and that they would meet up in Madrid as soon they could start work. That project, negotiated in an airplane flying away from New York, also deprived Leonardo of any need to return there. He wouldn't need a student visa and his career could achieve lift off under the Mediterranean sun with those close to him. The rest of the journey turned into a dazzling flamenco show. With all that *jaleo*, soul, dancing and singing, Leonardo had put his Cordoban sombrero back on and recovered his hunger for elemental art.

Of course, those flights were very expensive. It had cost Leonardo four years to save up, but, conversely, the airline company was very accommodating when it came to stopovers. If you wanted, it was possible to delay your journey and visit one of the cities where the airplane stopped. Balada joined the group of Rebés and La Chunga on a long stopover in Paris, and went out with the flamenco troupe. They all went to a party organized to celebrate the troupe's success in the United States. It was held in the famous palace of the Rothschilds.[3] That was where Leonardo saw La Chunga dance for the first time, a moment of great emotion which stirred his feeling for a genuine art born from the salt of the earth.

His homecoming was extremely moving. His family was waiting for him when he got off the plane. Pepito gave him the big hug that both had been looking forward to for years and his brother, Elíseo, looked at him strangely. Yes, that was his brother, the one who wrote every day and lived in America. Naturally he was sorry that Llucieta wasn't there; she was going through a patch of poor health, and was waiting impatiently at home. Leonardo soon adapted to the bustle of street life after he had recounted his adventures and misadventures to his family and friends. He did it so often, he couldn't remember if he had or hadn't told all the stories about those organs and their pedals. He was so happy that only a desire to keep learning enabled him to escape from that emotional catharsis and give himself a fresh objective for that summer.

The "Music in Compostela" summer courses were perhaps the most prestigious available in a Spain which was so impermeable to art. Every

---

3   A dynasty of German Jewish bankers who had acted as artistic patrons from the eighteenth century onwards. One branch was very important in Paris in the middle of the twentieth.

summer renowned figures from the world of Spanish music, teachers and musicians of international repute, came together. Leonardo signed up for the course on composition that was to be imparted by Alexandre Tansman,[4] a man with a past and importance that went beyond the narrow frontiers of Spanish music. Leonardo Balada stood out in Santiago. Regrettably, it was unusual to find a Spanish composer with a diploma from Juilliard and a good number of compositions already under his belt, even recordings of some. Balada was an out of the ordinary composer there and not only among the professionals giving classes. Tansman welcomed him warmly from the start, so much so that when he had seen and listened to some of his work, he suggested he should give them a special airing in front of a select audience, before the concert that brought the course to a close. Of note are those who attended: Gaspar Cassadó, Alicia de Larrocha, Conchita Badía, Andrés Segovia, Lazar Levin, José López Calo, Frederic Mompou. And those were only the maestros, since the student cohort included Narciso Yepes, María Rosa Calvo Manzano, John Williams and others.

It was the occasion when one of the first works that opened Balada's current catalogue was negotiated. The proposal was to collaborate with a member of his generation, the aforementioned English guitarist John Williams, who had come to the course drawn by the presence of Andrés Segovia, to whom the piece *Lento with variations* (1960) was dedicated. The six minutes of *Lento with variations* continued what was already a quite personal interpretation of the neoclassical that was by then veering towards a Spanish neobaroque that drank directly from the wells of the great century of the vihuela. In this work Balada exploits the concept of variation in terms of theme, and increases rhythmic and melodic tensions. To that end he doesn't skimp changes of beat and sources of sound that add intensity before rounding the piece off with a return to the calm waters of *tempo primo*. Williams premiered the work on his return to London and sent the good news to his fellow student. It was his first international premiere.

One afternoon during the course Tansman introduced Balada's music so it could be discussed by his distinguished colleagues, but there was an incident when Andrés Segovia rose angrily to his feet after five tense minutes and left the room, slamming the door behind him. Those present were dumbfounded, especially Tansman, who hadn't expected such a reaction.

---

4   Alexandre Tansman (1897-1986) developed a close relationship with Spain and the courses in Santiago. He emigrated to the United States as a result of the persecution of the Jews in Europe, met Schönberg there and worked in the film world. When he returned, his neoclassical style had become very outmoded and he took refuge in teaching.

He tried to calm Leonardo down and went off to find Segovia and discover what had happened. At the end of the session Leonardo was congratulated all round and Cassadó was so impressed he commissioned a work. They were talking about that when Tansman took Balada to one side and told him that Segovia was still very upset by that lunch when Leonardo had showed a lack of respect for the great Manuel de Falla. He had judged that to be so unacceptable and unforgiveable that when his music began, Segovia's latent indignation resurfaced and he walked out in a huff.

The great Andrés Segovia could be prickly. Days before Leonardo had slipped into one of his classes to learn something about guitar technique. On that occasion it was the turn of a short-sighted, bespectacled young gui-

tarist by the name of Narciso Yepes to feel his ire. He started to play an arrangement of Johann Sebastian Bach's *Chaconne* so brilliantly and fluently that it deeply impressed Leonardo. When he finished, Segovia looked insulted and rudely said goodbye to his student after asking him which arrangement he had played. In Leonardo's opinion, he had performed with great precision and subtlety. When he went to talk to Yepes, the latter wasn't at all disappointed; in fact, he felt flattered by the mae-

With Narciso Yepes during the rehearsals for *Concerto for Guitar and Orchestra no. 1* in 1967

stro's attitude. He had used his own arrangement and ignored Segovia's own arrangements of Bach's music, which at the time were considered to be unique and masterly. Segovia must have found that hard to stomach.

Frederic Mompou was the resident composer on the Santiago summer course in the sixties. A quiet, introverted man he used to walk along the city's winding streets on the arm of his wife, Carmen Bravo, absorbed in his thoughts about his *Música Callada* (1959-1967). As was de rigueur according to the course's rules, Mompou had to give a brief introduction to his music before it was performed, something that hugely taxed the Catalan composer.

The course encouraged the setting up of different size groups that rehearsed quickly and enthusiastically works they then performed. One orchestral grouping was formed with a view to performing works by students in the composition class. That opening led to Leonardo Balada's debut in Spain. Eight minutes were performed of the work for piano, *Música en cuatro tiempos*, played by the Belgian Pauline Marcelle and with a small *ad hoc* orchestra, the now out-of-catalogue *Música Tranquila* for strings conducted by Gabriel Rodó.[5] After the concert Mompou the maestro walked slowly over and congratulated the young Balada on his works, which made a great impact on the young composer because they were words from a genius at creating austere sound and spare expressiveness charged with emotion. "I always admire those people who do things I can't do," said Mompou, words etched by fire on Leonardo's memory.

Those concerts tended to gather a little from here and there, and created a space for composers, performers and teachers to bring an emotional conclusion to a time they had shared intensely. It was the middle of September when Tansman introduced one of the concerts with a speech that was completely different to what one might have heard months before Darmstadt. The composer referred to sincerity in language as the guarantee of high level work, even though that directly challenged the recalcitrant academicism and extremism of other sectors. His words stirred the thinking of Balada who was using those ideas to shape a unique aesthetic universe of sound quite removed from any copycat pursuit of prefabricated structures. The concert received striking press coverage including a long article in *La Vanguardia*. Critic Luis Santamaría made special mention of the program's two works by Balada and lamented not being able to hear more music by the Catalan. In effect, that was a first impetus, a promising start, the beginning of a career whose ups and downs have always been followed in the media.

The Compostela experience was extraordinary. That summer course was his best opportunity to take the pulse of Spanish music and reveal his own unique self, a new, original voice on the rise. However, it would be wrong to think that what was cooked in the musical kitchen in Santiago

5   Gabriel Rodó Vergés (1904-1963) had been taught composition by Tansman in the mid-twenties and used to collaborate with his teacher conducting the orchestra, where he started in the early forties. He was also a well-known cellist and taught at the Liceu Conservatory in Barcelona.

was a true reflection of Spanish musical life. The aesthetic gloss on the courses was quite traditional, even in the composition section. Except for Mompou, who was struggling with himself and his totally denuded form of expression, the rest of the illustrious teachers performed standard repertoire and some were wholly impermeable to new creative trends. The real battles were being fought in less flowery fields that received much less exposure in the daily press. In any case, Balada's style was a perfect fit for the musical panorama at that time, because he retained an element of the internationalist neoclassicism that was beating a retreat, although it was still very alive in Spain, at least among the generation of maestros who hadn't gone into exile. That situation jarred with the generations of young Spanish composers then starting to break their ties to the past, if slowly and more in theory than in practice, creating a *de facto* two-headed aesthetic creature whose mainspring came principally from performers who leaned on tradition. The Nueva Música group had been founded in Madrid in 1958 and their premieres initiated a hesitant shift towards the avant-garde. The music by Halffter, Pablo or Bernaola, that one could hear in concert halls, still fed on those materials. Conversely, Ramón Barce represented the avant-garde with an intellectual thrust that had actually broken free, and his aesthetic conviction was the cornerstone for the awakening of many young Spanish musicians. Juan Hidalgo and Walter Marchetti were, for their part, already making an impression in Barcelona, and soon after would go to Madrid and establish ZAJ[6] with Barce.

That was why what was on offer in Santiago de Compostela was somewhat different to what was being attempted in Barcelona or Madrid. But the hunger and pursuit of new paths began to perforate Balada's aesthetic criteria. He was a composer who had been shaped in the United States, although his roots weren't there. That was his strength and card to play: he could be an individual creator everywhere, with no recognisable tics, no debts to anyone, his own man. On the journey home he had plenty of time to reflect on the creative identity of artists, on their limits and ambitions. His hunger for music was experiencing changes that required time and human interaction to reach a happy outcome, in order to rethink himself and be reborn with a different face but the same depths.

---

6   The activities of Hidalgo and Marchetti in Barcelona met with no success at all. Only a series of presentations and happenings endorsed by John Cage succeeded in slightly catching the attention of Catalan composers. Given the lack of interest in Barcelona, Hidalgo and Marchetti sought to make an impact in Madrid. Although their ideas didn't meet with the success they anticipated, it was Ramón Barce who led the setting up of ZAJ and its launch in 1964.

When he was back in the family home, Rebés phoned to invite him to come to a meeting in Madrid. The *Los Tarantos* project was still simmering apparently, since Rebés had already spoken to Picasso, Dalí and Viola, who would look after the scenery and costume design for the three-act ballet. There was even a wage for Leonardo which would help cover the cost of his stay in Madrid when he worked with Alfredo Mañas. He quickly packed his suitcase and went to live in Madrid, with all its advantages, but with the one big disadvantage, that he would be alone again. The weeks went by, and from his brief conversations with Mañas, he gathered that the writer was working on film projects that were much more profitable and enjoyable than their project, while Leonardo went for a stroll in the Retiro Park on his empty afternoons. Christmas came and the flamenco idea was still only words and hot air. Leonardo tired of waiting and decided to go home. The dream of *Los Tarantos* vanished soon after, or at least in its original conception, coinciding with La Chunga's marriage.[7] Apparently her recent husband didn't want his wife to continue working and everything collapsed like a house of cards. It was yet another notch on the tally of failed projects.

Several years later refashioned as a film, the new version of *Los Tarantos* was finally premiered in 1963 with a screenplay by Mañas and directed by Rovira Beleta, but La Chunga had given way to Carmen Amaya and Antonio Gades, and Leonardo Balada wasn't among the credits. The film was nominated for an Oscar in 1964 in the category of Best Foreign Film and the music was in the end composed by a long list of musicians, with everyone adding their specific grain of sand, from the flamenco Andrés Batista[8] to the renowned Fernando García Morcillo,[9] and the guitar maestros, Emilio Pujol and José Solà.[10]

Back in Barcelona, Leonardo tried to rediscover the musical pulse of the city. One afternoon, he and Joan Guinjoan visited one of the few

---

7 Paradoxically, her husband, José Luis Gonzalvo (1939-1997), was a film director, producer and owner of the Debla production company. He shot four films in the sixties. For her part La Chunga had already appeared in the undervalued *De espaldas a la puerta* (1959), directed by José María Forque. She starred or was given a credit in four other films, including *La ley de una raza*, in which she appeared alongside her husband and daughter.
8 Andrés Batista is a flamenco guitarist whose approach is widely valued in Spain.
9 Fernando García Morcillo (1916-2002) was one of the most famous composers for cinema in the fifties and sixties. He specialized in Spanish music, which meant that his offering for *Los Tarantos* was along the most traditional lines. He wrote the famous "*Mi vaca lechera*" and over 1,500 of his works have been recorded.
10 José Solà Sánchez (1930) was a well-known composer for film and television, the author of various soundtracks and jingles. He retired from the cinema in 1986.

maestros whose ideas went beyond the blinkers of state frontiers. Cristò-for Taltabull[11] was extremely cultured and his aesthetic influence over his pupils was central to the musical development of the Catalan avant-garde. The always interesting Joaquim Serra[12] was on the same wavelength, as was violinist and great composer Rafael Ferrer,[13] whose work opposed the official line of Zamacois.[14] In any case, Balada found inactivity and his Spanish fatherland deeply painful. He made another big decision in February 1961. He would take advantage of his student visa and return to the United States. It was a decision he hadn't reached lightly. He would be leaving his family again, but the truth was his future lay on the other side of the Atlantic. Many things had changed, but on his journey back he didn't feel at all anxious but rather full of renewed expectations at being able to recover a style of life that had fulfilled him professionally and personally. He was now a composer. The absence of his family was alleviated by the pledge that he would come home every summer. It was a new start; he had now made the key decisions.

Leonardo opted for a long stopover in London. He had met a young violinist in the corridors in Santiago who lived and worked there, so when he decided to return to the United States, he wanted to renew that friend-ship. On his second day in the latter's house, they went to have lunch with the distinguished violinist Antoni Brossa[15] who put him in touch with no less a figure than Roberto Gerhard. Within minutes Leonardo was engaging in lively conversation with the maestro, who lived in Cam-bridge and worked for the BBC. As time pressed, Leonardo was unable

11   Taltabull (1888-1964) is one of the undeniable masters who stayed on in Spain after the civil war. Born in Barcelona, he was already a composer of repute. His first compositions date from 1907, before he went to study in Munich and Leipzig under Max Reger. He settled in Paris in 1914 whence he returned in 1940 in flight from the Second World War. Given the artistic scene in Spain, he went into teaching and was highly influential for Catalan composers born in the 1930s.
12   Though short-lived, 1907-1957, he became a central figure in the development of the Catalan *cobla* and the *sardana*.
13   Rafael Ferrer (1911-1988) was a violinist and conductor of great prestige in Barcelona and Madrid. His recordings of *zarzuelas* are still a point of reference.
14   Joaquim Zamacois (1894-1976) was born in Chile but then lived in Barcelona. He taught at the Liceu Conservatory and wrote a number of treatises on musical harmony and pedagogy. He founded the Municipal Conservatory in 1945.
15   Antoni Brossa (1894-1974) was one of the distinguished Spanish musicians who triumphed outside Spain and remained practically unpublished in his native land. From La Canonja (Tarrag-ona), Brossa enjoyed enormous prestige as a violinist as a result of his famous premiere of Benjamin Britten's *Concerto for Violin and Piano* in 1940 in New York's Carnegie Hall. He divided his time between the Royal College of Music in London and his world tours. He was always very interested in contemporary music. Balada remembers him as being extremely cordial. During his visit to London, Brossa showed him the Royal College. He played a Stradivarius for a long time.

to visit him in the university city, though he could accept Gerhard's invitation to the premiere of his Third Symphony "Collages" that was first performed in London by the BBC Symphony Orchestra conducted by Rudolph Schwarz. They were unable to have a lengthy conversation, but the maestro urged him to come to next year's courses in Tanglewood where he would be teaching, but time again pressed and Balada couldn't make that date planned so long in advance, because, by the time those courses began, he would be a married man.

14.
Dalí's Mustache

There are moments in life that mark us indelibly. Looks, words or gestures are etched on our subconscious and then surface unexpectedly, even remain incubating, waiting for the opportunity to reappear and mark our path at a crossroads against which we have no redress. That moment when Salvador Dalí rushed into the lobby at the Saint Regis was one such moment for Leonardo Balada. The *Temas* magazine had sent two Catalans, Carles Font-serè and Leonardo Balada to report on Salvador Dalí, the most universal Catalan of the time. Balada had a longstanding admiration for Dalí the artist, but found his character disconcerting. Every young artist is usually convinced of his creative truth until at some point he falls off his horse. In

Dalí and Balada in New York

the prime of youth a creative mind can't handle posturing, staged scenes, polite protocols or mannered courtesy. Unchallengeable axioms—transcendent art will always receive the recognition it deserves or that you only need youthful, brilliant ideas to achieve success—are but two of youth's utopian flights. But the truth strikes home eventually with the sober reality that it is the genius of agents rather than of artists that makes the difference.

Some of the media circus effects Dalí carried in his baggage could be amusing because they were so over-the-top, but could also be dangerous if the artist mistook fiction for reality. From the moment they saw Dalí enter the hotel lobby, Balada began to perceive other truths about the genius, the painter and the individual. His first words in Catalan were reassuring. The artist most in the media limelight was serious, thoughtful, profound and scintillating in word and gesture. He wore a ravishing black suit and his long, carefully combed hair was impressive too, but what stood out was his trademark, magnificent, sleek mustache. He was a celebrity in New York before that encounter; he appeared almost daily in the media, and enjoyed almost Hollywood stardom. After his first collective exhibition in 1932[1] and first trip to the city with Gala in 1934, and the *Fantastic Art, Dada and Surrealism* exhibition at the Museum of Modern Art (MOMA) in 1936, Dalí had even premiered the work *Bacchanale*[2] in the Metropolitan Opera House in 1939. His ballet *Labyrinth*[3] was also premiered on that stage to coincide with the first retrospective of his paintings at the MOMA, that had raised him to undeniable heights of fame. Apparently financial help from Pablo Picasso to the tune of five hundred dollars had enabled him to reach the United States in 1940, thus sparing him the world war and allowing him to settle down provisionally among the Big Apple's skyscrapers. He was always on the go and liked to mount genuine semi-street happenings at every event he attended, giving free rein to the much touted acts of delirium that affirmed his right to artistic madness[4] Dalí's persona perfectly matched the idea North Americans had of avant-garde

---

1   The exhibition of surrealist art in the Julien Levy Gallery.
2   Dalí's first work for the stage, *Bacchanale*, was premiered at the Metropolitan Opera House, with the libretto, costumes and scenery all designed by him; Léonide Massine's choreography for the Russian Ballets of Monte Carlo and music adapted from work by Richard Wagner, the painter's favorite composer.
3   *Labyrinth* was premiered on October 8, 1941 with the same performers and stage sets, but on that occasion with music *de pasticcio* by Franz Schubert.
4   It was during one of his stays in America, in 1939, when he published his *Declaration of the independence of the imagination and the right of a man to his own madness* as his response to the banning of his construction of an image of a Venus with the head of a fish.

artists, so that the presence of the painter from Figueres on television and in newspapers became ever more frequent. His openly conservative ideology, hot air rather than substance, was broadcast to the four corners of the land, enabling him to enjoy a reputation that was more suited to him in his old age. In any case, in that first interview, with friendly people and for a Hispanic magazine, posturing and grandiloquence were unnecessary.

Fontserè's photo lit up the room and immortalized seconds that would fill a few folios that night, which early the next morning, made their way to the *Temas* editor. Dalí displayed a knowledge and creativity that impressed Leonardo. The man couldn't stop creating whether he used paintbrushes, hands or words. Notebook in hand, the musician jotted with nervous energy, a white pencil in his right hand, next to a table littered with photographs and previous issues of *Temas* that Dalí glanced at sporadically as he talked. There was a bottle of sparkling mineral water and a jug of tap water on the edge of table; their expenses didn't stretch to anything alcoholic. Some fans of the painter suddenly appeared wanting an autograph as a souvenir. In a matter of seconds Dalí's relaxed, serious expression transformed into the familiar lunatic grimace of the eccentric character he liked to play.

Page from the Dalí interview in *Temas*

His hands drew circles and his voice became shrill and histrionic in an English that was very correct but carried a heavy Figueres accent. When the autograph hunters disappeared, Dalí switched back equally speedily, his body and face now regained their serious demeanor and he reverted to the "ultratypical Catalan countryman," as he liked to define himself.

That interview was the beginning of their friendship. They repaired to a department store where Dalí encountered a situation, that, in his view, he couldn't condone. The painter had designed a shop window for which he had been paid most generously, but the store management thought that some of the figures were immoral in terms of the ideals espoused by their business. In an outburst of moral fervor, they had changed those figures without telling Dalí. The media launch turned into an improvised happening when the painter started breaking windows. The hand of genius was unique and, like Juan Ramón Jiménez's rose, any tampering would remove the purple mantle he had bestowed.[5] Given the awful fracas that was brewing, Leonardo stepped aside and asked the police to come and keep the populace in order. Dalí was Dalí, period.

The following day he walked up to the door of Dalí's suite, knocked timidly, and Gala appeared, distant, elegant, almost invisible and ethereal. Dalí spoke about aesthetics, his idea of Dalinian surrealism, his concept of the mutable and the transformation of matter in every individual's brain. Leonardo soaked up the free lecture while asking about the real nature of the avant-garde.

Every year Dalí spent a few months in New York and was a frequent presence at parties, exhibitions or gala evenings. Leonardo's liking for painting, and for the avant-garde in particular, was gradually permeating his style and way of understanding artistic creation. It wasn't unusual to see Balada at the latest exhibitions in New York's most daring galleries taking notes and applying similar thinking to his staves. Obviously having Dalí at hand was an opportunity to participate in an extraordinary learning experience. His previously one-sided relationship with the painter soon became a creative dialogue. The idea of collaborating cropped up one afternoon. It was 1960. Dalí was working on the idea of a twenty-minute short—that were eighteen in the end—with a happening that was a sort of satire of Piet Mondrian. Dalí's destructive penchant went down well in the United States; apparently only geniuses were allowed to be iconoclastic and then only when they confessed they were half mad. Although it was clear that Dalí was no madman, he loved to act up and consequently the film was an act of creative madness. The tape was directed by a longstanding friend, the photographer Phillipe Halsman, and is now considered to be one of the first historical examples of video art. The plot was in itself an authentic surrealist painting. The mocking of Mondrian was enacted by

---

5 From Juan Ramón's famous poem, *No la toques ya más / así es la rosa* (Don't touch it anymore / that's how the rose is)

Dalí painting pigs (four were transported from the neighboring state of Pennsylvania), popcorn and even a nude model. Dalí appeared in the film with two models, Leslie Crane and Miriam de Cova. The movie was made on the understanding that it would be shown at the 5th Annual Convention for Visual Communication, but over time it disappeared and until recently was thought to have been lost for good. Only a few memories rehearsed by participants in the venture kept alive the myth of a film nobody had seen, but which everybody had heard about.

The idea was that Balada should be responsible for the soundtrack, or rather the music to be heard at a specific moment in the movie, since a fragment of Mozart's *Concerto for Flute, Harp and Orchestra in D Major K.299* is played at the end of the film. Dalí wanted Balada to compose a score inspired by one of his drawings. After seeing the short we deduce that Balada's presence was probably a requisite imposed by Dalí, since the short lacks dramatic continuity and his contribution complements the film's thesis, even if it is quite tokenistic. Balada was asked to put music to the concept, and that was a real challenge when it was an exercise in not particularly subtle aesthetic leg-pulling. It wasn't easy to come up with music to enhance a work of this nature.

Still of the credits for *Chaos and Creation*

It was an exercise that limited his scope for creativity, but as a young artist Balada had to accept that his was a secondary role. It was usual and even desirable for such invitations to collaborate to come at the level of suggested themes rather than precise images. A work with lines and dots by Dalí himself had brushstrokes that could very well have suggested musical notation—or at least shapes that appeared to—and that as such could be scattered over a Dalinian horizon. Suddenly, the great idea came. Balada asked for a photo of the work, then put his staves over the drawing and began to arrange the notes as a reference point for his later improvisation for piano. The work was an essay in the purest avant-garde and totally deserved the name it was given: *Chaos and Creation.* Some years later when the Dalí Museum in Figueres began

Still of Balada in *Chaos and Creation*

cataloguing his complete nonpainterly works, a few documents related to *Chaos and Creation* surfaced, but no more detail. Félix Fanés, among other Dalí specialists, salvaged the work that had been converted to celluloid from a previous video version. The production company went by the name of Videotape Productions of New York. In an article for the Instituto Cervantes Virtual Library Fanés commented on Balada's contribution:[6]

". . . A second leading collaborator in the project was musician Lleonard Balada (sic). Resident in New York at the time, Balada was a a student at The Juilliard School, and was commissioned to discover in the blotches and dribbles of paint on the work being created during the recording of the tape, images similar to notes, that he had to transfer to the staves and play on the piano, which is what he did . . ."

Whenever Dalí returned to New York, the two friends enjoyed many a leisurely afternoon and relaxed conversation when they chatted about everything and everybody. Although they met at parties organized by the city's Hispanic contingent, their quiet exchanges were much more interesting. After *Chaos and Creation* Leonardo asked Dalí for a reference

6   Fanés, Félix, "*Chaos and Creation*, un film inédito de Salvador Dalí," Biblioteca Virtual Miguel de Cervantes.

to support his working and residence in the United States, given he was now no longer a student, but a professional. As many distinguished composers and performers endorsed Leonardo's work, the prospect of a future in the United States with that longed-for residency permit seemed rosy. In the case of Dalí's extremely interesting document, it was sent by the painter himself and dated April 12, 1961. The reference recognizes Balada's "great musical talent," and emphasizes "the high degree of maturity and originality" of his scores. But the most important part of the letter was the mention of a future project, because, as well as citing their recent film collaboration, it pointed out: "I have some plans for the future in which he will again create the music. One of them will be an opera the outline

Letter of recommendation from Salvador Dalí

of which has already been decided and which we will start working on in the near future."

These future plans were possibly in the making at the end of the spring of 1961, when both artists got together again with a notebook and a bowl of peanuts. On that occasion, the interview was for an issue of the *Amigos* magazine, of which the July issue was the first and the last. On the front cover a baby played with a tin of talcum powder wrapped in a huge diaper and it contained, at a cost of 25 cents, an interview with Salvador Dalí entitled: "Salvador Dalí; half magic, half art": page 23 carried the start of that latest encounter between painter and musician in the "Arts Page" section. The newness of the magazine led to a few errors in the layout as the title now appeared as: "Salvador Dalí: Magic and Biochemistry." Balada's fascination for Dalí was laid out in black and white and this is how Balada saw Dalí:

"To speak of Salvador Dalí is almost to speak of magic and alchemy and—in no small measure—of art. Both the public at large and the press have viewed the famous painter's personality from a wrong angle, that has been astutely exaggerated by the wit and will of Dalí himself. People and newspapers only see his mustache, his eccentricities and his showmanship. But this isn't Salvador Dalí. As a private person, the Catalan artist is not like that at all: he is thoughtful, reasonable and—above all—a conscious artist. We have had the good fortune to know him for some time and could grasp and relish the intense humanity and sincerity Dalí hides behind his mask.

When he is wearing his mask, Dalí transforms the world and distorts sizes, making everything seem less sad and more fantastic. Let's continue, for a few seconds, with this fantastic Dalí and play along with his game of words and images . . ."

These introductory words clearly show that Balada wants to distinguish between Dalí in private and Dalí the actor. That interview came with an extra media element attached because it took place a few days after a public event when Dalí's mustache was attacked. An *espontáneo*, or at least that was what he was called, got close up to the artist with a pair scissors and cut off one end of his trademark, immaculate mustache.[7] In the quiet of

---

7   In effect, that act wasn't as spontaneous as it appeared; the perpetrator was Joan Gardy-Artigas

that hotel room, with Gala lurking silently in the background, Dalí turned that skirmish into an artistically meaningful event.

"What happened to your mustache the other day?" we asked.

Dalí pretended not to hear.

"Don't pretend. We were there."

"They say it was a joke; I think they wanted to preserve part of my mustache for the benefit of history . . ."

As payment for the article had been agreed by word of mouth and depended on the subscriptions and sales of the next issues, that was simply a pleasant conversation with a friend, since the magazine folded immediately. At one moment in the interview, Dalí grabbed a piece of paper, smaller than a quarto, and made a precise, quite abstract drawing with a blue pen that he dedicated to the *Amigos* magazine. It was the best payment Balada could have imagined, as the collapse of the magazine meant he kept a drawing that now adorns the white, Mediterranean wall of his home.

Artigas clipping one end of Dalí's mustache

Later, in 1967, a telephone call put the seal on that reference in support of Leonardo's application for a residency permit. The second collaboration between Dalí and Balada was in the offing. The painter, whose star was waning in New York as a result of the fierce competition for attention that existed every year in the Big Apple, tried to give a Copernican twist to his image. This twist was influenced by the endless alternative cultural spaces springing up in New York to boost its recognition throughout the world. It was a time when there was a great confusion between artistic and purely commercial events in the city. A time, in a word, of great creativity and imagination. The proposal was the following. The present-day Avery Fisher Hall, the former Philharmonia Hall, the right-hand side of the Lincoln Center and one of New York's most prestigious concert spaces would advertise a unique, exceptional, unrepeatable event.

(1938), son of Josep Llorens i Artigas (1892-1980), a famous potter, friend and collaborator of Joan Miró's. It is very likely Joan Gardy-Artigas had conferred with the painter about this "barber-shop" happening.

The great painter Salvador Dalí, immortal in his lifetime, would enact a happening on stage with Carles Fontserè as stage director and music by Leonardo Balada. To that end, an oval transparent structure was devised within which the painter would produce a series of paintings he would improvise by hurling objects at canvases the whole audience could see. As the act would be incomplete in itself, the musical contribution apparently wasn't merely an accompaniment, but merited a preeminent space in the event. Dalí decided to rely on Leonardo Balada, who was now well known and had a proven track record, to create the musical sound. Balada's idea was to litter the stage with a number of small groups making sound from a series of improvised phrases that would be perfectly articulated. From a point visible to each group, he would indicate the random entries for each set of improvisers, thus creating the right accompaniment to Dalí. In short, it was about expanding random painterly creation to the sonorous space within the room, retaining the same creative, aesthetic elements. It was really a *mano a mano* between two artists creating there and then, whose art would expand and recede in surprising ways.

The media impact of that duel no doubt gave a crucial boost to Balada's reputation and was a rallying point for the controversial figure of Dalí. There is little one can say about the work itself, since its genesis contained a depth and destiny that were inevitably fated to a momentary existence, however poetically charged that might have been. Dalí was to repeat that way of working which was even filmed in a few shorts, but it proved a beginning and end for Leonardo. It was difficult to repeat something that was so eminently unrepeatable.

The relationship between Leonardo Balada and Salvador Dalí continues to this day. Balada's creative style has continued to evolve and has led to a singular period of creation and consolidation that could be called Mediterranean Surrealism with Dalinian aspirations. One could trace the start of this sensibility in the opera project that took shape around 1994 as a commission for the Festival of Perelada, which was then consolidated in Madrid's Teatro Real, leaving some brilliant pieces in its wake, like the *Diario de sueños*, (*Diary of Dreams*), 1995, one of the most original Spanish chamber works from the end of the twentieth century. The illustrious figure of Fernando Arrabal appeared in a number of those projects as the potential writer of the text, since both met Dalí, though on separate occasions, in the Saint Regis Hotel in New York, a meeting they both revisited when preparing the idea of *Faust-bal*.

Dalí and Balada during one of the interviews

The stamp that Dalí left on Balada's work, as we said, has become more marked over recent years. Years characterized by a maturing of that strange, Dalinian surrealism that had led Balada to explore the fields of permanent sound transformation. Their essence is present on Dalí's canvases but has undergone an adaptation to musical sound, since Balada introduces well-defined creative lines that mutate into others that are also perfectly defined, that is, as if one recognizable object were to change into another that is equally recognizable following a direct, human, intuitive process of metamorphosis.

15.
Scores Are Not for Eating

New York greeted Balada with that mixture of freezing cold and gray damp typical of the beginning of a New Year. 1961 had just kicked off. The chill entered the bones thanks to a sea more imagined than seen. Many New Yorkers live in maritime conditions but have never been near the sea, which was always a real paradox that underlined other features. The pretext of the Mannes School had worked perfectly; Balada returned to the Redds' house with his student visa renewed and keen to resume his previous life. His work with Norman Dello Joio was no longer what was central; he had to make up time and look to the future with a new perspective. New York was no longer a stepping stone; it was an end in itself. The postgraduate courses sounded like frivolous offerings for the rich, but the tailor's son wanted to extend the unique training he had begun. Part-time jobs, the organ, friends and long conversations in which you could hear a pin drop when words like Barcelona, Mediterranean, and home were mentioned once more filled up most of his time. But something was very different now. The starting point for his existential anabasis was no longer Sant Just to New York, but quite the contrary, and that was much more than a clever turn of phrase, it had become a mindset.

When he entered his old room, Balada understood that nothing was as it used to be, his life as a composer was on track and now it was all about seeking and finding work and success on what was a complex road map. Before saying goodbye to Santiago de Compostela, Narciso Yepes had commissioned a work he wanted to premiere straight away. Balada sat at his desk and looked for a motif, a spur to get him started. The revision of his *Lento and Variation* was the spark. And here we find one of the keys to his creative process; rather than turning to diverse aesthetic moments or incidents, he has habitually tried to find a musical reference to initiate and organize the body of sound of any new work.[1]

Leonardo had learned a lot from the creative process of writing *Lento and Variation* and was keen to recover the pulse of the guitar in order to apply all the novel experiments he had seen Yepes was trying out. However, the new work dawning on staves could no longer be a student exercise; it was no longer enough to show enthusiasm and honest talent: this was a professional commission for what would be a professional premiere. The creative void was so terrifying for a moment he felt the need to plunge in with the instrument at firsthand, to feel its vibrations, complexities and live pulse between its strings; he went out and bought a guitar. He had to give material form to the sound he was weaving in his head, which his technique was failing to coalesce. When he was back home, he could only find chords to strum and a flamenco beat on the box drum. Absorbed in thought he observed himself in the midst of his own private Spanish fiesta and looking more bewildered than a chicken at a convention of pharmacists.

A young Andalusian guitarist whom he had met on the Santiago courses was honing his art nearby and he now clung to him like a red-hot brand. José Luis Franco had worked in New York for some time and had just married a vivacious fellow Andalusian. Mutual needs brought them together and that was how Balada received his first lessons in guitar technique and fingering. But every morning it was an increasingly uphill struggle. The music flowed in his mind in a distinct way but his fingers couldn't react at the same speed. The work would be a homage to Spanish Golden Age music, so echoes of the vihuela would lead into more contemporary sounds, revitalizing the specifically twilight neobaroque to be found in the later de Falla, the best Rodrigo and Ernesto Halffter. He was immersed in *Suite no. 1* when Yepes called. Their conversation focused on technical issues and musical inspiration. The work would have a revision of the Landini cadences as its purely speculative horizon. As usual Yepes personally would sort out the fingering, a taxing reality for someone trained as a pianist like Balada. Even so, the composer had purchased that cheap guitar

---

1   This doesn't mean that Balada has always had recourse to sonorous content to create his structure, but that such a recourse acts as the spark, a creative impulse that can sometimes be purely musical, at other times philosophical, and on other occasions an idea or completely abstract concept. In this respect, training in the United States tends to involve less speculation than his Spanish and European contemporaries would expect. While many members of his generation see creation as an intellectual challenge, when it comes to solving a musical problem a sonorous, communicative presence is present in the whole process in the American world of artistic creation.

to practice and immerse himself in the language of the instrument. Yepes advised him to sell the guitar and not worry about reducing or rationalizing technical problems: he would lose an artist's necessary freshness and freedom. It wasn't good for a composer to get bogged down in such detail, it was best to work with maximum freedom, and the problems would be resolved in due course.

That *Suite* had five movements (*Allegretto, Moderato, Andantino, Lento* and *Animando*) and continues to be performed, even though it belongs aesthetically to the period when Balada was still finding his way. The vicissitudes of the *Suite* seemed to find a safe landing. At the following year's course in Santiago de Compostela Leonardo slipped the score into Narciso Yepes's briefcase almost on the sly, and it rested there for months, and then years. Yepes reappeared and phoned in 1965. He was in New York and giving a concert at the Town Hall. The door of the Balada home opened wide for the guitarist from Murcia and they were able to rehearse properly before the big premiere. Concerts given by Yepes usually received lots of attention in the American media, as he was seen as the natural heir to Andrés Segovia, who was already a myth in his own right. That night the *Suite No I* was heard for the first time and it was one of Balada's first big premieres. From then on whenever Yepes played that piece, he would interrupt his concert routine to recount the story of the guitar Balada had bought and then sold. Many guitarists discovered Balada as a result of that anecdote which Yepes so liked to retell.

Leonardo soon stopped recognizing himself in the reflection from those nostalgic Landini cadences. The call of the contemporary had entered his thinking in the mid-sixties, a crucial period of aesthetic meditation as he edged his way to a very different universe of sound. However, as the writer said, that's quite another story. The *Suite*'s success led Yepes to initiate a more flowing collaboration with the composer, as well as an intense, complex friendship. Perhaps as the result of nostalgia or artistic challenges, the guitar stands out as one of Balada's favorite instruments, the one for which he has composed most works.

Following a similar pattern to what happened with Yepes, in that first course in 1960, Gaspar Cassadó[2] was another soloist who showed a lot of interest in Balada's work and he commissioned a cello concerto that meant

---

2   Gaspar Cassadó (1897-1966) was an internationally renowned cellist and a keen promoter of the contemporary repertoire, so it wasn't altogether surprising for him to commission composers as young as Balada. He died in Madrid.

he would again be working for one of the most important soloists of the day. Balada threw himself into the composition like a man possessed and it was soon ready and at the next course, two years later, he picked up the thread again. Cassadó, with Pau Casals, was one the world's great cellists; that was an honor he couldn't defer. Strangely, when Cassadó was only a boy he gave a concert which Casals attended, and that practically led to his discovery and the start of his legend. Before twelve months were up, Leonardo had finished the work. It was 1962. The following year the concerto was selected for the Spanish section of the SIMC (the International Society for Contemporary Music), as had happened previously with *Música Tranquila*, though that wasn't a premiere, but analyses and reading of works. That year's Festival was held in Copenhagen and the other Spanish composers selected were José Baguena, Carmelo Alonso Bernaola, Cristóbal Halffter, Jaume Padró and Enric Raxach. When Cassadó passed through New York, he worked on the fingering, intricacies of rhythm and flights of melody, but regrettably the cellist died before he could premiere the work and the concert had no immediate prospects. Balada completely revised the work and created the definitive version in 1967.[3]

It was an impressive creative return to the United States and the early sixties began to lay the first foundations of his catalogue. The imbricated ways of the guitar encouraged him to delve deeper amid its strings. The fruit of that endeavor was *Tres divagaciones* (*Three improvisations*)for guitar, a work from 1962 based on three themes from Castile. Balada was preparing the way for what would become the most personal area of his work as a composer with a piece based on elements from folklore.[4] *Tres divagaciones* navigates much more tonal language than some of his previous works, demonstrating that the piece was aimed at Spain and its most classical guitarists and not at the United States where contemporary musical language was dictated by other scenarios.

---

3   The *Concerto for Cello and Nine Players* reflects the paradox that it was composed for Cassadó, who commissioned it during Balada's initial phase (1962), but it was revised when he moved into his avant-garde phase. Structured in the classic three movements, the work locates the lyricism of the cello, Balada's favorite instrument, alongside a stringless instrumental ensemble with wind and percussion that engaged in an intense dialogue with the soloist. The work was finally premiered by Nathaniel Rosen with the Pittsburgh New Music Ensemble conducted by David Stock.

4   Although it's not one of his most important works, *Tres divagaciones* reveals an artistic reality that is very interesting as regards Balada's aesthetics and development. The work on Castilian motifs, even though it is a long way from the evident modernity of his later technique, marks out a line of discourse that shows that Balada found working with an ethnic resource to be extremely fruitful in terms of aesthetic drive. This is particularly striking given we are speaking about a work from 1962 and hence from his early, starting-out period.

Although 1963 was a very active year at the personal level, that wasn't the case in terms of creativity. He only finished one strange work for the organ *The Seven Last Words*, and the word "strange" used advisedly because the title has a very Christian ring. It was even stranger coming from an out-and-out atheist like Balada. But once one moves inside the score, it is seen that there is no religious content beyond the clear reference to Christ's words on the cross. The work was premiered by Montserrat Torrent[5] at the Religious Week in Cuenca, Balada's first participation in this event and his first collaboration with the Catalan organist for whom he wrote the spectacular *Elementalis* in 1972, where Balada scaled his greatest heights with the concert organ. The scintillating way he plays with the stops and uses full clusters make his composition a key piece within contemporary writing for the organ. The latter work had the honor of being the first music to be played on the new organ in Barcelona's Palau de la Música on February 21, 1973.

As paradox seemed to be Balada's constant companion in the early sixties, he ended 1963 on one of those chance occurrences that makes one wonder whether fate does or doesn't exist. Every year New York organized a big concert for the best young composers of the moment. Media coverage was huge because the critics on the daily broadsheets went in force. Success in such Composers' Forums guaranteed years of commissions and perhaps even offers of employment in the country's most prestigious universities. Balada was one of those invited in 1963. The works selected were old acquaintances, *Música en cuatro tiempos* and *Sonata for violin and piano*, a sample of almost thirty minutes that would act as a noncontroversial introduction, given the aesthetic followed by Balada in his early works. The concert went very well and the performances were excellent, but heavenly choruses were telling Leonardo to bring his language of sound into line with contemporary musical reality. Everything had gone swimmingly, but a problem arose the following day. When he woke up early, he ran to buy all the city dailies. He got to the kiosk and repeatedly looked at his watch before asking the newspaper seller why the dailies hadn't yet arrived, to which the reply came that there was no press—there had been a strike the previous day. Heavens, the first newspaper strike in decades, and it had

---

5   Born in Barcelona in 1926, Montserrat Torrent was a pupil of Taltabull and is today one of the world's leading organists. Her work with contemporary music is worthy of note as her instrument can look to a glorious past that barely leaves room for new contributions. Balada wrote for her the two organ works that appear in his catalogue, *The Seven Last Words* (1963) and *Elementalis* (1973).

to happen on that day! Leonardo's first big professional success received no reviews or critiques. He would have to wait for another opportunity.

As stated, in previous years Leonardo's personal life had been circumscribed by the boundaries that safeguarded his creative universe. Friendships and amorous skirmishes had come and gone in previous months and years, but a stable, serious commitment hadn't materialized. One night Balada donned his best suit and overcoat, pocketed his international journalist card and walked to Lincoln Center. That night promised to be a classy night out at the Metropolitan Opera House, and so it was, but not for what you might imagine. It was freezing outside, Christmas was nigh and December was buzzing. Balada had been waiting for some time in the famous Standing Room, when he spotted a girl in the distance who looked as if she was waiting for someone or something. He went over and they began a pleasant conversation that continued to the end of the performance and the way home. They agreed to see each other at a party she was organizing shortly. Though he didn't realize it at the time, that elegant venue would give a new twist to his life. After the usual polite introductions, Leonardo began to meander around the impressive room until his eyes met those of an Irish beauty who captured his attention for the rest of the evening. He now all but forgot his hostess, the air in the room rushed to the same spot.

Her name was Monica McCormack, an actress—meaning she worked at everything but that—and was indeed Irish, although she had a U.S. passport and dual citizenship. He immediately felt she emanated energy that was unheard of among Anglo-Saxons. In her way, Monica was intense, the epitome of the Irish, and in effect, very Spanish. They were an item when they left the party and within a few months, in early summer, they were married in New York. That was June 1962.

The young couple shared a series of unusual features that

Balada and his first wife, Monica McCormack, at the Met in 1966 made them stand out. A budding composer was settling down with an actress in search of openings and both were surely in one of the most competitive places in the world. The international center for artistic creativity had shifted from Paris to New York, now the mecca for all those who craved to be somebody. That forced the young marrieds to work on two different levels, the emotional and family, and the purely professional, not to mention the urgent need to pay their bills and live with a degree of calm. Pursuing the professional trail, days before their honeymoon, Balada went to see Victoria de los Ángeles, who was the most famous living Spanish singer. They had breathed the same air of their Barcelona birthplace and been taught within the walls of the same Liceu Conservatory, so they hit it off immediately. Leonardo needed money, he had just married and knew you couldn't live off scores, so he was looking for commissions, now that marriage had solved the problem of his residence permit. No sooner said than done, the great soprano commissioned a work for voice and piano. The sound of Leonardo's music had entered a kind of interregnum, where the diaphanous, bordering on tonal, tradition, was being enriched by a range of dissonances in keeping with contemporary taste. The main challenge of that commission was to satisfy the singer's melodic identity—her training and technique were clearly marked by the language of the nineteenth century—without reneging on his own idiosyncrasies as a contemporary composer. The dichotomy between the composer composing bespoke and the composer who felt compelled by an aesthetic challenge to create something new, would become Leonardo Balada's constant traveling companion. In the event, the contemporary language would belong to the piano while the voice took off in free flowing, *cantabile* form, unblinkered by the past or the recycling of anything stereotypically Spanish. He finished the work quickly, before they returned to Europe where the couple would spend their first holidays together. The initial title was *Cuatro Canciones de la Provincia de Madrid*, (*Four Songs from the Province of Madrid*) but Victoria de los Ángeles proceeded to forget all about it or simply couldn't find the time to premiere the songs. It would first be heard in Spain sung by another internationally renowned singer, Teresa Berganza. Balada later revised the work and gave it a different title, *Cuatro Canciones Españolas* (*Song for Holy Week*, *Wheel of Love*, *Lullaby* and *Child's Song*) although it is still rather ambiguous in the catalogue. Years later, Victoria de los Ángeles gave a concert in Pittsburgh. Balada, *noblesse oblige*, went to the dressing room to offer to be her guide to the city. She admitted she hadn't behaved well towards him, since she had commissioned a work that she hadn't paid for or premiered. An occupational hazard, thought Leonardo to himself, as he responded with a perfect smile.

Monica and Leonardo Balada departed on their honeymoon to Europe. First destination was Barcelona, where Monica Balada met her husband's family—amazing, very different people. She also managed a glimpse of Barcelona, the only corner of her husband's heart she had yet to scrutinize. One afternoon, the young couple went to a gathering of Catalan composers attended by Xavier Montsalvatge, Manuel Valls and Xavier Turull,[6] amongst others. The first was busy writing his opera *Babel 46*, an intense, multilingual work about a concentration camp at the end of the Second World War. Monsalvatge must have been misinformed; he was so excited to meet Monica because he thought she was a singer and insisted she would have a role in the opera he was finishing. Balada was always on friendly terms with contemporary composers, which amounted to admiration when it came to patriarchs from previous generations. The case of Montsalvatge was particularly meaningful. Whenever Balada returned to Barcelona, he visited the composer from Girona, thus nurturing a close friendship. But to return to the historical moment in our narrative, the reality was that *Babel 46* received its premiere forty years later, when Monica McCormack was no longer Leonardo's wife, and had yet to become a singer. The couple's independence and modernity was clear from the start. No one in their relationship was striving to dominate; it was based on mutual need.

Leonardo went back to the courses in Santiago, though he could see that, like the old stones of the Obradoiro, nothing had changed. The same people, the same geniuses, the same limp, rather dog-eared aesthetics. The experience of the previous round, enhanced by the expectations of the brand-new composer returning home to show off his achievements, enabled him to establish closer links with the individuals he admired, who were now his colleagues in the trade. That new situation for Balada launched a broad period of aesthetic reflection from a creative point of view. As we have seen, the early sixties are years when Balada composed little, whenever he was commissioned, and wasn't ready to unleash the creative storm heading his way; he still wasn't sure of his convictions.

The 1962 summer course, "Music in Compostela," confronted him

---

6   Xavier Turull (1922-2000) spent eight years in South America teaching violin and chamber music in various universities. He studied under Massià, Menuhin and Casals. As a musician he was committed to contemporary music.

with an urgent need to look beyond the mirrors of the Spanish music that passed as the official repertoire, but didn't reflect the real state of the art. That definitely wasn't the sum total of Spanish music, or at least that was his hope; he increasingly began to lose interest. Balada didn't stay on to the end of the course but left for Ireland where his new wife had been waiting for weeks. However, he did make a stopover in Paris to slake his thirst for that *other* Spanish music. He had a telephone number he had been longing to ring for some time; it belonged to Salvador Bacarisse, another of the great maestros of the Generation of the Republic who lived in sad exile.[7] He enjoyed an unforgettable hour with the friendly composer in his house in the Quartier Latin, a dwelling next to the house once inhabited by George Sand. His intelligent gaze stared out from behind thick spectacles, and his slow, thoughtful way of speaking couldn't hide the suffering caused by his enforced exile. A cultural activist under the Second Republic, he had been the visible head of the short-lived Junta for Music and Lyric Theater set up by the first republican government. He had been forced to change his modern, polytonal, neoclassical style back to the one he hated in his youth, an old-fashioned, worn-out folkloric Spanish style that put food on his table. Many Spanish musicians from the avant-garde past were compelled to carry that cross which they had so violently rejected when they were artists on the rise and musicians appearing in the dailies and in neon lights. If they wanted to have a hot meal every day, as long as exile lasted, they had no choice. In effect, exile strangled a brilliant intellectual vein in modern Spanish music, while at the same time other inevitable obligations never took them away from a path that was somewhat closer to the general public. In any case, the figure of Bacarisse was more than simply a composer from a previous generation; he was the symbolic image of a music that had been denied, an extinct aesthetic, that soon or later should be reborn. They aired many topics in that visit, above all, Leonardo's admiration for that individual and his actions, since his work was so undervalued in a world like the present that is so cauterized by the culture of the standard repertoire.

---

7 Salvador Bacarisse (1898-1963) is a paradigmatic example of the unfortunate musicians of the Generation of the Republic. His early work revealed an extraordinary aesthetic quest, that he crowned with an opera, that has yet to be performed, *Charlot* (1932-33), with texts by Ramón Gómez de la Serna. Fate, changes of government and the civil war plunged the avant-garde strain in this generation into oblivion. Necessity forced them to compose music full of Spanish local color that they themselves had rejected in their youth. Bacarisse spent his entire exile in Paris, where he died without ever being able to return, though he was always a point of reference for young Spanish composers visiting Paris.

Dylan Balada (the young couple's son), Monica and her parents in Ireland

When he reached Ireland, it was now Leonardo's turn to meet Monica's family, a very close, very Irish family who were instantly welcoming. It was a happy time, time for the famous "Guinness and stew with you," though naturally it couldn't last. On their return to New York, pressure from his wife meant that Leonardo, as head of the family, had to seek daily sustenance in the form of a stable job. Temporary jobs as an organist with sporadic payment no longer sufficed; nor did the scant pay from arty magazines. Commissions came, but little money was ever advanced on account; art was a labor of love. It wasn't that money was delayed, it simply never arrived. After they had lived in Jean and Margarita Redd's house for a few months (they were now living in Andorra), Monica decided she wanted her own home, and that involved a huge outlay because house ownership was a luxury in New York. As he went in search of regular, remunerated work, the variables were clear and well defined. He needed a well-paid job related to music that gave him enough time to compose. Monica went to lots of castings but her forceful character clashed with directors who didn't see her as at all malleable as an actress. In the meantime, she worked as a secretary in a private detective agency, so when they conversed over supper it felt as if Dashiell Hammett had joined the family.

However, an opportunity came much earlier than anticipated in Manhattan. A private high school, with a quite unusual philosophy, needed a teacher of Spanish who could complete his timetable with the occasional music class and lead the school choir. It was a perfect fit for Balada. His nationality and qualifications must have made him the best candidate to fill that post. On his first day at the Walden School,[8] the headmaster told him about the school's ethos. It was a private institution without religious or political affiliations, although marked by a modern educational trend according to which there was barely any hierarchy among members of the educational community (teachers, concierges or pupils). Some former pupils of the Walden School went on to become stars in American popular culture, like the hippies Peter, Paul and Mary—singers who become famous for their antiwar activities during the Vietnam war—or Elmer Bernstein, the iconic composer of music for modern Westerns. As that was no time for niceties, the first day of classes presented the young teacher with a series of existential doubts. His level of Spanish was quite acceptable in use—he worked as a journalist—but it wasn't so good grammatically. Spanish friends, particularly, Met Miravitlles, helped him clear away the grammatical cobwebs. From the beginning, interaction with pupils was a tough business. It was quite usual for them to put their feet on the table and call him Leonardo, a familiarity that clashed with more formal Hispanic traditions. Although he was now a married man and twenty-nine years old, his rather boyish face didn't play in his favor. But the main problem arose where he least expected it: from the children's choir. From the start that was a boat he couldn't control, where nobody did anything and the din made by the kids drowned any musical sound. One day he wore dark glasses hoping to intimidate those insolent youngsters and that put jokes about the blind on the agenda from the first recess. The management was so annoyed they took away his music classes, much to their relief and that of pupils and teacher.

An opportunity came in the middle of those battles to teach in the high school that the United Nations had established to offer a good education to the children of ambassadors and administrators posted to the

---

8   Walden School was a reference point for so-called progressive education, with an unconventional methodology that was effective judging by the students that finally emerged. The project had been started in 1914 by Margaret Naumberg, who was committed to the ideal of an individualized relationship between teachers and pupils (teachers were addressed by their first names), the elimination of competition, no divisions according to ability and no preparation for later entrance examinations. The philosophy was quite similar to that of Ferrer's Modern School. Artistic education was a cornerstone. The school suffered from the exodus of the middle classes from Manhattan in the mid-eighties and went into liquidation in 1987.

institution. As one must strike while the iron is hot, Leonardo managed to divide his time and complement his half-time teacher status at the Walden School with a full-time position at the United Nations International School (UNIS),[9] where he gave Spanish as well as music classes. Those last words brought a frisson of horror. He accepted the suggestion with the utmost tact and soon saw that the students were extraordinarily well behaved and the music classes were thought to be an essential part of the education of those youngsters and not a simple time filler to keep them occupied for a while. Music classes now became an oasis where he could apply his

Dylan Balada

knowledge of the history of music, and that also spilled over into practical classes that were general in nature but ended up fostering choral performances and even theater musicals and happenings. This multiple tasking lasted for a year thanks to the good faith of the directors of studies, who allowed him to combine the Walden with the UNIS, even though the to-and-fro was constant and Leonardo found he was spending half the day underground getting on and off the subway. The UNIS finally became his only place of work. The Spanish classes were very demanding, because the degree of excellence was much higher and he was teaching at levels that were preparing for pre-university examinations, which brought the additional pressure of the need to achieve good results in public tests. Everything went so well he kept that position until 1970 when he left to take up a post at Carnegie Mellon University in Pittsburgh.

It is clear that those music classes became increasingly important and

9   An educational service offered to the families of those working at the United Nations, this school was inaugurated in 1947 and its main feature has always been the variety of nationalities, races and languages that fills its classrooms. Nowadays it is a highly prestigious center linked to an array of national and international satellite organizations.

helped guide his vocation as a teacher towards arts teaching. In the mid-sixties, New York was possessed by a surge in multidisciplinary happenings and Balada applied those concepts to his classroom practice. Painting, musical or theatrical improvisations fused in the avant-garde performances that rounded off every academic year. Though he wasn't a teacher of composition, he taught students who later became renowned composers who remember him affectionately in their autobiographies as their first grand maestro. They included a tiny, chubby, lively boy by the name of Stephen Hartke. From the start that boy showed great interest not only in musical performance, at which he was already almost a professional,[10] but in creation. One afternoon he asked Leonardo if he could continue studying composition, but in private classes. As the boy had no money to pay for such lessons—not that Leonardo wanted him to—they came to a curious agreement. Hartke looked after little Dylan, the Baladas' son, on the days when Monica and Leonardo went out, and he repaid him with private tuition. Soon after, at the age of sixteen, Hartke won a prize for composition, a Broadcast Music, Inc. Award, with a work for string orchestra,

Stephen Hartke

that initiated a brilliant career. That plump little boy, now a professional musician, later performed as the pianist in the premiere of Balada's *María Sabina* at Carnegie Hall in 1970. At the time he was studying composition at Yale, and today he is a well-known composer who has won a great number of prizes and premiered in the most prestigious concert halls in the United States. But Hartke wasn't the only one. There was another boy by the name of John Zorn.[11] Unlike Hartke, Zorn was just a normal member

---

10   Stephen Hartke (1952) is currently one of the American composers with the highest international profile. From the age of nine he sang as a soprano in numerous choirs in the heartlands of New York musical culture, the Metropolitan Opera House, Juilliard Opera, etc.

11   John Zorn (1953) is undoubtedly one of the most important eclectic musicians in the United States with an impressive trajectory and interesting mestizo mix of sounds that singles him out as a unique voice in the world of American music.

of the group. He was always open and eager for new possibilities and over time became a fusion artist whose music incorporates elements of jazz, contemporary and Jewish music. Zorn also collaborated in the premiere of *María Sabina* as a member of the choir, which was made up of singers from New York University and the UNIS where Balada taught.

The following summer they initiated the custom of returning to Europe for their summer vacations, though in 1963 there was an additional, very different motive. Monica was pregnant and wanted to give birth in Ireland. The big event happened in September. The Balada family gained another member, Dylan.

16.
Necessity and Conviction

Tradition—avant-garde, individual—audience, creation—recreation, imitator—imitated, spirit—reality, hunger—conformism, action—reaction, explosion—implosion, lights—shadows, risk—tranquility, I—you, applause—success, one—thousands. How to be unique, inimitable, different, individual, radical, living on the edge, an anarchist intellectual. . . . The Baladas traveled to Ireland in the summer of 1964. It wasn't just another journey. Crossing the Atlantic, Balada reflected, matured, reinvented himself every five minutes. For years he had been an outright fan of all the avant-garde painting that made its mark in New York and his knowledge of the avant-gardes, that was quite haphazard as a result of his old-fashioned musical education, had led him to nurture the occasional twelve-tone work that had literally been born on the first outward journey, when he climbed on to that airplane, minutes before falling into a kind of nervous doze. Painting, sculpture, theater and of course . . . music. He was an assiduous fan of the most outrageous concerts, of the most way-out happenings, of the most impossible leaps into the void of sound. Meanwhile, his own musical language was spluttering its last in a suffocating aesthetic quagmire, in a struggle between his intellectual mindset and his communicative training and needs. It was this inner, uncontrollable conflict—since he rarely found the right match in most of those extreme manifestations of the avant-garde—which forced him to focus on his own expressive needs. Years ago, his father had emphasized that he should be different, separate himself from the crowd, and that was also relevant to his artistic bent. At the same time Leonardo was convinced the avant-garde should adapt to him, that he shouldn't be adapting to the avant-garde.

After a few days in Ireland, the family met up with Pepito and headed to London where one of Monica's sisters lived. In her sickly, if resistant, state of health, Llucieta couldn't risk going on such a long, wearisome journey, and, besides, someone had to stay and look after Elíseo, the youngster in the family. Once in London, Leonardo decided to do something he'd been wanting to do for some time. He resolutely picked up the telephone and called the house of Roberto Gerhard in his best Catalan. Gerhard lived in Cambridge, so that meant it would be a mixture of work and pleasure. Balada father and son caught the train to the historic university city. They were warmly welcomed by Gerhard and his wife, who also spoke in an exquisite Catalan that she had learned and loved with her husband. While she finished cooking a wonderful paella, the Mediterranean party was completed by lively conversation airing all kinds of issues, though the principal focus was music. Balada had brought several scores and a few homemade recordings of his work, and Gerhard took his time to review each page in detail. In the end the clear advice from him was to stop looking back to the orchestra of the Romantics and open himself up to new contemporary sounds.

Those words hid many other implications. It wasn't simply a question of instrumental fabric, but rather an aesthetic slant, a creative pulse that was livelier, more contemporary and less predictable. That was the drop which made the cup run over and confirmation of all his inner struggles. On the return journey father and son were soon locked in an argument that focused on aesthetics from a solely existential perspective. Whether to be a composer who belonged to the past or the present, with all the associated connotations, was a difficult decision many artists had to confront in those decades. When their stay in London was over, all the Baladas boarded the ferry and traveled to Paris where they had purchased a car from the United States. By then the problems over visas and leaving and entering New York had been resolved, so those references from the famous urging the authorities to renew Balada's residence permit were now unnecessary and part of the family archive. He was able to take possession of that SIMCA 1000 with its New York license plate, a brand-new vehicle which they drove across France to Barcelona. A time for reflection, a time for conviction.

Leonardo was preparing to compose his first *Concerto for Piano and Orchestra*, a commission from pianist Pauline Marcelle, whom he had befriended on the Santiago de Compostela course.[1] Like all projects, it

---

1   Pauline Marcelle, a Belgian pianist, had numerous links to Catalan music. According to Joaquím Homs in his monograph on Roberto Gerhard, Marcelle sought refuge in Barcelona during the

was ambitious and testing. Marcelle intended to premiere it in Brussels with André Cluytens, but the concerto kept being delayed and the conductor died. Pianist and composer lost contact and Leonardo Balada's *Concerto for Piano and Orchestra no. 1* began to sleep the sleep of the just and has never premiered. The fine fruit of an external commission, the concert shifts aesthetically in that struggle of Titans where traditional and avant-garde fought to win the foreground. However, far from prompting an understandable mood of sadness, that frustrated premiere led to positive outcomes. As Balada listened to his previous work, he began to realize that his music needed to change and the problem was finding a pretext, a trampoline from which he could make the leap to a new style, and open those windows Gerhard had referred to. Balada now believes that this first concerto is obsolete, an old dinosaur he needs to revisit to ensure it is suitable to remain in his catalogue.

His first *Concerto for Guitar and Orchestra no. 1* was finished in 1965. After all the good feeling and success generated by his first *Suite*, Narciso Yepes had asked him for a guitar concerto. When he thought back to how well received the *Suite* had been, he felt morally obliged to compose it in similar style, since his desire to please was more powerful than his commitment to change. As the notes for the concerto flowed from his pencil, Balada became increasingly convinced it was an epitaph to a style which no longer made any sense. Both concertos represented his first attempts to write for a large orchestra, an instrument he never abandoned since it contained all the palettes for his paintings in sound. However, the guitar concerto, like the piano concerto, wasn't premiered after it was finished, though that did happen a few years later. During its complex genesis, Balada discussed his aesthetic conflicts with Yepes who enthusiastically encouraged him to make the leap to the avant-garde. When he could see the way forward, he would commission a work that took many more risks and later on a concerto for guitar and orchestra. Balada was now receiving lots of advice and it all spurred him in the same direction. Even though the 1965 guitar concerto was a commission, there was no sign of any money, which he no longer needed, or at least less so than in previous years, and he had learned his lesson—now it was all about being patient and cultivating

---

Second World War, because she was Jewish and started meeting musicians there. Homs himself wrote music for her, that she performed and recorded, alongside her French repertoire. She also performed Balada's *Música en cuatro tiempos* in Madrid, as is evident from the review published in *ABC*, on January 21, 1962, page 76, where critic Federico Sopeña describes Balada's work as ". . . interesting music, expressive and successfully pianistic . . ."

Narciso Yepes, Leonardo Balada and Odón Alonso in Madrid, 1967

his garden. In any case, premieres would enrich his vita, but the works he had composed, driven by feeling and inspiration, brought much more. Conversely, commissions from institutions brought secure remuneration, and they would only come if he had a lively track record.

Time passed, and the guitar concerto wasn't premiered. Yepes insisted he really liked it and *would* play it, but he hadn't found the right opportunity. Finally a call went out from the Second South America and Spain Festival that would take place in Madrid in October 1967. Lots of money, an international event and on the home front. Narciso Yepes was going to play the concerto with the Madrid Philharmonic Orchestra conducted by Odón Alonso. As it was a contemporary music festival, the context was eminently suitable for the work. Leonardo Balada's *Concerto for Guitar and Orchestra no. 1* was premiered at that important event where it launched his work on the big stage and acted as a swan song for a style he had now put behind him. The composer arrived in Madrid, no longer the Balada who had written that work, but a composer committed to an intense, personal avant-garde vision. He had already written *Geometries no. 1* and *Guernica* and was now a completely different artist. As the festival progressed, he realized that his concerto, though contemporary, wasn't on the same wavelength as the music he was hearing, it didn't breathe the same experimental air . . . but there was no going back. Rehearsals were dreadful. Yepes came to Madrid after a long tour and a recording session in London and was practically sight-reading, while the orchestra's situation was even more calamitous. Everything pointed to a disaster of historic proportions in the presence of seasoned colleagues and critics unhappy about his aesthetic coming and going. The much-awaited day of the premiere dawned shrouded in mist for Balada, who took one look at his new suit and imagined it sprayed in tomato sauce. The concerto began. The work was definitely out of kilter with his present style, but the performance hardly helped, as one mistake followed another. The orchestra was almost sight-reading too and nothing much seemed to have improved since the previous day, though not entirely, as Yepes displayed his huge talent by playing the score professionally, accurately and practically from memory. Musicians didn't grasp, and still don't, that contemporary music requires much more care and rehearsal than anything from the repertoire. The crime was recorded, but the work wasn't performed again. Reviews weren't all bad; quite the contrary, *La Vanguardia* praised the work and never criticized the aesthetic abyss so obvious to Leonardo's ears. If one listens to it today, putting aside the problems of performance, it isn't a work to be disdained. It is personal, more modern than it must have seemed at the time and, despite the late-Renaissance echoes, it is an interesting piece of music. Gerhard's advice is evident in the much more contemporary treatment for the orchestra: a vibraphone stands out, and the orchestra is more percussive, a feature that will be taken on board by Balada in the rest of his work. Formally, the work is in a quite classical style with three movements structured by leitmotifs, but the guitar resonates with a new, richer sound full of chiaroscuros that represent an important technical advance.

The return to New York in 1965 was confirmation of many changes. The personal ones were obvious: the family had grown and the income from his teaching was vital, but Monica also played an important role in the family's well-being. After she had worked as a secretary in a detective agency, her artistic career registered a fleeting, though important, lift-off in the 1965-1966 season. The courses in Stanislavsky method she had taken and that had made stars out of a good number of actors, had left her with a particularly irascible temperament, experiencing moments of great euphoria followed by periods of depression and insecurity. The famous agent William Liebling was present at one of the castings she showed up for. Liebling's prestige went before him; he was already steering the careers

Scene from *The Hogan's Goat* with Monica McCormack (fourth from left)

of big stars like Marlon Brando, Montgomery Clift, Paul Newman, Audrey Hepburn, Elizabeth Taylor, Natalie Wood and Elia Kazan. Bill Liebling was very struck by Monica's communicative ability and expressive range. On November 11, 1965 William Alfred's *The Hogan's Goat* was premiered at the St. Clement Church theater. Ralph Waite and Faye Dunawaye were in the cast and the work was a total success from day one. There were 607 performances, as well as many prizes and adaptations for television and the theater musical version.[2] Monica played a secondary role as a maid, which she wouldn't keep in subsequent adaptations after the first production run ended.

Monica was a Pandora's box and also had a talent for writing, which led Audrey Wood, Liebling's wife and a literary agent, to offer her the chance to publish a collection of short stories. Wood was up there with her husband, since she represented Tennessee Williams, Carson McCullers and William Inge among others. However, the idea never came to fruition. Nonetheless her writing talents did contribute to the creative process that led to *María Sabina*; Monica was an important influence on the writing of the text and creation of the character of its powerful protagonist. *María Sabina* was probably her most lasting contribution to the stage. And as a

---

2   The musical adaption, premiered in 1970, was *Cry for USA II*.

reward for her input, both Camilo José Cela and Balada agreed to dedicate the work to her. She and her temperament *were* María Sabina.

Family success had fortunately become a byword in the Balada household. While Monica was conquering the stage, Leonardo was playing his part in places as unexpected as Paris. The Paris Biennale was held at the end of October 1965, and the music section was a *tour de force* for audiences, who were required to listen extremely attentively to almost twelve hours of nonstop music with sixty-two composers from twenty-two countries from all over the world. The essential requisite to participate was to be under thirty-five. Balada triumphed at the Biennale with two works from his first period. *Música en cuatro tiempos* and *Sonata para violín y piano* were performed under their original titles, that had been simplified by a publisher bent on not scaring people away. It wasn't Balada's first appearance at the Biennale, because he had presented his ballet *City* there the year before.

Once he had written the guitar concerto, Balada took time out to meditate on his composition. An exhibition by one of his former flatmates put him on track to challenge himself, and transformed conviction into necessity. It was an exhibition of abstract paintings where geometric figures dominated the spaces. In 1966 that need to communicate led him to finish *Geometries no. 1* for instrumental ensemble. He gave form to the most striking features of those paintings on his staves: physical, sonorous lines and spaces between instruments. Unlike most works of a similar structure, today it seems fresh and communicative. Giving form to graphic sources on a stave

First page of score of *Geometrías no. 1*

usually involves a loss of humanity. How Balada ensured that *Geometries no. 1* didn't lose the breath of life is very straightforward. He simply highlighted the lines and dots, the graphic ascents and descents of the lines of sound, and to that extent the work's structural element, but there is also a physical component shaped by repeated motifs and reoccurrences of elements with a melodic content (anathema in that period as a consequence of the last throes of Integral Serialism) that help guide the listener across the canvas of sound. Finally, there is also a rhythmic charge, something that had also been discarded by the gurus of the art of music, but which right away distinguishes Balada's approach to the avant-garde with his own individual reading and irrevocable stamp.

We all have a series of recurrent obsessions that struggle to come to the surface throughout our lives and that only do so when they find the right time and right place. That was the intriguing case of *Guernica*. After *Geometries* Balada felt relaxed and aesthetically satisfied by the leap he had made, but something was still needed for him to be completely himself. He had to take that one step further, a step that signaled his commitment, with an emotional intensity as powerful for the audience as it was for the performer, a blow struck for human awareness. Periodically, Leonardo stood before an artistic masterpiece that sent a shiver down his spine whenever he discerned it at the other end of the room: Pablo Ruiz Picasso's *Guernica*. Ever since the painting had come to New York, it was a must-see work for every emigrant and exile—or "escapees" in the words of Carles Fontserè—as it represented a cry from the depths of genius, a mixture of disenchantment and contained anger at the time and lives lost after the bloody war. Picasso had created an icon of rebellion, a furious assault on fascism and the repression of ideas, an incantation to a time that had perished. All who felt that rage believed the painting to be much more than a painting in black, white and an infinite range of grays; it was visceral, dramatic, living, pure communication, the evanescent nature of sadness caught on canvas. How could anyone simply walk past that work? How could some ignoramus reveal their mediocrity by criticizing it? Of course, they didn't grasp what lay behind those expressions. Its rule-breaking aesthetic spoke directly to the individual, it was the work of art that could most move an exile or a marooned sailor, which amounted to the same thing. *Guernica* taught Balada a fresh, invaluable lesson in his quest to find himself as an artist; that painting poured out emotion, an emotion so intense it crossed cultural barriers, though only a Spaniard could feel that stabbing pain

Fragment of score of *Guernica*

before the twisted hand piercing the wall and the flower fleeing from its fingers. He put *Guernica* to music so many times after that cold afternoon when he first discovered it in New York!

A call for submissions was published one morning in 1966: "The deadline is announced for the presentation of orchestral works to be read by the New Orleans Philharmonic Orchestra." It was a short deadline and gave hardly any time to write anything new, but Leonardo already held *Guernica* in his head. Every morning he got up early and started on his trek from the Upper West Side to Downtown East that ended with a decent walk to reach the UNIS. The school wasn't next to the UN building; it was ten blocks further on. That whole journey served as time for creative introspection when Balada composed continuously. Three trains and almost three quarters of an hour on foot gave him ample scope. As he concentrated his thoughts, *Guernica* sounded seamless, though he hadn't yet had time to commit it to paper. When he arrived home, darkness had fallen and playing with Dylan took up the rest of his time. *Guernica* was still struggling to emerge at the beginning of the Christmas holidays and the deadline was only a few days away. He needed a couple of weeks without the subway and school and a pile of staves to pack with lots of music. One week to write and one to revise were, in effect, all he required. *Guernica* was an unquenchable volcano, an intense, brutal, original masterpiece. Before the ink had dried, the composition was on its way to the New Orleans Philharmonic Orchestra in a wax-sealed envelope, as were a hundred others competing to win the prize of a reading by one of the country's great orchestras. *Guernica* was one of the twelve lucky scores to be selected and would be conducted by none other than Werner Torkanowsky[3] who had turned the city of jazz's symphony orchestra into one of the country's most prestigious. After reading the work, the conductor was so interested by the score he called Balada personally. The work was so truthful and personal he wanted to premiere it in the next season, not as an event within the competition cycle, but as a work in the season's general program! That was the first great prize, the first great success, and the confirmation of much else.

Today *Guernica* is undoubtedly one of the most personal and ambitious compositions in Spanish symphonic writing. It has the form of a single orchestral piece, with no divisions or recurrent leitmotifs, and it is a work with undeniable descriptive aspirations that starts with Picasso's painting, and transcends it with a harsh denunciation of all civil wars and cruelty against kith and kin. That was the exact image Picasso and his painting suggested to Balada. There is a clear, concise dedication at the beginning of the score: "To Pablo Picasso." It was the modest tribute that the composer, the son of a loser in the civil war, made to all the losers who had fallen, stabbed in the heart by the fate of their people, and who saw themselves reflected in Picasso's masterly brushstrokes.

---

3   Werner Torkanowsky (1926-1992) was an important figure in Leonardo Balada's career. He not only became his main endorser as regards his first premieres, but continued actively to support the Catalan composer throughout his career. A German Jew, he suffered persecution at the hands of the Nazis and reached the United States in 1948 from Israel. His work leading the New Orleans Philharmonic Orchestra was so extraordinary that it went from being second-tier to become one of the country's leading orchestras, with a large number of recordings. He was a sought-after conductor of operas, and worked on operas by G. Menotti and S. Barber, among others. He failed in his attempt to replace Antal Dorati as conductor of the Detroit Symphony Orchestra, and that led him to take up a position with the Bangor Symphony Orchestra in Maine, which he coupled for years with the post of conductor of the Carnegie Mellon University Orchestra that he applied for at the suggestion of Balada.

In his *Guernica*, Balada soars above the dramatic aspects of the subject, and does something more complex: He concretizes the poetics of the
painting, the bitter impulse that sears and inflames each figure, making
the painting and hence the music new at every glance, from first to last
brushstroke, from first to last note. The textures play with a range of timbres where we already hear the mature Balada, the indisputable master of
orchestral writing. The presence of percussion adds a local feature to the
work, since it was commonly used in the fabric of American music, whereas
its tonal presence in Europe was restricted to filling the empty gaps with
heterogeneous chamber groups, given there was a lack of orchestras. *Guernica* contains the essence of much that Balada would develop in the immediate future. That defines the work, but it isn't at all a trial run or timid
dithering with a "let's see what we can do with this" attitude—quite the
contrary. His control of options, tempi and tensions reveals a maturity one
can only grasp if one sees it as coming from a composer who has reflected
long and hard and succeeded in transforming necessity into conviction and
conviction into necessity with no erasures or doubts, with a fully fledged
message and personality.

The work was a huge success. Leonardo Balada had finally managed
to find his path, the way he wanted to work and the natural space for his
bursts of creativity. The orchestra was his instrument, the field waiting
to be sown, the canvas wanting to absorb all the ideas he could put out.
Over time, *Guernica* has become emblematic of Balada's music and has
benefited from important performances and recordings, though a new
interpretation always comes along and surprises us—like the frustrated
premiere in Spain planned by William Steinberg in 1972. Leonardo had
known Steinberg from 1970, when he came to Pittsburgh to conduct the
Symphony Orchestra, a post he complemented with the Boston Symphony
Orchestra. The orchestra was about to tour Spain and Steinberg thought it
would be opportune to perform Spanish music in their concerts, but not
realizing that *Guernica*'s content meant it couldn't be played in Spain, he
programmed it to be performed by his assistant Michael Tilson-Thomas.
Obviously, when they realized it would be impossible to perform it under
its original title, they changed it to *Música en Rojo y Negro* (*Music in Red and
Black*).[4] Problems with a Mahler Symphony in pretour rehearsals then meant

---

4   This title that never reached the printed program, is still quoted by Tomás Marco in the fourth
volume of the *Historia General de la Música* published by Alpuerto, 1978.

Balada during the course in Santiago in 1966

that there wasn't time to prepare *Guernica* properly and it was replaced by something easier from their repertoire.

In any case the story of *Guernica* was far from over and continued to advance inexorably towards that unique moment Balada had dreamed of. He had often fantasized about the day he would knock on the door of the genius from Málaga and personally hand him the score and recording. When General Music published the score before the premiere and the Louisville Orchestra First Edition with Jorge Mester produced the recording, the publishers asked if it would be a good idea to send Pablo Picasso a set of scores. Leonardo replied that he went to Spain every summer and would find a moment to go to Mougins near Cannes and deliver the package in person. Negotiations got under way thanks to Camilo José Cela, since during the gestation of *María Sabina*, Cela and Balada had spoken at length about almost everything and everybody, and obviously about Picasso, whom the future Nobel Prize winner knew well. After he had heard *Guernica*, the Galician writer had no hesitation about writing Balada a letter of introduction to Picasso. Picasso lived in his private re-creation of Spain under the French Mediterranean sun, closer to the sea than his previous house, following instructions from his doctors. Cela told him he should give Picasso a record and the artist would almost certainly give him a painting. After a first attempt that was frustrated for professional reasons, the longed-for summer return to Spain came around again. It was 1969. The car was almost loaded with scores and vinyl hoping to reach the hands of Pablo Picasso, when Monica and Leonardo had a vicious row that turned into a huge marital crisis. The trip had to be postponed much to the disappointment of Leonardo who could see that his opportunity to meet the painter was fading. Regrettably, there was no journey to Spain in 1970 and that was Picasso's final year—he died April 8, 1971.

However, looking back over the previous five years, something was clear in the composer's trajectory; after *Geometries no. 1* and *Guernica*, Leonardo had established himself in the avant-garde, perhaps in its most extreme form, almost with no escape route, but worst of all . . . that's what he wanted.

17.
An Aesthetic of Commitment

Returning to Balada's creative impulse, at the end of the sixties he was a composer who is beginning to recognize himself and to be recognized, an individual with an evident ethical integrity, a paterfamilias with an identity fighting to be and exist in two habitually impermeable worlds. With *Guernica* Leonardo was really thumping his fist on the table and claiming a unique space for his aesthetic thinking. At the end of the sixties, New York was torn by great moral and artistic conflicts as it constituted itself as the city of the avant-garde, and its universality was sidelining the key center of avant-garde musical sound in Darmstadt. War had questioned a whole way of seeing life and everything had begun to change so much and so rapidly that there was hardly time to stop and think. Culturally, the world of economics had taken over key sectors of American life, including the very sensitive one of advertising.

From the end of the fifties, the companies that had made their profits from an almost entirely domestic business had assumed control of the mass media with the clear aim of democratizing everything, including culture. They created and imposed idols and dictated what one wore, ate, saw and felt. The United States had experienced a breakdown within its own tolerant, multicultural identity. This created an abyss and the small groups that dominated intellectual life distanced themselves from the media, became hermetic, and gave up on the aim of communicability as a final goal, although, conversely, their obscurity also clashed with the so-called post-avant-garde or European post-modernity that they accused of eclecticism. It is true that American intellectuals no longer wanted to be offshoots of what was being done on the old continent; they too had thumped their fists down on the table. What they didn't grasp was that those punches had alienated them from their own audiences and imprisoned them in the wonderful watchtower that was New York in the sixties.[1]

With different scales of values based on that perspective, on that independent identity, one of the great gains in American society after the world war, was an element of opportunity, youth and inhibition that opposed the would-be transcendence of the European. The young generation in the sixties claimed its space differently and called for a different kind of world, and succeeded in patching together one of the most complex aesthetic scenarios in history. By the mid-sixties, the boundaries between popular culture and high culture started to be seen as diffuse, if not, nonexistent, pushing away the great U.S. artists of self-absorption and opening the doors to a *mestizaje* that was complex in its make-up. John Cage and Meredith Monk, Bob Dylan or John Lennon shared sensitivies and even aims, though their projects differed in essentials, in their logic and execution. That period of rare fusion had no parallel in Europe, except for the movements linked to Fluxus and Zaj that consciously took their inspiration from Cage. But the rest of society remained in the shadows on the other side of the room, passively enjoying something it felt was harmless, proper and well meaning, but because it remained on the outside, it hived off its contents to the highest bidder. This was the breeding ground for European critics who accused the whole *mestizaje* movement of being vacuous and simplistic. The almost transparent space of complicity between both worlds was now shattered by the fear that one group's manipulations and the other's intellectualism would mix and allow fertile cross-fertilization on both sides. That process of *mestizaje* was also embodied by Leonardo Balada, not so much in his work of that period (located in the most experimental avant-garde), as in the process of reflection that led to his next creative phase. It is important to grasp this process or one will always fall into facile criticism of an eclecticism that is both empty of content and patronizing, something that is quite the opposite of Balada's real aesthetic thinking.

But from Europe that cultural and sociological journey was seen as having other, less diaphanous features. Access to that knowledge was restricted to a minority and that minority, mainly intellectuals and politicians, were either horrified by the definitive drawing to a close of a lengthy nineteenth century or were won over by those siren songs. The values of Schopenhauer's aesthetics, the functionality of art or the ethical

---

1 Perhaps this specificity is still evident in the artistic world, since New York continues to present itself as an island within the cultural development of the rest of the United States.

framework of human creativity were in danger of disintegrating at their very center. Consequently, it was necessary to hold onto the transcendent schema of a world that was going downhill fast by salvaging what was immortal in human beings. Evidently, the logical circuits for these paths were radically opposed on both sides of the ocean, so the United States and Europe began to generate completely opposed cultural spaces. The points of contact between the two worlds were *rara avis* in both places and the gurus of the new tendencies in America deplored the musical art from the Darmstadt School because it was inhuman and deliberately hermetic, while the champions of contemporary European serial music laughed at the new tendencies as an employer might mock the clowning of an old employee. Where did Leonardo Balada stand in relation to this dialectical morass? Who was he? What was he doing? Which was his identity?

Leonardo Balada Ibáñez wasn't American, but lived in America. His artistic sensibility had been shaped alongside Gaudí, Dalí, Picasso and Mompou, but he had been trained on the opposite side of the pond. He wasn't white, but nor was he black. He was creating an avant-garde form of music, but . . . which avant-garde? *Geometries* and *Guernica* sounded like European music, which could be a double-edged sword in the United States. The way he understood music was decidedly European and was considered to be so in the U.S., but what was happening in Europe? How was Balada's music received on the old continent? Balada's work was hardly a presence in Spain at the time, which wasn't surprising given the grayness of a culture that only lightning flashes from Nueva Música or Alea, among others, had managed to color. By the time echoes of the Catalan's successes in America reached Spain, Balada was beginning to experience another change, another process of crisis and aesthetic reflection. And *his* horizons were more sensitive to what he had only just superseded. For him, it wasn't a question of deciding between avant-garde or tradition, between easy applause or the shock of commitment—the issue was subtler and riskier. The gains of the avant-garde were nonnegotiable, but . . . did that music truly reflect his real self? The much-debated, thorny problem of personality, a conflict that remained dormant during the bloodiest wars of the twentieth century, was now strikingly renewed in Balada. The expressive content of avant-garde creation didn't seem valid. Its approaches were no doubt a means, an important means, but not an end. Leonardo had listened to a lot of contemporary music over those years and had seen lots of projects born and die, from the most outrageous to the most reactionary, from the most European to the most genuinely American. However, sadly, yet reasonably enough, he could see himself nowhere. The music of the sixties seemed to hunger after that breath of human energy that transformed Michelangelo's statues into something living. He wanted to be able to finish a work and tell it to stand up of its own accord. Music, that longs to have a life, should be able to engage human beings without them having to become prisoners of an aesthetic. People who thought Rachmaninov reached people were wrong; it wasn't him but the halo that surrounded him. You couldn't do that anymore, society had changed, had grown older and people no longer trusted their neighbors.

One afternoon when he was walking energetically along the city streets, he bumped into a friend, the soprano Helen Phillips.[2] She persuaded him to go and listen to a speech given by someone who was about to become a myth: Martin Luther King. At the end of the event, Helen, a famous singer influential in some spheres of African-American opinion, grabbed Leonardo and introduced him to King. That strange electric feeling, only sparked at highly important moments in life, ran down his spine when he shook that man's hand. He had always been interested in black culture, and it had influenced his own work, something that often happened with whatever implied a minority situation.[3] Thanks to the painter Josep Benet Espuny's girlfriend he met a black woman he went out with several times and one of their dates became Balada's own introduction to the Spanish Society of New York, that was then a meeting place for socialites. Félix Lequerica,[4] the then Spanish ambassador in New York, gave him some strange looks, not because he didn't know Leonardo Balada, because they had already met at some party or event, but because it was highly unusual to see a black woman at the Spanish Institute. But, of course, some like to be on the winning side all the time and belong to the most powerful

---

2   Helen L. Phillips (1919-2005) was one of the great lyrical sopranos of her generation. She was the first black soprano to join the choir of the Metropolitan Opera House where she made her debut as a soloist in 1947 in Mascagni's *Cavalleria Rusticana*. She was renowned as a singer of German *lied* and negro spirituals.

3   Balada's interest in understanding and assimilating specific cultural tendencies is partly the reason for his interest in the ethnic as artistic avant-garde. He doesn't differ in this from other great artists like Picasso. His catalogue includes references to Afro-Americans, to American and Latin American Indians, to the Irish and to Spanish folklore, and, one should add, to ideological minorities and to nature itself.

4   José Félix de Lequerica (1891-1963) had been the Franco government's ambassador in the United States from 1951 and from 1956 held the post of Spain's permanent first ambassador to the United Nations.

team; others prefer lost causes. The emotional impact King made on Balada exploded when he heard the news of his murder on April 4, 1968.

That was when he received a commission from Spain. His first important commission, or at least that was what Balada thought initially. Enrique Franco, musical director at Spanish National Radio, proposed he should write a work for a big orchestra. Balada immediately discovered he could make that new style his own in which contemporary techniques came together with ethnic resonances. Though it was nothing conscious, he had already set out on that singular path, and it was precisely what was needed for that commission. The ethical conflict between anarchist philosophy and unfettered capitalism had been dormant at least as a spur to creation, and was still waiting for its moment to surface. The permanent repercussion of ethical problems had coalesced in Balada's music practically from the start. War, tyranny, inequality, greed . . . all that was capable of imbricating notes in an avant-garde key, but with a lever which made it human, alive, diverse and *his*. Leonardo Balada's work began to assume its own unique features with that commission. He would write a symphony that was a homage to Martin Luther King, it would be his first attempt at a score for a big orchestra, and it would be *Sinfonía en negro*.

As he composed, Balada encountered a few problems of language prompted by the subject matter driving him. The concern was how he could create a work to give form to King and his ideals, that would speak about the black population, its struggle and its misfortunes, using a specific language that wasn't totally alien to that culture but at the same time belonged to the avant-garde. That strange, complex fusion came wonderfully together in the course of the symphony's four movements. The most extreme textures gradually shone brightly in a rhythm here, an interval there, this chord, that coloration. It wasn't a mixture, it was something much more natural, since that impossible equation was pure *mestizaje*, European, Mediterranean and American. Black culture was being read from within the parameters of contemporary orchestral music and it seemed to be working.

An amusing problem arose when it came to paying for the commission. Apparently, the invitation had been to compose a chamber work, not a symphony, and he was paid as such. Paradoxically if this key work had been a chamber work, Balada's orchestral vocation might have changed and he might have devoted himself to small formations. In any case, the premiere was performed by the Spanish Radio and Television Symphony

(RTVE) Orchestra conducted by Enrique García Asensio, and Balada checked several times to make sure they didn't think it was a work for string or wind quartet, as stranger things have been known. Despite its challenging language, the symphony was a total success in Madrid. It was June 1969 and Leonardo's first big success in Spain had also been broadcast on national radio, ensuring it received a large, supportive hearing. So much so that Camilo José Cela for some time would refer to Balada as the composer of the *Sinfonía en negro*, which is indicative of the lasting impact the work had on the country's intellectual elite. At the end of the concert, he was approached by Carles Santos, whom he had met previously in New York, and who was now fully established in Spain in terms of savoir-faire, profession and minimalist practices. Santos assured him he had achieved something that was almost impossible in that country: he had won over both the most recalcitrant traditionalists and most hard-line avant-garde.

When the RTVE Orchestra went on an American tour in 1971, becoming the first Spanish orchestra to do so, they took that work with them. The *Sinfonía en negro* received its American premiere in New York's Carnegie Hall on the emblematic twelfth of October, and was first on the list of works programmed to be played on the tour. The symphony met with great applause and praise in all the other concert halls where the orchestra played, from Washington to Mexico City. It was evidently a fruitful path, but the horizons then blew winds towards other places that weren't far from the Mexican capital.

Before Balada could be swept along by a new phase of genuine creative energy, he felt the need to exhaust all the recourses of the extreme avant-garde. His new style, his success with audiences and consequent quest for an aesthetic identity led him to compose six works in two years. They all recreated an individual universe, in a determined move to find the right path to engage with that great creative, emotional moment. In this specific interlude between works for big orchestras, Balada explores smaller compositions and their possible adaptation to his new language. A substantial, tried-and-tested literature already existed on this front throughout the world, but Balada was tackling the difficult equation of how to achieve something distinctive in his orchestral compositions; it was a tough nut to crack for heterogeneous ensembles. Two cycles of three songs emerged, written for the Mexican tenor Salvador Novoa,[5] who that same year had

---

5   Salvador Novoa (1937) was born in Mexico City. After studying in the city of his birth, he made

triumphed in the premiere of Alberto Ginastera's opera *Bomarzo*[6] in Washington alongside Isabel Penagos. Novoa was a spinto lyric tenor who was used to working with the contemporary repertoire and thought to be a very expressive actor, so Balada's application of his new avant-garde style to song was to be a great success. The *Tres Cervantinas* was also premiered in the same concert, with texts by Cervantes, though none, curiously enough, from *Don Quijote*. The second cycle of three songs was *Thres Epitafios*

Salvador Novoa and Isabel Penagos, *Bomarzo* (1967) by A. Ginastera

de Quevedo, a very important, dense, attractive work for any contemporary singer, since Balada's style is particularly attentive to prosody and musical breathing, something that would be a great help when he took on his great operatic challenge almost twenty years later.

1967 climaxed with the addition of two unique works to Balada's catalogue. On the one hand, was his first and only work for a pure string quartet, *Miniatures*, premiered by the Spanish National Radio Quartet—an agile, direct piece of under ten minutes that is a rare exception in his oeuvre. Conversely, there was a work that was long in the making and on which much hung for composer and dedicatee, namely *Analogies*. After the first premiere by John Williams of *Lento and Variation* (1960), *Suite no. 1* and *Tres Divagaciones* (1962), Balada had written the now aesthetically old-fashioned concerto that would be premiered that same year in the America-Spain Festival with Narciso Yepes leading the way. In order to compensate for the longed-for premiere, realizing that his change of style was by now very well

---

his debut in 1960 as Pinkerton in Puccini's *Madame Butterfly*. He soon began to take on spinto lyric tenor roles, as well as premiering *Bomarzo* and *Beatrix Cenci*, by Alberto Ginestra.

6 This opera is based on the novel of that title by Manuel Mújica Laínez, who wrote the libretto himself, premiered in Washington D.C. April 19, 1967 and a year later in New York. Its frustrated premiere in Argentina, scheduled for August 1967, was censured by the Argentinian president Juan Carlos Onganía who considered it to be pornographic. Isabel Penagos, who starred in the premiere and the recording with Salvador Nonoa, commented that she wore a very thick leotard, but it caused a stir among the more puritanical sectors of the audience. This detail was remembered by the singer and Balada himself, who was present at the premiere, on the occasion of the premiere in Madrid in 2006 of *The Town of Greed*. Of course, shortly before General Onganía had banned the performance of the ballet version of *The Rite of Spring* in the presence of the Japanese emperor Akihito. Alberto Ginastera's score is from his most avant-garde period and is one of the most significant operas of the twentieth century.

known, Balada had composed this work, *Analogías*, that Narciso Yepes had commissioned, with the idea of adding a work with a more contemporary sound to his repertoire. The piece is no doubt the most significant and ambitious piece written by Balada for solo guitar. It was composed expressly for the ten-string guitar Yepes had begun to use in 1964 and together with *Minis* from 1975—a much longer work now fully suffused by a new artistic style—*Analogías* is to a great extent Leonardo Balada's masterpiece for solo guitar. Although it lasts for around ten minutes, the work has four movements that are significant in terms of the aesthetic abstractions used by Balada: I. *Propulsions*, II. *Oscillations*, III. *Outlines* and IV. *Abysses*.[7] Yepes recorded the work for Deutsche Grammophon, and it was a great leap forward in writing for solo guitar. Yepes continued to play this work during the rest of his career,[8] and always used to introduce *Analogías* with the curious anecdote of how Balada purchased a guitar to familiarize himself with the feel and technique of the instrument.

Cover of the Narciso Yepes recording for Deutsche Grammophon

Two other unusual works also arose from Balada's relationship with a distinguished musician. Alejandro Barletta[9] was the first great bandoneon player who strove to create a contemporary concert repertoire for the instrument, by commissioning work from leading composers of the time. Argentinian and Catalan soon reached an understanding that found its expression in *Geometries no.3* (1968) and *Minis* (1969), both premiered by Barletta himself in New York and published by General Music-EMI.

The range of timbres is extraordinary but is difficult to hear, given that the repertoire has been ungenerous with these works that straddle Balada's most avant-garde moment and the features of a personal style that he was then forging. Writing for unusual instruments on the world stage tends to be linked to dynamic leading instrumentalists. The case of works for bandoneon represents a wager aimed at generating a repertoire that, linked

---

7   The impact of *Analogías* in the version recorded by Yepes has been huge. The recording has been used in a number of contemporary dance choreographies.
8   For example, in the concert Yepes gave in New York's Carnegie Hall in 1984. In the review written by Bernard Holland, *Analogías* is marked out as a "singular," "complicated and anxious" work.
9   Alejandro Barletta (1924-2008) is considered to be the leading bandoneon player of his generation. He has been the key figure promoting the presence of the bandoneon in the contemporary concert repertoire.

to a specific musician, always run the risk of being limited to its historic context and the subsequent oblivion that follows. *Minis* can be understood as a work that probes the use of the instrument's resources, the exploitation of timbres and their potential in a kind of laboratory of experiments in possibilities that finally shaped a concerto for soloist and orchestra that was finished in 1970.

Leonardo Balada at the end of the 1960s

18.
Cela, María Sabina
and the Mushrooms

It was not altogether unusual for leading Spanish cultural figures to come to New York and give a lecture, open an exhibition or perform in concert. The Spanish community greeted such moments as almost a moral duty, a way to find out at firsthand how things were going back home, given that news about Spain in a country like the United States was scant, if not completely nonexistent. Then some of the most distinguished exiles gradually returned, thus reducing what was once a select band of illustrious names.

In 1966 New York University's Spanish literature department advertised a lecture by the Spanish writer Camilo José Cela. Cela was then a key figure on the Spanish literary scene and despite his slippery ideology, his literary talent was beyond dispute. Nor was he an unknown quantity in the U.S. where Syracuse University had given him an honorary doctorate two years before, so his figure and presence could count on significant support from Spanish intellectuals in America, something that wasn't always the case. Cela's visibility was also high because of his fondness for outlandish behavior, sometimes pure happenings, making him a worthy continuer of the tradition established by Dalí and later pursued by Fernando Arrabal. That image, however, was in striking contrast to the solemn presence of a tall, imposing man, whose stentorian voice underlined a rich, direct use of language. Inevitably, Balada went to the lecture intending to speak to the maestro and introduce himself as a composer, as he knew Cela considered himself to be an influential figure in Spanish culture. He had long been turning over in his mind a substantial composition in the form of a semistaged oratorio with orchestra, soloists and choir on one of those prickly, provocative issues that appealed to his conscience. At the end of the lecture, Balada approached Cela and polite introductions soon led to the project the composer had in mind of writing something like an opera. Opera wasn't a genre that was generally well regarded by the avant-garde, so Balada focused his idea more on the hazy world of a semistaged cantata, with texts that were sung and recited. Cela asked about the libretto he was intending to work on, and Balada replied he would write it himself. Cela looked at the table, thought for a moment, then looked up, waved his index finger and exclaimed: "Cobbler, to your last."

That expression stuck in Balada's memory and sparked off an interesting collaboration. It all happened immediately. In the summer of 1967, Monica and Leonardo Balada visited Cela in his house on La Bonanova, in the historic neighborhood of Son Armadans in Palma de Mallorca, that was the premises and title of the famous literary journal *Papeles de Son Armadans* that Cela published. Both he and his wife, María del Rosario Conde, welcomed them, showering them with all kinds of attention. Cela had just finished his first work for the theater that was about to be published, a formally unconventional piece, part of a genre that had little in common with what was thought of as writing for the stage. The work centered on the then notorious María Sabina,[1] folk healer,

María Sabina

shaman or *chjota chjne* ("one who knows"), an expert in hallucinogenic mushrooms from the area of Oaxaca in Mexico. Shortly afterwards, Beatles John Lennon and George Harrison visited her in Mexico in search of new experiences with natural drugs, as she had become a veritable hippie

---

1   María Sabina Magdalena García (1894-1985) was an illiterate indigenous woman who, thanks to a series of studies in the 1940s on hallucinogenic mushrooms, leapt onto the world stage of shamanism. Many books were written about her, most notable of which were Cela's iconographic recreation and the biography by Álvaro Estrada published by Siglo XXI in 1989 entitled *María Sabina, la sabia de los hongos* (*María Sabina, the Wise Woman of Mushrooms*).

icon. Cela had started writing this work in 1965 and Balada's proposal allowed him to adapt the text for a novel kind of staging. Robert Graves had probably introduced the writer to the world of María Sabina, but Cela didn't restrict himself to the indigenous woman's actual life or her gifts as a shaman; he also extrapolated his character to a trial that ended in a death sentence because she inhabited a world that was alien to the official status quo because she was free and demanded a space beyond the harsh realities around her. The work had a strong meditative thread focused on the nature of being, justice, transcendence and the many faces of the divine; it went much beyond a simple theatrical event. With *María Sabina*, the writer was revisiting a modern Quixote, a woman laden with symbolism. Cela never renounced that vision and his dedication to the text published by Destino was emphatic in that respect: "To the children who smoke flowers of magnolia. With well-founded expectations." It can be assumed that, as on other occasions, Cela was positioning himself in a polemical space, as if it were almost a pose, because of a desire to provoke that only someone who was almost untouchable could allow himself. In any case, the work was there and is what we can read now.

They started work in Cela's house when Balada visited Palma de Mallorca for the first time, and continued over the next two summers up to 1969. In the time they stayed in Son Armadans, Monica became very involved in the adaptation of the text and words to the music. The cantata preserved Cela's original structure, a proclamation and five melopeas, which had overexpanded according to Balada, but that, despite reasonable requests from the composer, Cela refused to trim. The eternal conflict between text and music hovered in the background. The words of Monica, who would act out María Sabina's role, were carefully noted by Cela who was anticipating the definitive version and eventual publication of the text. Judging by the original text published in *Papeles de Son Armadans* in 1967 and, later by Destino, very little or nothing at all changed. After every copious meal Cela retired for his siesta, while Leonardo and Monica enjoyed the island's Mediterranean light and beauty. One anecdote will suffice to show the degree of closeness enjoyed by both artists. The moment Monica entered La Bonanova she fell in love with a tapestry that hung royally in the Celas' lounge. She showed such an interest that, before they left, the writer took the tapestry down and gave it to her. That was how the Baladas left Majorca with a text that was almost finished, a set of agreements to fix a premiere and a tapestry.

As the second America-Spain Festival would take place in Madrid in 1967, Balada frantically wrote the score for *María Sabina*. There was an additional problem in the Galician writer's original text: punctuation was completely lacking, whether in the form of commas or full stops. Only the presence of a capital letter indicated where a new verse began. The unravelling of the lines in the text consumed a lot of time in their exchanges in Majorca, even though they brought an avant-garde touch that would be lost in the final musical version.

The premiere of *Concerto for Guitar and Orchestra* with Yepes and Alonso was so removed in its aesthetic and time, Balada had lost interest. At the festival he met the most influential Spanish composers of the moment, including Gerard Gombau, a small, interesting, meticulous man who had made an approach to contemporary music in his mature work. Established Spanish music seemed to be in a decent state of health and Balada was keen to participate. For the first time the process of writing the cantata[2] challenged Balada to write for voices and a large orchestra. A number of features required close attention; for example, he was certain the dense texture of the words needed clarifying, so that the solo voices, that belonged to actors and not singers, were understandable within the complex, entangled weft of orchestra and choir. Cela's text, the dramatic thrust of which was so direct, should be intelligible at every point and Balada assumed his responsibility and directed his efforts and technical resources to ensure that was the case. One decision was soon taken: María Sabina would declaim at times in an expressive mode that wasn't exactly *sprechgesang*,[3] but was more than simple narrative. Thanks to the use of controlled improvisation—there were indications to María Soledad Romero for when she should start and stop—the protagonist's interventions happened in what we might describe as a controlled free narrative. The choir would define itself alongside by means of repeated, highly chromatic and atonal melodic motifs, using homophony to guarantee intelligibility, as when the protagonist's name or key words necessary to understand the feelings of the populace were employed. Finally, *María Sabina* betrayed a discreet, if very obvious ethnic element, not only in the use of the distinct Indian rhythm of the drums but also through the rhythm in choral and solo interventions, something that the *philistines* of contemporary sound culture found anathema.

---

2   In the text published by Cela in 1967, the Galician writer uses the term "Oratorio" to refer to *María Sabina*; it was written October 13-17, 1965, that is, before he started working with Balada.
3   A German term used by Arnold Schönberg to define the concept of "speaking in song."

The avalanche of lines in Celas's initial version meant the score grew exponentially. There were multiple possible solutions to the problem of length, but they always started from the same premise: the integrity of the text was nonnegotiable. That was why Balada decided to remove the musical content from a large number of the protagonist's interventions, thus saving time and losing none of the theatrical impact of Cela's writing. There would be a minimal musical backdrop that would act as a continuo, a musical pretext lightening that interminable succession of interventions characterized by similar half lines with slightly different endings. Cela's idiosyncratic writing style for *María Sabina*, with a content that was at once poetic and rhythmic rather than dramatic, created its own musical beat, so Balada could limit himself to supporting that theatrical sound. Even so the work lasted over ninety minutes. In spite of all the solutions that were found, he tied one loose end only to loosen another. *María Sabina* would be judged by its music, not only by the text, so María Sabina's bare, long tirades might seem too long without some kind of musical backing. That was one of the features that influenced the audience's reaction at the Madrid premiere, since it had come to witness a musical, not theatrical, work.

It was 1968 already, a turbulent year that saw the failure of a revolution in social ideas, and *María Sabina* slowly met its deadlines. The technical name, *Tragiphony*, was explicit enough to describe the force driving it. It worked as a cantata that allowed for stage effects, which could be static or purely theatrical, and under that heading, and quite unintentionally, it was subsumed within a genre that was problematic for composers at the time: opera. For Tomás Marco,[4] *María Sabina* is Balada's first opera and he isn't far wrong in terms of the purely dramatic movement the work has from the very beginning, even if the relation between text and stage doesn't amount to an operatic treatment. It was regarded as an opera in New York and Madrid, even if the static staging differed from what was considered to be normal in the genre. Naturally one doesn't necessarily have to conjure up the romantic concept of opera when using the term, but something much more complex and dynamic.[5] This ambiguity was

---

4   The text we refer to appeared as an article in the theater program for *Hangman, Hangman!* and *The Town of Greed* at the Teatro de la Zarzuela in Madrid, for the 2007-2008 season.
5   We mustn't lose sight of the purely sociological aspect of the term and its relation to the times. It is obvious that an operatic spectacle looks back to past eras when the genre was filled with content additional to what was purely musical. Once that specificity was lost for composers, programmers and audiences didn't necessarily see it the same way, so a real demand for opera existed at a social level, whereas composers themselves didn't see the genre as at all viable. This led to a series of disconnections that need to be studied if we are to grasp the abyss that still exists today between opera

adroitly used to launch the premieres. *María Sabina* was premiered in New York and Madrid quite differently and almost simultaneously, something that would be highly unusual today. The process of managing those first performances was certainly odd. It was much more complicated than one might imagine in the Spanish case, whereas in New York it followed an easier path thanks to private sponsorship.

The first performance of *María Sabina* in New York was negotiated by the Hispanic Society of America, headed at the time by Theodore I. Beardsley, who years later would write about the work in *Papeles de Son Armadans*.[6] In previous years Balada had contacted the society for various reasons, and their proposed support was warmly welcomed. First news of the future premiere appeared in the Madrid daily, *ABC*, May 31, 1968, when a review of a Spanish music concert in New York whose program included several works by Balada mentioned in passing the composition of *María Sabina* and even hazarded a date for the premiere in the Big Apple for the spring of 1969.

Although Cela had clout in the world of official Spanish politics, things were rather more difficult on the other side of the Atlantic. Cela was the first to be interested in setting up a big premiere for his first incursion onto the stage. That process of reinvention implied a different kind of participation, since the stage required a greater range of collaboration than a novel. Cela had to resort to his most political friendships to find a space for *María Sabina*. The support of Manuel Fraga Iribarne as Minister for the cultural sector was vital for putting the premiere on the right track. There is a significant correspondence which in part is transcribed as:

Palma de Mallorca, 9 March 1969
Exc. Sr.D. Manuel Fraga Iribarne
Minister for Information and Tourism
Madrid

Dear Manolo:

. . . Leonardo Balada, a Spanish musician resident in New York, a very modern composer and winner of several awards in the United States,

---

audiences and composers. Consequently, we shouldn't dismiss the obsession with premiering an opera that reached the extreme of forcing a semistaged cantata into an operatic straitjacket.
6 Beardsley, Theodore, "El estreno mundial de María Sabina. Apuntes bibliográficos," in *Papeles de Son Armadans*, vol. 180, page 371, March 1971.

has written the music for my oratorio—our "tragiphony," María Sabina, that will probably be premiered in the Carnegie Hall in that city in October.

Both he and I would naturally like to perform the work in Spain, but that would be an absolutely impossible dream without official support and without the orchestra and choirs of Spanish Radio and Television that, as Balada says, are magnificent. I am writing to you in case you can see fit to give your support.

It lasts 75 to 80 minutes. The choirs require a minimum of 80 voices and the orchestra, another minimum of 52 musicians. It needs a lead actress (not a singer) and three male characters (not singers either). I can assure you that the work will make an impact worldwide. The decision is yours.

Very warm regards from your friend,
Camilo José Cela

Madrid, 17 March 1969
Exc. Sr. D. Camilo José Cela
Palma de Mallorca

My dear friend,

. . . I am pleased to hear that Leonardo Balada has put your "tragiphony" María Sabina *to music whom we know and admire.*

I will pass this matter on to my immediate collaborators in the area. . . . I gather that it will be feasible . . .

Warm regards from your good friend,
Manuel Fraga Iribarne.

Independent of the more or less friendly tone of these two letters it can be deduced that Camilo José Celas's input to help the programming of *María Sabina* involved treading very carefully. It's evident that Cela was well informed about Balada's work and that honors him, given the scant interest shown by Spanish writers towards musical composers. Letters were exchanged for a whole year between Cela, Balada and the deputy-director of the sector who rejoiced in the name of General Deputy-Director for Popular Culture, within the Ministry for Information and Tourism.

It is noteworthy that in the course of the negotiations one deputy-director was sacked, which didn't prove to be a problem, given that Minister Fraga was involved in the process. Enrique de la Hoz and Antolín de Santiago y Juárez assumed responsibility together with the Head of the Section for Cultural Campaigns, Álvaro León Ara, who filled the position in the interregnum. In terms of the content of the exchange of letters, the first issues focused on the definition of the work as a genre in order to decide whether to slot it into this or that festival or season. The first reaction was authentically Spanish, invoking the excuse that it was proving difficult or impossible because of dates or lack of time. Then, with that most theatrical definition of "tragiphony," the work began to enter the frame of the Madrid Opera Festival that was usually held between April and June each year at the capital's only musical theater, the Teatro de la Zarzuela. If one takes a glance at the profiles of previous editions of the festival, one sees it relied heavily on repertoire, since it was the only opportunity to see and hear operas in Madrid. The year 1970 suffices to illustrate that point—the year when *María Sabina* was premiered, the season's program included *Fidelio*, *Loengrin* (sic), *Fausto*, *La Boheme*, *Otelo* (sic) and *La Sonambula*. The new offerings at the festival were *Bomarzo*, by Alberto Ginastera, and the special pairing of *María Sabina* and *La Púrpura de la Rosa*, by Torrejón de Velasco, the first ever South American opera, premiered in 1700. As it was an operatic festival, it seemed obvious the project would necessarily be a theatrical one, and the theater director suggested was Adolfo Marsillach, with Balada himself conducting the orchestra. In a letter dated February 27, 1970, the new deputy-director notified Balada that Marsillach couldn't do it and that the stage director would now be Cayetano Luca de Tena.

When Leopoldo Hontañon published his review of *María Sabina* in *ABC* on May 30, 1970, it was full of praise for Balada and harsh words for Cela—who also wrote for the monarchist daily—and it opened the way for another problem that should be seen as quite usual in the Spain of the time. Hontañon denounced the censuring of the text (Cela maintained that nothing was censored though Balada insisted the text was), which greatly upset Cela who responded to Hontañon's criticism a few days later in the same newspaper. But the most interesting part of the review isn't that polemic but the direct way the Francoist cultural apparatus came under attack, when he affirmed that only the intervention of nationally renowned figures made the premieres of contemporary work possible.

When the arrangements for both premieres had been sorted, a paradoxical situation was created: the New York premiere preceded the Spanish one. The world premiere of *María Sabina* took place on April 17, 1970. The expectations around what was an intriguing premiere for New York's Hispanic world were palpable in Carnegie Hall. It was the first complete premiere of a Spanish work in New York since Enrique Granados's *Goyescas* in the old Metropolitan Opera House

A rehearsal session for María Sabina in New York

on that wretched day in 1916.[7] Previous months had required an unusual effort on the part of Balada, who worked with the Manhattan School Orchestra and a combination of the NYU choirs and part of his own UNIS choir. As already noted, John Zorn sang in that choir and Steven Hartke collaborated as pianist and assistant to the conductor. Obviously, as it was the world premiere, rehearsals were marked by the score's complexity; it was decidedly not a straightforward score. The avant-garde tendencies of the orchestral writing and the difficulty of the choir's role made for intense, exacting, rehearsals. Everything Balada had learned in conducting courses at Juilliard and in Santiago de Compostela with Igor Markevitch in 1966 now surfaced to help. Cela arrived in New York a few days before the premiere and after attending a general rehearsal emerged extremely happy with the work. Not so, Balada. And for one very simple reason: the work was overlong thanks to the proclamation and five monotone soliloquies, over an hour and a half of a work, that was not mostly music, punctuated by an excessive repetition of the grammatical structures voiced by the

---

7   Because the work was so successful, it was suggested to Granados he should change his return boat to Spain, a change that meant he traveled on a boat that was bombed and subsequently sank leading to the composer's tragic death.

Camilo José Cela and Leonardo Balada outside New York's
Carnegie Hall. Photo: Carles Fontserè

protagonist, never mind the content of what she was saying. Length and
language pointed to a turbulent premiere in Madrid.

Balada in his tails entered his dressing room at Carnegie Hall relishing
the special atmosphere. It was undoubtedly the highpoint of his career, or
at least the first of many. The backstage manager knocked to indicate it was
ten minutes to the start. He looked at himself in the mirror several times,
straightened his bow tie, smoothed his jacket and took a deep breath, enjoying that moment to the full. Five minutes later another knock at the door.
Balada asked Hartke for the score and the baton. An icy silence descended
on the room as they exchanged blank looks. There was no sign of a baton.
The work was already complex enough: a platform had been built for the
premiere where María Soledad Romero would stand and perform the

role of María Sabina, with the choir and huge orchestra, piano and electric organ on either side of her. This meant that physically there would be a lack of contact between the performers and that the conductor's presence was essential to coordinate the tumult. Hartke turned a deathly pale as he frantically searched every corner of the dressing room, but Balada's was more

like a freshly white-washed Mediterranean wall. They knocked again . . . two minutes to go. The young pupil shot out like a rocket to look for a baton while Leonardo, who had found a clothes hanger in the dressing-room, started to bend it into shape to use as a device to signal entrances into the work. Nervous footsteps were heard outside when the stage manager opened

Original poster of the New York premiere of *María Sabina*

Premiere of *María Sabina* in Carnegie Hall

the door and caught Balada with one foot on the hanger trying to break it in two. He had brought three batons. There were now three too many—two in reserve—and a new, original hanger-baton that had yet to be patented. Everything went wonderfully well as tends to be the case when prior moments augur disaster. It was a great success, Balada's first great success in the Big Apple. The concert hall was completely won over by Cela's powers of expression and Balada's masterly

María Soledad Romero in a rehearsal of *María Sabina*

display of musical sound. The resonances from the premiere were such that the work filled the front page of the Mexican daily *Excelsior*'s Sunday supplement.

Balada reached Madrid a few days later with a victory under his arm: recognition in the United States. A new orchestra, a new choir, but he was now convinced that the cantata worked. Madrid promised an even better outcome and that was what he anticipated as he began work with the Spanish Radio and Television choir and orchestra. There is no doubt that the orchestra for the Spanish premiere was more professional than the one in New York, and the same could be said of the choir, but would the venue be an improvement? The soloist was the only one involved for a second time: María Soledad Romero, a Puerto Rican actress who radiated the South American magic that seemingly imbued the protagonist and she had thoroughly thought herself into the role. The rehearsals went smoothly as did his understanding with Luca de Tena. With an orchestra in the pit and a choir on stage with María Sabina, the town crier, the constable and the executioner, that really did seem like an opera, as did the length. It was startling to think that *María Sabina* lasted for an hour and a half and would be followed by a baroque opera with every solo aria followed by the requisite applause. A marathon night that would have its premiere on May 28 and a second performance on Saturday, May 30, 1970. The great day came. The *Sinfonía en negro* had already won over even the noisy, reactionary Thursday audiences for the RTVE orchestra; this would be the moment to crown Balada as a composer fully at his peak. Success in New York could only augur well for the premiere on the home front, but neither Cela nor Balada had thought how the Carnegie Hall audience had barely understood the text, whereas in Madrid the words might provoke a more robust reaction from the fellows in bowler hats who sported conventional mustaches, who were upset by Stravinsky and Bartok and frantically applauded any uniform that appeared on stage. Leonardo walked into the pit with a case that contained several batons.

The first chords struck up, and the bowler-hatted in the hall began to mutter and shift uneasily in their seats. When María Sabina began to say that she was a whore, a whore's daughter, "a woman who breeds vipers and bracken in her armpits" or "a woman with six nipples like a bitch," the muttering turned into continuous whistling and foot-stomping. Balada was extremely patient, stopped the orchestra and choir and waited for the shouting and exiting from the hall to stop. The performance resumed, and the dissonances clashed like knives as María Sabina said:

Poster for the operas

"*Hey, sewer rat,*" while more indignantly left the concert hall.
"*Hey, you bum,*
"*Hey, you pampered strumpet that allows a bum to suck her blood. . . .*"
"*I couldn't care less if you're impatient.*"

And now the jeering drowned everything. Balada raised his hand and stopped the orchestra again. He waited patiently until the noise lowered to a tolerable level and the protagonist continued:

"*You know I am a woman that spits in your face*
You know I am a woman that pisses with raunchy glee. . . .
You know I am a woman who spews in disgust on your heads."

Then the key moment came when Leonardo feared he might not emerge physically unscathed. The score stated that after María Sabina's execution, the chorus should simulate retching, vomiting and coughing at a fearful rate. "We'll cut that . . . we cut that. No vomiting."

The work finished with a spectacular finale while Balada checked that no knife, false teeth or other projectiles were lodged in his back. After that raucous performance, opinions were divided. Balada spotted Cela in one of the boxes that overlooked the front of the stage and urged him to come down and share in the acrimony. Camilo slowly crept behind a column, mouthing that he couldn't, he was wearing a new suit. The composer looked at the audience and the performers, bowed and that was it!

A big scandal like that was apparently the key to opening the gates to the heaven where the great reside. Few ever escaped that, whether in the shape of reviews or audience applause/booing/catcalling. Mozart, Beethoven, Chopin, Liszt, Wagner, Puccini, Stravinsky, Schönberg, Bartok— Leonardo Balada had now joined that illustrious group, and *María Sabina* was an exceptional work.

A few days after Cela recounted his version of the facts in *La Vanguardia*, September 26, 1974 to his son Camilo José Cela Conde. He wrote:

> *There was one hell of a shindig; you should have seen the ladies in their mink coats and Majorica pearl necklaces bawling and stamping they were so annoyed. For sure they directed their ire at me most politely; one shouted wildly: "Be more respectful, Señor Cela!" I stood and waved courteously from my box, so they could see that I am well-behaved. There was what is known as a difference of opinion, there were even fisticuffs, and with one thing and another, the performance was interrupted for over a quarter of an hour. I really had a different opinion of the contented, opera-going bourgeoisie, I don't know why, but I did . . .*

After the performances in Madrid were over, Balada commented to Cela that the work was overlong. Disappointed by the scant success of his

work on home territory, the future Nobel-Prize winner, said fine, it was his work and he could do what he wanted with it. A few days later the scissor literally went into action eliminating two of the monotone soliloquies and many of the repetitions and excess passages. *María Sabina* was reduced to a definitive version of thirty-five minutes and that is the

Balada, Espert and Cela in Madrid

version in circulation today, whether in concerts or recordings. If one looks back at the original extensive score, the cuts or areas blacked out or changed testify to a search for a more reasonable length for a singular work that had been adapted to a preconceived literary idea that gave little flexibility in terms of the needs of the stage.

In its reduced version, *María Sabina* has been very successful, thus endorsing the unwritten adage: a work booed at its premiere will be applauded long afterwards. The role of María Sabina has been performed magnificently by many great actresses, but possibly one of the most significant was the one staged on the occasion of the Balada retrospective that the National Music Auditorium in Madrid organized in November 1995 with the Spanish National Orchestra and Choir and Núria Espert in the leading role. Cela came to that performance and was much happier than he had been at that rumbustious Madrid premiere.

19.
Paradoxes in Equilibrium

A phone call from one Joseph E. Slater changed Leonardo Balada's immediate future almost overnight. Who was Joseph E. Slater? He was the
father of a pupil at the UNIS, but was also one of those influential men
who dominated a country from behind the scenes by appointing and dis-
missing leaders. Balada was or had been his daughter's Spanish teacher, or
at best, her music teacher, so he imagined the conversation would follow
the routine for that kind of exchange. Nothing of the sort, Slater had come
with a proposal he couldn't reject. The previous year, 1969, Slater had
been appointed president of the Aspen Institute, one of the most important
centers for generating new thinking in the United States.[1] Aspen acted as
a kind of summer spiritual recharge center for businessmen, intellectuals
and others of the great and the good, where they could think through
and debate everything and everybody as they sought human solutions for
matters that had been dehumanized in the rest of the year. For a few weeks,
those financial tycoons discovered they were human beings, capable of
laughter, and that even the select few could be moved and excited.

From the day it was established, the Aspen Institute had encouraged
artistic creativity in the course of its encounters and to that end a festival
and music school were initiated in 1954. The idea that art was essential
for the fulfillment and improvement of the individual, plus the presence

---

1   Aspen is an idyllic place in the state of Colorado, a winter sports center and summer haven for
elites. In 1948 a businessman by the name of Walter Paepcke fell in love with the place and decided
to create a site that could be an intellectual point of reference for ideas and people. He began his
project by commemorating the two-hundredth anniversary of Goethe's birth, and invited individuals
of the stature of Alfred Schweitzer, José Ortega y Gasset and Arthur Rubinstein to be among the
over two thousand participants. The wealth of ideas and emotions generated was such that activities
at the Aspen Institute began in 1950 with the support of Chicago University.

of a large source of money, had generated a prestigious, unique space that would have been unthinkable in Europe. In 1965 Aspen began to create chairs for artists-in-residence across all branches of knowledge, that were awarded to leading international figures. The list of musicians linked to Aspen is impressive: from Rubinstein to Stravinsky via Benjamin Britten. Slater's proposal was none other than to offer the chair of resident composer to Balada for the following course in the summer of 1970.

The start of that institutional relationship was a commission to compose a piece for an instrumental ensemble that would be resident that same summer: the renowned American Brass Quintet. Leonardo accepted the commission there and then. It was undoubtedly an enviable high point for any contemporary composer and public recognition by a social stratum that acted as patrons in a country where art survives on the basis of the checkbooks of private individuals. The first thing he was forced to do was rethink his holidays, since he wouldn't be able to return to Sant Just that summer because he would be off to enjoy the blessed cool of Aspen's snow-topped mountains. At the time Monica was involved in a play and stayed in New York with Dylan, promising to meet up a few weeks later among the mountains. The second was to sit in front of his staves and begin to compose *Mosaico*.

The work turned into a study of the potential for chamber composition focused on odd and even beats and the role of stresses. He had already begun to explore that path with *Cuatris* in 1969,[2] but on that occasion an ensemble of such heterogeneous instruments didn't allow him to probe the textures of similar instruments. In a way, *Mosaico* marked the conscious beginning of a stylistic recourse soon to become a feature in his compositions: sequences of similar notes, stressed in an irregular pattern, delineating a human cycle where rhythm recovered part of its lost identity. *Mosaico* finally received its premiere in Aspen and was a great success, even though it was a work that one could describe as challenging in its aesthetic texture, quite removed from any kind of recognizable melodic pattern. However, though it might seem paradoxical, *Mosaico* wasn't the first work by Balada to have been performed in Aspen. The previous year, the music school orchestra had played *Guernica*, thanks to the Mexican conductor Jorge Mester who had been performing it across the country. The invitation to

---

2   *Cuatris* for flute, clarinet, trombone and piano had a strange premiere in New York as part of a concert commemorating the Day of the Americas. The Spanish contribution also included *Concert Irregular* by Joan Brossa and Carles Santos.

go to Aspen must have been prompted by that success, rather than by any teaching connection with Mr Slater via his daughter and that did wonders for Balada's self-esteem.

Aspen brought something else apart from professional opportunity. When Leonardo reached those mountain landscapes, he grasped perfectly why that place could generate what it generated. He was so impressed by those peaks he was soon asking how much a small house would cost in the area. The response ruined any dreams of a happy night's sleep, but he tried to recreate that environment nearer home by purchasing a plot of land with a house in the Vall d'Aran. All that was extraordinary both at an emotional and a creative level. As resident composer he had to lead a few seminars on his work for those executives who wanted to soften their razor-edges and showed a remarkable interest in every session. Speaking about his own work enabled him to explore in depth features that related to his personal style and the terrains where he intended to locate his next creative challenges. He had come to Aspen with a few more commissions in his bag, the most important being from Spain and, in effect, from a subsection of the Ministry for Information and Tourism, the one for the Fine Arts. The proposal had come from Antonio Iglesias, whom he had met on the Santiago de Compostela courses and who had a certain leverage to take decisions in the area. It was for a work to celebrate Saint Teresa of Avila with texts by the mystic. It was an ambitious composition for choir and instrumental ensemble with the form and acts of a nonstaged cantata that sought to relive the success of *Sinfonía en negro,* rather than the furor caused by *María Sabina.* He also composed *Concierto por bandoneón y orquesta,* a natural consequence of the solo works he had written for Barletta in previous years but which had regrettably been a short-lived collaboration.

As if a cumulus cloud of paradoxes had somehow found equilibrium on the steep slopes of the Aspen mountains, one afternoon, when he was strolling through one of the art exhibitions, he struck up a friendship with a very active, determined and eccentric individual, who interrupted the flow of Leonardo's thought opposite a painting. He was Sydney Harth[3] and in their short conversation he mentioned how interested he was in Leon-

---

3   Sydney Harth (1925-2011) was one of the best-known violinists in the United States. He began to forge his reputation after becoming the first American violinist to win the International Henryk Wieniawsky Competition in 1957. He soon conquered the U.S. concert circuit, started giving master classes and began an important career as conductor. He was assistant conductor and first violinist under Zubin Metha in Los Angeles and in the New York Philharmonic Orchestra. He was musical director of the Duquesne University Orchestra in Pittsburgh until his death in February 2011.

ardo's music and the way he had assumed more contemporary avant-garde perspectives. Balada immediately recognized who the man was, one of the world's leading violinists, who was also giving master classes in Aspen and had attended the premiere of *Mosaico*. They hit it off straightaway and their conversation ranged amicably and at length over many topics. At the time Harth was director of the music department at Carnegie Mellon University, a prestigious center of learning in the gray city of Pittsburgh. The university directorate was searching for a reliable and renowned teacher of composition. Private university centers tried to attract students by dint of their tried-and-tested faculty. After fourteen years in New York, Balada had been wanting a radical change for some time. Returning to Spain was one option, but a post in the United States implied he could continue to stay on the crest of the wave, at the top of the world, as James Cagney might have said.

When he returned home, war broke out. Monica, whose career was weathering the storm without really taking off, knew that if she moved away from New York, it would be goodbye to her dreams of limelight and stage fame. For Leonardo, Pittsburgh was the great opportunity to devote himself exclusively to teaching composition and secure a post that was both more prestigious and economically advantageous. That city with its three rivers had a renowned orchestra and several universities, as well as being a city that was expanding economically, given that the United States steel industry was located between its three rivers. On the other hand, the decision involved severe drawbacks. New York was the center of the world, it was his home and he had a social life there that was often a source of distraction but also of frequent highs. Any premiere there had an immediate impact in the rest of the world. One issue was whether there would be any more premieres in the Big Apple, since competition was in a ratio to the huge number of composers pullulating down its streets. It was the eternal saga of the lion's tail and the mouse's head, of staying plumb in the center or watching the action from the sidelines. Balada's dual cultural identity helped him reach a decision. Balada had forged a reputation on the old continent that wouldn't be diminished if he swapped New York for Pittsburgh, and while his professional options there would remain intact, he would lose a presence that had been in decline recently. He decided to make the leap and did so timidly. He asked for temporary leave from the United Nations and joined Carnegie Mellon University as a teacher in 1970. Monica and Dylan didn't accompany him, and weren't to do so for nine months. It had been a difficult decision to take, but absolutely vital in his view.

When he arrived in Pittsburgh, he realized that the idea of a breath of fresh air was a crassly inane joke. As he walked alongside the River Ohio, he began to see the first skyscrapers of downtown Pittsburgh emerge from a black cloud. He soon understood it was no storm cloud but a permanent canopy preventing the sun from ever warming the city floor. The level of activity in the steel industry was so great the quality of life was frankly poor. If you took a short walk, mud rained down on you, or so people said. It wasn't exactly a place to enjoy breathing and certainly not suitable for a young boy. On the other hand, Carnegie Mellon University was located in a greener, more residential area a long way from the industrial zone. The most important buildings of the University of Pittsburgh were next to its campus, and it was an institution that acted almost as a public center with a history of teaching that went back to the late eighteenth century. Balada started off by living in special housing for teachers on campus, and soon noted the first effect of the change in terms of the time he saved. It is common knowledge that hours seem longer in small places, but in Pittsburgh they increased threefold. An hour's tortuous commute underground was replaced by a few minutes stroll from door to door. Everything else was composition. He had made the right choice.

Balada's labor status was that of a full-time associate professor. Nicolai Lopatkinov[4] had just retired, a distinguished Estonian composer who had taken U.S. citizenship and was one of the most prestigious music teachers of the day. He was a real institution at Carnegie Mellon, since he had occupied his post from 1945 until retirement in 1969. Balada's presence was highly valued, since distinguished foreign teachers were a vital element in guaranteeing a high student intake, with the subsequent economic benefits that brought. The Music School functioned like a European conservatory. A practical approach predominated over theory, and entrance wasn't subject to previous qualifications, but to an independent test of ability. Such a system ensured a flow of high-quality students who were committed to

---

4   Nikolai Lopatnikov (1903-1976) was born in the Estonian capital of Tallinn, although he studied in Saint Petersburg. After the victory of the Russian Revolution he went into exile in Finland and soon afterwards to Germany where he was taught by Ernst Toch. In 1933 he returned to Finland to work with Jean Sibelius, although he finally settled in the United States in 1939. He taught composition at Carnegie Mellon University until 1969. He wrote an opera, *Danton* (1930-32), four symphonies and a big catalogue of concertos and chamber music. His musical and teaching style was traditional and he soon assimilated the neoclassical trends within American music and nowadays is thought of as an American composer.

With Sydney Harth and Harry Franklin in Carnegie Mellon University, 1970

their studies because they knew they were privileged to have a place, and filtered through both musicians who were naturally gifted and ones who were diligent and focused. Given the fees they had to pay, there were few unmotivated students.

From the start Harth was Balada's main champion within the university, and from his position as director of the music section, his backing was so influential that Balada was appointed a full-time teacher without the usual national call for applications. He soon began a fruitful collaboration with pianist Harry Franklin for whom he would write the *Concerto for Piano, Wind and Percussion*, that opened the doors to the Pittsburgh Symphony Orchestra. Although he had quite a full teaching timetable, since he gave classes in composition, harmony and instrumentation, his new post allowed him to devote himself almost body and soul to composition. In only nine months, Leonardo dedicated all that time to fulfilling the multiple commissions he was engaged in. The composition classes released enormous creative energy. The explanation of particular issues in composition, far from making him dogmatic, made him freer and more consistent, as he found solutions suitable for his pupils and for himself. He received an interesting commission soon after stepping foot in Pittsburgh:

Downtown Pittsburgh

a major work for a band. Traditionally, music bands in the United States have been an essential component in the education of high school pupils, independent of their musical studies. That is why brass sections are so good in those parts. For Balada, as for anyone from the Iberian Peninsula, a music band was synonymous with bandstands, *pasadobles* and Sunday hops, but after he heard the Carnegie Mellon University Band, he radically changed his perception.

The ensemble's prestige was such that it received an annual request to perform in New York's Carnegie Hall. The premiere of the commissioned work was programmed for 1972 and was naturally paid for professionally and scrupulously by the university. Balada conceived a markedly avant-garde symphony, one that distanced itself from any hint of a military or dance hall tune. The idea of a symphony for a band was formally daring, and a clearly North American contribution to the classical formulations of a catalogue. Today *Cumbres (Summits)*, with all its merits, is the second symphony in his catalogue and it was a real testing ground for new resonances, new combinations of timbres, and agogic and dynamic elements.

1971 was so intensive in terms of composition that he had five works ready to premiere in 1972. Solitude was transmuted into creative activity to the detriment of emotional life. There were even three new commissions from Spain: *Voices no. 1* for a mixed a cappella choir, premiered by Luis Morondo and the Pamplona Choral Chamber Group: another for the organ that would bid farewell to the style of *The Seven Words* from the aesthetically distant 1963, and was premiered by Montserrat Torrent in Barcelona's Palau de la Música; and finally a project that was long in the making and aimed at Narciso Yepes, which like the organ work, represented an avant-garde riposte to his previous concerto for guitar and orchestra.

The history of the concerto was highly significant. After the disappointing premiere of the *Concerto for guitar and orchestra no. 1* at the 1967 America-Spain Festival, Yepes had expressed interest in a concerto in Balada's most avant-garde style. The composer liked the idea because the first concerto had left a bitter aftertaste. The aesthetic concept was clear, but Balada wanted to solve a problem inherent in twentieth-century guitar concertos: the scant projection of solo instrument above a steamrolling

Opening page of *Cumbres*

orchestra. For some time the sound of guitars had been amplified in a curious attempt to endow works in the repertoire with a fresh dimension. Balada also believed amplification had its uses, since it could shift the mass of orchestral sounds, dynamically liberate it, without any loss of textures or melodic detail on the part of the soloist. The problem was the kind of amplification in use at the time. The idea of geometric amplification implied a considerable loss of color and resonance, which was something that Yepes's sophisticated sense of sound couldn't allow. Before starting the composition, Balada tried to investigate the range of possibilities on offer, and creator and re-creator headed to New Jersey to see Les Paul.[5] A renowned jazz guitarist, Paul also invented amplification systems for live performances, so all they needed was there in one individual. However,

---

5 Les Paul (1915-2009) is considered to be the father of rock and roll sound, thanks to his tonal development of the solid-body electric guitar. He was a huge success in the world of live performances because of his application of white American sound to jazz at the end of the thirties and beginning of the forties. He was a tireless experimenter in the field of musical acoustics.

Narciso Yepes didn't put much faith in a jazz musician and preferred to rely on a well-known Argentine expert, a close friend he felt much more respect for as a professional. While they waited for a solution the guitarist liked, they made a list of minimum elements the amplification must have and that would allow Balada to start composing. And that is how *Persistencies, Sinfonía concertante for Guitar and Orchestra* was born. The work was signed off in 1972, meeting the terms of the commission from Narciso Yepes and, to place it on a professional footing, they signed a contract of payment for the score in the form of a fraction of the advance on the completion of the work. That was why Balada was never fully paid for the concerto; the problem of amplification was never resolved, not only over the coming months, but the coming years. Soon after, in the mid-seventies, Balada reminded Yepes that they had a work awaiting its premiere, but the ten-string guitar and guitarist ignored him. When Theo Alcántara became musical director of the Grand Rapids Symphony Orchestra in 1973, a formation that, despite its picturesque name, was based in Michigan state, Balada found a way to program the concerto with Yepes included. Days before the long-suffering premiere, he heard that Yepes had switched the work and was now going to play the *Concerto of Aranjuez*, no less! Anger overrode friendship and Balada called Yepes several times to lambast him for his attitude. He had put the concerto on the program and Yepes had jilted him. Time passed rancorously and by 1978, tired of waiting for a premiere that had long gone cold, Leonardo called Jesús López Cobos[6] who was then conducting the National Orchestra of Spain, and recounted the series of upsets this score had brought him. Within days a telephone call revived hopes that it would happen, as the conductor had spoken to Yepes and the concerto would be premiered first in Madrid and then in Tokyo, where the orchestra was about to tour; it would alternate with the Rodrigo. The orchestra invited Balada to go to Tokyo and listen to the much-deferred premiere. But as happened in the case of the previous guitar concerto, Balada's style had moved on in the eighties. History was fated to repeat itself.

While he was composing these works, there was a significant change in the leadership at Carnegie Mellon. A new dean was appointed to the Collage of Fine Arts, where almost all the artistic disciplines were grouped. The post was given to a literary figure of Syrian origin by the name

---

6   This conductor, born in Cuenca in 1941, trained in Madrid and Salzburg before moving to the United States. He had conducted leading orchestras in Europe and America and has always had a special rapport with the figure and work of Leonardo Balada.

Yepes, Balada and López Cobos
rehearsing *Persistencias* in Tokyo

of Akram Midani,[7] a man who was very interested in music, and who supported Balada on every front from the beginning of his mandate. Their friendship started right away and soon extended to Watfa, Midani's wife, an Egyptian painter with a distinct artistic profile of her own. In 1973, when Balada's three-year term as associate professor came to an end, it was the moment of truth. To give tenure-track status, a public call for applicants had to be posted to ensure the best candidates were convened. Sydney Harth had left Carnegie Mellon for Duquesne University, also in Pittsburgh, so his previous mentor had departed. Leonardo was confirmed in post in record time, on a better salary, a lighter teaching load and for life. Years later Midani told Leonardo he had accelerated the process because he knew how good he was and was sure that if he hadn't secured him, he would soon have flown to a place of greater repute. From that moment to the present, Leonardo Balada has been an international point of reference for the high quality of the composition department at Carnegie Mellon University.

---

7   Akram Midani (1928-2001) was a dramatist and philologist born in Damascus, educated in Cairo and New York, where he was his country's diplomatic representative at the United Nations. He came to the United States in 1955 and began his teaching career at Carnegie Mellon in 1965 as a drama teacher. He was a writer and essayist, and collaborated with Balada on the libretto for the opera *The Town of Greed* in 1997.

20.
Too Human

Llúcia Ibáñez, Llucieta, had died. The mother of Nardo Balada Ibáñez, the girl who played in that house on Calle Bonavista in Saint Just Desvern, who married a tailor, who lived in Barcelona, who had three children, who rarely traveled because of her poor health, was always a voice of common-sense and always made the most of everything. . . . It was 1971, a sad year for Josep, Nardo and Elíseo. They were bereft. The matriarch's bad health had passed a point of no return long ago. Those months caught Leon-ardo in a phase of personal and professional consolidation very far from home. No doubt Llucieta's decease ended a key part of his life. All those memories soon pounded his temples tinged with the black and white of photos. The Balada family experi-enced harsh, cruel times that soon impacted in surprising ways.

Balada's emotional sensitiv-ity had deepened in Pittsburgh. In that city of soot and huge factories, money flowed from office to office while the vast contingent of steel-workers breathed poisonous air. The consequences of that period could be seen in a city with a black population that had been living on hand-outs for the last twenty years, sleeping in dilapidated houses and queueing on

Josep Balada and Llúcia Ibáñez

cold December mornings outside a former hospital hoping to get toys for their children and grandchildren. It was very different to the bustle and glamour of New York where going for a walk was outlawed because it might interrupt the development of something useful. All that led a man raised in a humanist tradition to meditate profoundly.

One summer afternoon Balada was invited to the home of the conductor of the Pittsburgh Symphony Orchestra,[1] William Steinberg.[2] It was usual for composers resident in the city to contact the orchestra the moment they arrived. In the case of Balada that invitation had been preceded by the performance of *Guernica* in 1969. Steinberg was a quite an institution in the city, as he had been resident conductor of the Pittsburgh Symphony Orchestra for several decades. Over recent years he had begun renewing the personnel with a view to laying the foundations for an orchestra that was to be a leader in the United States and internationally. Like most conductors of his generation, he wasn't keen to dismantle the established repertoire. Attendance at symphonic concerts in a small city like Pittsburgh was a vital ingredient of social life and subscriptions were necessary to ensure the survival of the cultural fabric of the area, the so-called purple belt, so one had to keep the punters happy. Patrons often left huge sums for the orchestra's development, and bequeathed their subscriptions to their heirs, thus creating a solid network, that surprisingly wasn't at all elitist. In fact, Americans aren't too fond of that kind of attitude more typical of nations whose societies are defined by inherited titles and other such paraphernalia, rather than by hard work. Given that framework, it was difficult for Balada to imagine a regular collaboration with that institution, since repertoires

---

1   The Pittsburgh Symphony Orchestra was founded in 1895 by Frederic Archer the conductor, and was led during that period by Victor Herbert, Edward Elgar and Richard Strauss. It disappeared for financial reasons in 1910 and was reborn in 1926. Antonio Mondarelli and Otto Klemperer refloated it in the thirties when it became an orchestra of distinction under Fritz Reiner. Steinberg's arrival was important from the point of view of stability, that continued with André Previn when it peaked in terms of media visibility. Lorin Maazel took over the orchestra between 1984 and 1996, securing tenure from 1988, before passing the baton to Mariss Jansons, Andrew Davis (as principal invited conductor) and Austrian Manfred Honeck at present.
2   Hans Wilhelm Steinberg (1899-1976), was born in Cologne, Germany. After his graduation as conductor, he was the protégé of Otto Klemperer and settled in Frankfurt. 1930 saw the premiere in his opera theater of *Von heute auf morgen*, by Arnold Schönberg, but the Nazis removed him from his post in 1933, forcing him to conduct orchestras exclusively made up of Jewish musicians. In 1936 he left Germany for Palestine that was still under British mandate. He was the first conductor of the Symphonic Orchestra of Palestine, subsequently of Israel, where he met Arturo Toscanini, with whom he came to the United States in 1938. In 1952 he became permanent conductor of the Pittsburgh Symphony Orchestra, a post he retained until his death in 1976.

were fixed by demand and entrenched by inertia, meaning that any new projects must adhere to the maxim of not displeasing too much.[3]

William Steinberg was a Pittsburgh musical myth—he even has a star in the Hollywood Hall of Fame—and was almost as well known as the Pittsburgh Steelers and the Pittsburgh Pirates,[4] to which one should add he had a steely gaze and pensive brow. As spokesman for the orchestra's sponsors, Steinberg indicated that the institution was interested in commissioning a piece from him for the next season. It would be a way to greet and bond with the great musical family within the city. Balada had a great orchestra at his disposal and a contemporary music specialist, maestro Donald Johanos.[5]

That commission was a great opportunity to work on an ambitious symphonic project, an extraordinary beginning that would secure Balada's roots in Pittsburgh. Balada created a harsh, raucous powerful score that aimed to embody that steel city. He composed the work in a short period of time, between September 10 and November 12, 1972, including composition, writing and revisions. As was the case with *Guernica*, creativity exploded straight from his head onto the staves at an unusual rate: The city, factories, machines, steel, the people coming and going, the three rivers, huge cargo boats and gray sky. *Steel Symphony* was definitely not going to be an ode to nature, but a reflection of the powerful machinery that meant that city alone produced more steel than many advanced countries throughout the world: Interwoven textures, harmonies charged with tension and a surreptitious rhythmic continuo, like a natural echo of the city. The work emerged as dense, brilliant, compact and shot through with multiple rhythms, almost like steel itself, but with the sheen of contemporary music as its benchmark. In under twenty minutes *Steel Symphony* introduces elements of manufacture that are a far cry from the anecdotal features one finds in Honegger or the futurists. The symphony is a most striking example of Balada's extreme avant-garde style.

In 1972 the work appeared on the music stands of a full orchestra led

---

3   In fact, Steinberg had devoted part of his career to twentieth-century music since most of his recordings are drawn from the repertoire of that period, though not to works we might describe as heavily avant-garde or post-avant-garde.

4   The Steelers and Pirates were champions in their respective leagues in 1979, so the city became known as the City of Champions. This sporting prominence coincided with the break-up of the steel industry.

5   Donald Johanos (1928-2007) was William Steinberg's assistant conductor from 1970 and permanent conductor of the Pittsburgh Chamber Orchestra. He specialized in conducting contemporary music.

by Johanos. It was an important day, success would be key to establishing a fluid relationship with the orchestra. Despite their fears and the music's strange textures, the whole audience grasped from the start the almost descriptive aim of the work and became fearlessly immersed, and even intrigued by its tempi. The work was an unexpected success. Reviews were favorable, writing: it was "a hugely well-delineated work"[6] or "an original, daring work."[7] Very quickly the work began to fly of its own accord, and was performed across the planet, giving prominence to the names of both composer and city.

The general concept behind the work goes beyond purely interpretative questions and penetrates a strange world outside the music itself. *Steel Symphony* is a work that surges from the orchestra's tuning where it returns and disappears like a shifting dune rising from the sand, from the earth, from pure sound, developing, exploding and disappearing once again. What is magnificent about all this is that it isn't an interpretation, that *is* how the work is written. At the beginning of the work, Balada writes literally that "the orchestra tunes us." The entire beginning is a spectacularly haphazard sequence framed by quasi-metallic chords that stand out in the chaos generated by the tuning. That is where the essence of *Steel Symphony* lies, like nature or even a city, it emerges from the earth, and is set between foundations or natural boundaries—in this case those marked out by the Allegheny, Monongahela and Ohio rivers—and starts to create its industrial base and product. From steel forging to manufactured wheels, Balada harnesses the spirit of a work that transcends the descriptive, where the parameters of thought, chaos and order are fused in a work full of minute detail. It includes, nonetheless, a literal description of the string of actions machines generate transmuted into intelligent music. That leads to extraordinary effects, even melodic ones, and fascinating sequences of the diverse rhythms and colors that are there, natural sounds produced by unnatural machines. For a moment Balada succeeds in making us forget that we are listening to an orchestra and the impact is so real we actually see the industrial process.

The whole creative range finds its starting point in the subtlest control of the material for the orchestra, that later develops into an ability to transcribe musically noises that in principle aren't at all musical. The development of that content is episodic, that is, we move from one section to

6   *Pittsburgh Post-Gazette*
7   *The Pittsburgh Press*

another, from one machine to another, from one factory to another, each possessing its own colors, melodies and specific rhythms, an entire garden of sound enveloped in a dark, dirty fog that, of course, is far from poetic. In the course of composition, Balada is usually a master when it comes to pinpointing moments for climaxes and anticlimaxes, but the shocking nature of this work posed a technically complex problem. So much tension built up that just before the end the array of timbres available to add even more tension had been exhausted. The solution to that riddle, similar to the one proposed by Ravel in *La Valse*, was to introduce a change in beat. After an episode of extreme tension marked by random excursions, he reasserts the brutality of the orchestra and invents a 10/8 beat that brings the necessary extra tension for the orchestra to proceed to the final climax.

But, as we already mentioned, the work appears and disappears into the polyphonic morass of the orchestra; Balada holds in store a finale unrivaled in contemporary music, another turn of the screw that veers away from anything that is purely musical sound. In a fresh random period when each instrument repeats *ad libitum* preestablished notes, everything fades into a new tuning session. At the end of the line for each instrument the score indicates that "they should stop playing, though not before reaching *pianísimo*," which is followed by an exclusive instruction to the conductor inviting him to end at a specific point. While this happens, the orchestra

Lorin Maazel and Leonardo Balada during the recording of *Steel Symphony*

Balada during a recording session of *Steel Symphony* in 1986

gradually fades away, and that's where the natural end to the work lies, though it is never performed like that, with the composer literally offering the option of a return to tuning up and, without a break, continuing on to the next piece in the program. Obviously this option is never chosen, but we need to take it into consideration if we are to evaluate Balada's overall conception. The composer is literally asking for his work to be fused seamlessly with the one that follows, whether it is Beethoven, Mozart or Webern, thus sacrificing his own applause. What prevails then is a natural creative space, that we can admire and enjoy, but, because of its natural flow, one we cannot necessarily appreciate. This ethical dimension is developed in quite a special way in the agnostic requiem *No-res*, (*Nothingness*).

The *Steel Symphony* put Balada on the map and there is no doubt that, in the symphonic terrain, it is the peak of his extreme avant-garde period. It was recorded in 1986, in a landmark version, with Lorin Maazel conducting the orchestra to which the work was dedicated in 1986 and was performed all over the world, but, unsurprisingly, the last one to find out is the guy next door and the Spanish premiere of *Steel Symphony* took place on October 16, 2003 played by the RTVE Orchestra conducted by Adrian Leaper. Media reaction to the Spanish premiere wasn't at all enthusiastic.

The abstract descriptive focus continued to drive Balada's creativity in another commission from a symphony orchestra in 1972. It came from Rafael Frühbeck de Burgos and the Spanish National Orchestra and inspired the symphonic poem *Auroris*, centered on the aurora borealis, and was also given a lukewarm reception by the Madrid audience. Ongoing contact with New York also led to a commission for the May Festival, an annual event held in the Composers' Theater. Balada wrote a strange chamber work for guitar, flute and cello, that in the Schirmer edition posited the possibility of replacing the flute with a violin, in order to widen its appeal.

In the early seventies chamber music seemed less present in Balada's work, and that makes the three movements of *Tresis* all the more interesting, along with their titles, *Spirals, Interruptions* and *Rebounds*, that refer to features of the form and mode of each section, and also gives coherence to the whole piece. *Tresis* contains elements that will distinguish Balada's creations in the future.

In 1972 Leonardo tried to update an area of his expertise that still remained pending—electronic acoustic music—or what we might describe as electronic acoustic thought. At the end of the sixties, he had attended initial courses at Columbia University whose approach he found excessively technical, leaving little scope for the creator's personality to make an impact. Synthesizers and thousands of buttons were enough to frighten anyone, as indeed were the outcomes. Once he had settled in Pittsburgh, he attended courses specializing in electronic creation at the University of Pittsburgh. It was there that he grasped the pros and cons of that kind of sound-making and tried to apply it to his own work. In any case, as Carnegie Mellon didn't possess a suitable laboratory, he tried to draw out the positive sides of electronic sound and apply them to the orchestra, as if by analogy. That search for new sounds brought an increase in orchestral coloring to his compositions. But how could he adapt all that to a small ensemble? *Tresis* is a good example. The use that Balada makes of harmonies, *ponticellos* and even the haphazard and clusters suggest that he found a refashioning of sound was simpler to coax from instruments than by resorting to synthesizers. Something similar happens in the *Concerto for Piano, Percussion and Band*, and above all in *No-res*, as well as in later works. Balada has a curious relationship with electronic music. Though seen as important from an intellectual point of view, its actual application is only endorsed when included instrumentally within a work or even opera, where we shall see it play an interesting role in the future, as if it was useful in specific musical compositions rather than in the pure creation of electronic sounds. That was Balada's way of restricting the coldness and unnaturalness he found in those concertos for loudspeakers.

When personal issues become critical, work can be an important therapy in helping overcome them. Something of that sort happened with Balada. The death of his mother and the process of the breakup of his marriage were two deeply upsetting occurrences that were almost simultaneous. On the other hand, commissions kept coming, and that seemed essential, as his time was filled by the impetus to create and he didn't have time to become self-absorbed or depressed. 1973 saw two projects of the same genre that preceded Balada's definitive entry into the tempestuous world of opera. The first came as a consequence of a party held at Carnegie Mellon. Akram Midani was the host who introduced Balada to the French writer Jean Paris, who happened to be visiting the university at the time. Both hit it off at once and the recent losses of their mothers brought them together in a project that was to be a posthumous gift and proper homage to them, *No-res*.

But a project with music and words also arrived from the other end of a telephone line. When he was talking to Werner Torkanowsky, who was married to Teresa Romero[8]—a flamenco dancer who partnered Luis Pérez Dávila[9] "Luisillo" in the Ballet Español de Teresa y Luisillo,[10] the conductor informed him that José Ferrer[11] would be involved in their next season. A proposal quickly emerged and Torkanowsky encouraged Balada to write a work that could harness the actor's voice. Leonardo's neurons went into action. He identified the figure of the great actor with the image

---

8   Teresa Romero, later Teresa Torkanowsky, was the conductor's third wife and a renowned flamenco dancer in the United States. She ran a restaurant in the French Quarter of New Orleans by the name of Flamenco Room. She worked as a choreographer of flamenco ballets, for which she was awarded a Gambit Weekly for the best ethnic choreography for a dance to J. S. Bach's *Tocata in D major*, a prize that she had previously won in 1999.

9   Luis Pérez Dávila "Luisillo" (1928-2007)

10   The Ballet Español de Teresa and Luisillo, dancers of Mexican origins, was set up in 1950 and forged its reputation mainly in America. They toured their flamenco dancing throughout the world including Spain, a place where they were probably misinterpreted. Although Teresa left the group after marrying Torkanowsky, Luisillo remained in the breach until 1976 when he retired to live in Spain.

11   José Ferrer de Otero (1909-1992) is possibly the most famous Puerto Rican actor of the twentieth century. With a doctorate from Princeton University from 1933, he made his debut on Broadway in 1935, and tried his hand at all manner of genres. His first film with a secondary role was *Joan of Arc*, with Ingrid Bergman, in 1948, for which he was nominated for an Oscar, an award he won the following year for his performance in *Cyrano de Bergerac*. Only a few weeks later he was summoned to declare before the Committee for Un-American Activities accused of being a communist. In 1952 he was nominated once again for *Moulin Rouge*.

José Ferrer

of the Hispanic community's struggle for dignity, since he had asked to receive his Oscar for *Cyrano de Bergerac* in his own country, Puerto Rico, and was one of the many individuals persecuted in the anti-communist witch-hunt led by Senator Joseph McCarthy and the so-called Committee for Un-American Activities. Given the level of the actor's commitment to his Hispanic background, Balada was quick to research a subject that had always interested him emotionally. He proposed a cantata for narrator and orchestra on the Nuremberg trials and to that end reestablished contact with a Spanish scholar and member of the Spanish Language Society in New York, Theodor S. Beardsley, with whom he had collaborated over the English translation of the *María Sabina* text for the premiere of the shortened version. The scholar's great interest in texts from the Spanish Golden Age channeled the original idea towards the lives of the Spanish conquistadors. The subject they finally chose, taking into account it was a role for José Ferrer, was the life and person of Ponce de León,[12] the conqueror of Puerto Rico and discoverer of Florida. Obviously, the text was written in English, not to help Ferrer, but out of deference to the audience. The work was premiered in 1974 with a superb performance by the New Orleans Symphony Orchestra, that was then considered to be one of the country's leading ensembles, and an acclaimed contribution from José Ferrer as narrator. Unlike other similar works by Balada, *Ponce de León*, had immediate repercussions in Spain and was performed in Madrid and Barcelona with dazzling success. Enrique García Asensio conducted both premieres in Spain, with journalist and presenter Pedro Macía as narrator. The work was enthusiastically received in Barcelona and in his review in *La Vanguardia*, Xavier Montsalvatge applauded Balada's tonal imagination, although he criticized what he saw as an excessively descriptive score.[13]

Greater visibility and a longed-for return home followed the com-

---

12   It is noteworthy that Juan Ponce de León (1460-1521) possibly made his first journey to South America with Christopher Columbus in 1493, and that opens up a line to Balada's later opera. Moreover, the polymorphous, demystifying image that Balada creates of the Spanish discoverers is never far away, of men who brought Western culture with them, but were bloodthirsty in the way they prosecuted the conquest.
13   "Hindemith, Shostakovich and a Leonardo Balada premiere, conducted by García Asensio," *La Vanguardia*, Tuesday, January 21, 1975, 51.

mission and premiere in Carnegie Hall of *Concerto for Piano, Percussion and Band*. As noted previously, the university band was first-rate and performed annually in New York. The commissioning of a piano concerto was a gift that Balada fully exploited. Harry Franklyn had taken on the challenge of the demanding soloist part with Richard Strange as conductor. It had been some time since Balada had written for the piano and whenever he did so, he seemed to be possessed by demons. In this case the piano became a sharp-edged percussive weapon for an intense piece that is especially inspired and brilliant and which deserves to be performed much more. The concerto, the second in the Balada catalogue, published by Schirmer in 1983, had two performance options: there was a version for wind orchestra that acted as a heterogeneous instrumental ensemble with one instrumentalist per line and another, the original, for band, requiring two of several instruments. Three percussionists are also involved and each ensemble performer has moments when he must dialogue with the piano as a soloist. The work unfurls in a single movement and is a composition that draws on the techniques of contemporary compositional writing, with an ad hoc symbolism subject to systems that had been agreed worldwide at the time. Given that any event in New York attracted media attention, even though it

Pedro Macía, Leonardo Balada and Enrique García Asensio

was a music ensemble from an educational institution, reviews were highly favorable. That 1974 harvest was particularly fortunate.

Similar in format to *Ponce de León*, but very different in terms of depth, intentions and final outcome, the symphonic tragedy *No-res* was the second project in that academic year. The work with Jean Paris proved to have an interesting genesis, since the latter used a text that was formally very contemporary and allowed the composer lots of scope. Balada went in search of financial backing for a score that promised to be taxing and was awarded the grant for composition the Juan March Foundation awarded annually. Before a blank sheet of staves, Leonardo decided to push his avant-garde style to the limit for narrator, large chorus, full orchestra and electronic tape. The composition had a more intensely felt conception than previous ones and was defined formally by the two parts of the text. The first focused on death, not from religious or merely human parameters, but from a universal perspective as the end without exception for all living beings. Diverse texts in various languages were mixed with sounds from nature. The void that death represents is communicated by a sense of the ultimate futility of our own lives, or at least of a life that doesn't try to project itself. Nardo Balada reappears at the end of the first part, when the words of his mother, Llucieta, find eternity in her son's music, immobilized in an implacable temporal space only musical sound can sustain. Each performer must stay still for a time in a kind of silent tableau.

Conversely, the second part follows a more linear path and uses English in its furious rejection of all the fears and impositions provoked by terror at the idea of disappearing forever. The music flows in a polymorphous manner until that point, then transmutes into a powerful Baladan atonal cannon. Of course, in the eyes of a convinced nonbeliever, the composition of a work structured like a requiem was extremely striking, so much so that in the course of writing Balada felt compelled to assign to the work the significant title of *No-res*, (*Nothingness*). The agnostic requiem begins with a wolf howling at the great beyond, and receives an appropriate imitative response from the choir.

The work was finished in 1974 and was naturally dedicated to Llúcia Ibáñez: a son's homage to the memory of his mother; paradoxically, *No-res* won the 1981 City of Barcelona Prize for Composition, and the reward was a premiere in that city. As usually happens with these things, excuses started to rain down. The main obstacle was the city's lack of a sufficiently professional choir to take on such a premiere. Time was moving on and

Balada started to revise the score, which was in danger of disappearing under the dust on the shelf. He arrived in Madrid with the revised version, full of renewed hope and optimism. Odón Alonso was keen to premiere the work, but on that occasion Schubert's one hundred and fiftieth anniversary intervened. Now well into the eighties, *No-res* and Leonardo continued on their painful quest for a premiere. The Pittsburgh Symphony Orchestra also looked kindly on the idea of a work for a narrator and orchestra, since it had just begun a project to premiere ambitious works by living composers. The work was to be conducted by Michael Lankester, then deputy to Maazel, who had just recorded *Steel Symphony* to great effect. The programming committee finally decided that they couldn't risk another premiere of that magnitude, after a similar premiere of William Schumann in the previous season had flopped completely. *No-res* was back on the shelf. In the nineties, Balada inquired again about the premiere he had been promised in Barcelona. He paid the orchestra's manager Abili Fort a visit as if he was applying for a teaching post, and reminded him of the prize and the contract that had been signed for the premiere they all must surely remember. He must have been thinking—so much energy expended by a well-known composer—what must it be like for those starting out! The response was no different, the orchestra was experiencing a difficult period and it was hard to justify such a demanding work, but a light soon flickered. Leonardo and the manager surreptitiously entered the office of the orchestra's permanent conductor, Lawrence Foster, and dropped the score on his upholstered chair. Leonardo received a call a few weeks later. Foster had come across the score of *No-res* in a drawer, had glanced at it leisurely and was highly impressed by what he had found. It would get its premiere next season. However, the problem of the choir remained. Was there a professional choir in the whole of Catalonia able to handle a score that complex, though, at the end of the day, it could be sung? Fortunately, a policy of sharing formations existed between Madrid and Barcelona and that year the National Choir was due to come to Barcelona, so that would be D-Day. Twenty-three years later, with one revision made, *No-res* was premiered at the Palau de la Música. The homage to his mother and that painful period of his life finally had closure. Unfortunately, such premiere issues are only too familiar to composers across the entire world and there is only one thing to say: "Sow the seed, nourish it and its time will come," *dixit* Leonardo Balada.

The magical harvest of 1974 ended with an unusual work, which,

At the premiere of *Apuntes*, Leonardo Balada and the Tarragó Quartet

conversely, has enjoyed a prosperous, successful life: *Apuntes* (*Sketches*) for guitar quartet. The work won first prize in the City of Saragossa Composition Prize and was premiered by the Tarragó Quartet, and was the genesis of the later *Concerto for Four Guitars and Orchestra*, the same ensemble commissioned in 1976. At the prize-gathering Leonardo and a cloud of military smoke sported their suits and bathed in the glory. *Apuntes* explores the expressive potential of a guitar quartet, illustrates its range of subtle, surprising timbres while never losing sight of elements of *ostinato*, percussion and even, finally, the use of the performers' voices.

That period, which had been only too human, had led to the composition of several great works in a short space of time, which was the only therapy possible. Did this mean he had taken his extreme avant-garde style as far as it would go?

Balada at the beginning of the '70s

21.
My Transparencies and I

And what would happen if we woke up one day, looked at ourselves in the mirror and found we had two almost identical noses? Which would we think was different, the usual one or the new one? Could we distinguish our nose from a hundred similar items? What *is* a nose at the end of the day? Is your nose you or are you your nose? What defines us best?—what we are, or what we want to be? There are people who tire of their noses and decide to change them, just like that, as if they were having a brain-change. One might go to the butcher's and ask for three quarters of that brain that seems to be overflowing with ideas. Unlike such nonsense, Leonardo Balada was experimenting with a new aesthetic process in his quest for a common space with which he could fully identify, a place where he could find a sufficient degree of depth from which to develop his longing to communicate musically. He experienced the same symptoms as before. Doubt hovered over his shoulder, asking him to take a fresh step towards his true self, his pure self, his genuinely creative self. When he looked backwards, as he often did, an offshoot of his work as a teacher sitting on the other side of the table, he reviewed his creative personality. Initially, he had adopted a style he had learned as a student, a phase when materials silted together, then he entered new terrains, that were naturally freer, although they also meant he had to sacrifice his own creative personality, but . . . was Balada still Balada? Reviews said he was, that his style was intense, personal and different, but Leonardo felt a *je ne sais quoi* was missing, a grain of salt, an axis on which his creative personality could turn. There were gains one couldn't surrender, techniques of composition from the past that, as the old musicians *au fait* with the repertoire thought, always represented an improvement. That is reasonable enough. I live today, consequently I know about yesterday's deal, which is what composers in the past knew, but I have the knowledge and freedom to make choices now. Conclusion, today's music must be better than yesterday's.

Hitherto Balada had always generated music with a capital M, personal music and music that moved audiences and performers. All his works, independent of their aesthetic location, enjoyed a solid foundation on which to erect an edifice of sounds. Sometimes it had been the Landini cadence, others a formal structure, or an inspired text, or a theme, or a city, or a individual performer. Would there ever be a time when there wasn't an incentive? What would happen if pretexts lost their mystery? Ethical and professional training occasionally journey down opposite paths. Balada, the professional, felt at ease in his creative development, but Leonardo, the individual, obsessed daily about his own emotional and creative identity. That surge of ideas in 1974 had been a strong statement of intent. Today we can understand that his creative hunger was a desperate race to close doors that had opened. Balada wanted to stay alone at home looking at himself in the mirror, and, after he had said all there was to say, he wanted to emerge as a new man. His personal and emotional situation also channeled part of the current in the same direction. His time in New York was at an end, with its bright lights, his first premieres and the troubles of a life he had enjoyed to the full, but now the pressure of logic took him along other roads and new paths to which he felt irrevocably drawn.

But this third turn of the tiller wasn't really that or at least not in the global sense of the term. Balada's music had previously sought itself in pockets that belonged to a common suit, in aesthetic mechanisms the avant-garde had put in place to consolidate a new space. That change for Balada, his transition to maturity, wasn't so dramatic; nobody needed to fall off their horse, all it needed was a change of hat, of motivation, of initial resources and point of gravity. It all began as a rather amusing wager. What could one do with an existing melody one subjected to contemporary textures of sound? Despite the fact that post-Darmstadt, pre-prepared postmodernity had condemned certain practices as quite uncontemporary, a period had now begun when creators were calling it a day and allowing their individual personalities to explode.[1]

The news of Pau Casal's death in Puerto Rico in October 1973 sym-

---

1 Inevitably we must turn to the great statement from Ramón Barce, first published in *El Urogallo* in 1973 and, later, in *Fronteras de la Música* (1985) and now in De Dios Hernández, Juan Francisco and Martín, Elena, *Las Palabras de la Música. Escritos de Ramón Barce*, 210-216: ". . . for twenty years we composers have been ingenious and clever. Now we must write music . . ."

208

Score of *Homage to Sarasate*

bolized the disappearance of a myth, of a standard-bearer, one of the last musical heirs to Romanticism. That was why Balada decided to return to that paradigmatic melody within Catalan culture, *El Cant dels Ocells*, (*Bird Song*) that the cellist from El Vendrell had immortalized and played throughout the world, and use it as a pretext. However, that might seem abusive, almost cannibalistic, but then it developed, entered a crisis until finally its flexibility and feasibility were confirmed. That creative act concealed a need to move on personally, to communicate in a mature, expressive mode. It was the gestation of a new way to view the act of creation, a new departure in order to explore new spaces. Balada immediately started on a work that was almost the exact opposite, a more dynamic, colorist piece that could act as a counterpoint to the lyricism of Casals' cello. Surprisingly, he also tackled *Zapateado*, by Pablo Sarasate, a reworking of a popular Spanish tune written by another immortal Spanish composer. That brought to fruition *Two Transparencies for Orchestra*, a decisive move en route to a new musical personality, a new twist on Leonardo Balada's aesthetic journey.

Despite the dissolution of General Music Publishing and its takeover by EMI, Balada continued to publish almost all his scores, from his first phase as well, though that happened later. In 1975 Leonardo spoke to Mario di Bonaventura, at the time head of G. Schirmer Inc., the publishing division of one of the world's most powerful publishing houses and he expressed an interest in having exclusive rights to publishing Balada's work and controlling performance rights. Schirmer was rather more than a publishing house, since, as a big company, it looked after rights, commissions and acted as manager, as well as fulfilling its mission as a publisher and promoter of scores.[2] Balada's music was now being performed in the most surprising places, so that was an important step to take. He had met George Sturm in the offices of G. Schirmer, one of their heads of publicity, and when Sturm left the firm, he became an independent agent for various composers including Leonardo. The publishers and Sturm himself, were above all interested in selling the product, and thought that the word "transparency" was ambiguous, too abstract and not meaningful enough, so the work came to be called *Homage to Casals* and *Homage to Sarasate*,[3] titles that were more powerful to a degree but they hid the real formal reasons behind the composer's decision to elaborate those two themes. The work brought Leonardo the City of Barcelona Composition Prize for the second time in 1976, in the orchestral work category, which was perfect for G. Schirmer that began to hear the delightful ring of the cash register.

So what is a *transparency*? The term "transparency" essentially holds the key to understanding Balada's period of creative maturity. Appealing to a previous, preestablished, inspiring source, whatever its form, was a spark to creation, a challenge in sound that appealed to the composer's creative drive. It wasn't about portraying or salvaging the existing theme, the aim was to superimpose diverse angles on this motif by applying every possible technique, as if it were a macrovariation intent on generating a universe that drank from the same spring, but wasn't the same water. Occasionally, that "transparency" might appear almost in its original form and gradually transmute in a continuous variation, while in others it appeared very distantly and required an effort of the subconscious. It follows no preestablished structure; it is volatile, brilliant and above all highly personal.

As we mentioned, the premieres of both scores, that were unpublished at the time, took place not long before. It was the Pittsburgh Symphony Orchestra's 1975-1976 season,[4] and the works were energetically conducted by Donald Johanos. When the first transparency began to unfurl no one could have been aware of what was going to hit them. A first chord, a

2   G. Schirmer Inc. is still one of the world's most important music publishing houses. Established in 1861 in New York by the German Gustav Schirmer, it gradually published the most important American composers of the twentieth century. Balada became a Schirmer author when the company no longer belonged to the Schirmer family but the Macmillan publishing house. After the publication of *Christopher Columbus*, Balada created his own publishing house, Beteca Music, even though he continues to be published by other companies.
3   The Schirmer edition came out in 1979 with a prologue by Balada and a transcription of the original melody of *El Cant dels Ocells*. *Sarasate* is dedicated to his father, Josep Balada.
4   The premiere was on May 7, 1976. In line with the stipulations for the composition prize, the European premiere took place in Barcelona and was conducted by Salvador Mas on December 2, 1978.

highly dissonant cluster *in divisi* for string and wind, were followed by an unexpected development. Those who hated the *Steel Symphony* could be heard coughing loudly. But then the way opened up for a melody, a melody that much of the audience didn't recognize. As the then director of Juilliard Peter Mennin exclaimed at the score's premiere in New York: "Heavens, a melody!"

El Cant del Ocells could only be heard in a fragmentary fashion, but it undoubtedly added a special, evocative thread to those expressive, resonant textures. The work opened with features similar to the most rabidly contemporary Balada, but with a distinct sheen. That all came and went and finally even allowed itself the luxury of throwing in a touch of neotonal, nostalgic lyricism in F minor, as a homage to Casals. At that point, the Catalan's cello refused to disappear into the dominant chord that refused to go away. When the echoes of Sarasate resounded in the concert hall, the battle was won and a new way to be avant-garde had been successfully negotiated. In his explanatory note to the Schirmer edition, Balada states that he was trying to apply avant-garde techniques of composition to Sarasate's music in the same way that Picasso had done years before with Velázquez's *Las Meninas*, revamping for contemporary eyes. In short, a fruitful contrast between old and new alongside a disruption of traditional values that were challenged by a surge of immediacy that brought a new reading and gaze to the traditional, to what had been classically or culturally taken for granted. All that cut a new, surprising path for the composer himself, but, of course . . . the work might be misunderstood by the mandarins of the avant-garde.[5] In effect, numerous critics were full of praise, and some complained about the aridity of some sections—and that was quite normal in the American music press—but an inertia was palpable in more intellectual circles that was difficult to explain.

Nobody can ignore the fact that the world of musical creation is complex and highly competitive. Sharks fill its waters waiting for prey to shred to pieces. For a long time access to the avant-garde had been managed by an entrance ticket denoting a "suitable manipulator of sounds." The old maestros didn't hold this ticket, particularly those in Spain who remained faithful to the nationalist tradition, and a small American avant-garde group known as the minimalists. What happened when an author in the so-called scholastic avant-garde switched to the side of the "baddies"? Usually it was seen as someone abandoning the system, and was welcomed

---

5   This is a term that Ramón Barce habitually used in his writing about aesthetics.

with a mixture of sighs of relief and a backwards look over the shoulder. At last, one less. Balada was given an epithet more suited to a grocery than a large department store on the golden mile. The composer of *Guernica* and the *Steel Symphony* had finally sold out to the Americans and was writing music to please the old dears who loved Chopin. Of course such a conclusion could only be reached from a state of ignorance and shouldn't be overcriticized in the case of a living musician, since channels of information were and usually still are precarious, thus limiting a deeper appraisal of a rival's aesthetic features, and descending, on the contrary, into the worst Manichaeism from the lips or pen of anyone set on filtering and evaluating the transcendence of contemporary art.

The route chosen by the composer had been risky and complex inasmuch as there was no way back, but it was absolutely necessary as a response to his own self. His subsequent doubts were reasonable enough: should or shouldn't he continue along that path? And if the answer came in the affirmative, with popular tunes like *El Cant dels Ocells*? Or memorable works that could easily be identified? Naturally, the composer plumped for the first option. The line marked out by *Sarasate* could evolve into an elaborate mannerism that entailed a degree of aesthetic self-denial. Recourse to the elemental, popular or ethnic, always represented a fresh take on the motivation of a new avant-garde that was more worried by issues of sound, while the second forded more turbulent folkloric, rather than meditative, streams. A third stage started then in his compositional style, a brilliant, personal, flexible phase that could be catalogued as ethnic internationalism or the subjective ethnic, based on the filtering and decontextualizing of popular tunes, stripping them of their playful, anecdotal features in order to explore their essentially human content.

To reach this perspective on the use of the popular, Balada tried out many a chord and a few more transparencies. Bach and Chopin were his next targets, and were so in unusual, distinct ways. Pau Casals' death moved the whole world of music, but Francoist Spain continued to see him as anti-patriotic, an unreconstructed supporter of the Second Republic and an exile like so many others. Nonetheless, in 1977, while the dictator's corpse was still fresh in everybody's mind, the Ministry for Education and Science, from its General Office for the Fine Arts, commissioned Balada and other composers to create works that rendered homage to the hundredth anniversary of the cellist's birth.[6] Just as he was going to place the score for

---

6   The works were published in the format of a book of scores with the title of *Homenaje a Pablo*

his *Homage* in an envelope, Balada discovered that the commission was for cello and piano. As he had already worked on *El Cant dels Ocells*, he had to look to other iconic works for the maestro, *The Prelude to the Suite No1 BWV 1007*,[7] by Johann Sebastian Bach. The work, whose title would be *Three Transparencies on a Bach Prelude*, was written between September 6 and November 9, 1976 in Pittsburgh, and was divided into three sections. The first blatantly recreates the Bach prelude that comes more from the piano than the cello. The work's structural development leads into a sequence of transparencies that seem to dovetail before, finally, in the second and third movements, moving irrevocably away from Bach, of whom only a few inflections and breaths remain, and transmuting into a purely Baladan journey. The work was premiered in Barcelona in a concert in homage to Casals; Pedro Corostola played the cello.

Paradoxically, in the following year another posthumous homage generated the *Transparency of Chopin's First Ballade*. The commission for this work caught him at home wielding castanets. The director of Dartmouth College was at the other end of the line,[8] an old university located in Hanover, New Hampshire. Apparently, one of the college's best loved piano teachers had just died and the teachers had decided to pay homage to her. They wanted to commission Balada to write a work for piano. The implicit downside was the general idea that should inspire the commission. The homage was for Paeff Silverman,[9] renowned for her performances of Chopin, and they wanted the work to relate to her expertise. Evidently that request wasn't met altogether enthusiastically by the composer who wasn't prepared to write anything in Chopin's style. It was finally agreed that the late Mrs Silverman would get her homage, but that Chopin's role would be to generate a new transparency.

In October 1976[10] Balada took out a sheet of music and began to write. It was the first work he had written for piano solo since *Música en cuatro tiempos*. This transparency, generally inspired by Frédéric Chopin's

---

Casals, which gathers the scores together. Apart from Balada, other contributors to the volume were Carmelo Bernaola, Manuel Castillo, Joaquim Homs, Frederic Mompou, Xavier Montsalvatge and Joaquín Rodrigo.

7   This prelude, that begins the cycle of suites for solo cello, was a standard in the career of Pau Casals. It is in G major.

8   This institution was founded in 1769 and is still renowned for its contribution to the arts.

9   The piano teacher's full name was Sonia Paeff Silverman and the Schirmer edition notes that the work was commissioned in memory of the deceased by a group of her friends. It was premiered by Anthony di Bonaventura at Dartmouth College.

10   The work was finished February 14, 1977, and was a complex piece of writing, which explains why it took almost four months to write.

Ballade no. 1, contains such electric, complex, brilliant music that it should belong in its own right to the repertoire of all contemporary pianists. The beautiful start to the piece comes from Chopin, as do a few fragmentary references, the passionate texture of the writing and the equally passionate performance the piece demands. *Rubato* is essential to the piece, since the initial stress of each phrase is vital to grasp the idea imbuing the work. In brief, to play Balada's transparency, one must be able to play a Chopin ballade and, after mastering all *its* technical aspects, one must fully master the techniques the contemporary avant-garde has applied to the piano over the last fifty years.

The lure of the piano didn't go away, but in fact intensified with two less unusual but equally distinguished commissions. The first also came in 1978 and was instigated by John J. Sommers, the founder of the Three Rivers Piano Competition, an international competition that enjoyed huge prestige at the end of the eighties. Balada's work would be the obligatory core test piece for participants in the 1979 competition and there would be a special prize for best performance. A ten-minute long score was needed, with technical rather than performative challenges since competitors had only a short time to prepare. To solve that conundrum, Balada took yet another unexpected turn and wrote one of the few works in his catalogue that displays traces of minimalism. Balada developed a ten-minute piece that was generated by a series of precise motifs that follow a minimalist route. That path sought to use repetition to create movement via the displacing of beats and stresses in the style of the innovations of Steve Reich or even Conlon Nancarrow, without losing the essence of Balada's own language. The title is already significant in terms of intention, *Persistencies*, a title that recalls the recent, happy *Persistencies Sinfonía Concertante for Guitar and Orchestra* written for Narciso Yepes, but from a radically different perspective. On this occasion, recourse to repetition is quite restricted by Balada and almost reduced to a recourse to help resolve problems of technique through performance.

And this cycle of piano works at the end of the decade concluded with a long-awaited commission from Alicia de Larrocha,[11] one of the finest Spanish musicians of the twentieth century. The great Catalan pianist used to visit Pittsburgh every year, one year to offer a recital and another to perform

---

11   Alicia de Larrocha (1923-2009) was the most important pianist of her generation and a permanent presence on the American concert circuit. She often drew on contemporary composition, and many great composers wrote for her including Xavier Montsalvatge. Larrocha's last tour with *Preludis Obstinants* took place in series of concerts in the U.S. in 1996.

With Alicia de Larrocha in Pittsburgh

with the orchestra. On one of those visits the possibility arose of writing a piece to fit her dynamic presence at the keyboard. The project couldn't have been more attractive, since Larrocha was a sure way to guarantee visibility, and implied a recording that would have an international impact because of her contract with BMG. The work was finished in 1979 and launched with the title of *Preludis Obstinants*, an eloquent title behind which are found five preludes where Balada exploits one of his most common techniques—the cluster or bunch of notes. However, Balada was now off the leash and the five preludes were technically demanding, so much so that Larrocha's tiny hands couldn't manage two of them and she was unable to play the premiere in public. In any case she was sure the problems could be resolved in a recording studio and the complete cycle would be recorded. The idea, approved by BMG, consisted in putting together a record where the musician would perform different pieces written for her, including *Preludis Obstinants*. But once again a cloud intervened between Leonardo and international visibility. Alicia de Larrocha tore up her recording contract and the project was back in a drawer.

Preludis Obstinants is a work that develops concepts relative to the passing of time in music and life. There are five preludes, with a basic driving motif that is the use of clusters from different perspectives alongside rhythmic, melodic or sustained chords. The main movement is generated between the lines and the pianist is required to display a subtle balance in the playing of chords, which was one of de Larrocha's great gifts. The second prelude contains a reminiscence of Frederic Mompou in an exercise aimed at catching atonal lyricism via changes in tempi and dynamics. The remaining three require a constant control of rhythmic beat and the horizontal and vertical flow of sounds from the cluster, a human game in which time and the circumstances of life reflect on the paths to take.

The composer met in some unexpected place another unique performer from the twentieth century, since few instruments were as identified with a single performer as castanets were with Lucero Tena.[12] An opportunity soon came for them to collaborate in the form of commission for a concerto. The writing of any other option was really

Balada with Lucero Tena and Mistlav Rostropovitch

difficult given that the great performer didn't know how to read a score, let alone a contemporary one. So that was how Balada came to write *Three Anecdotes, Concertino for Castanets and Orchestra* between 1976 and 1977. As such a unique, elemental instrument wasn't part of his extensive technical knowledge, Balada had to work with the most similar instrument he could find in an orchestra—wood percussion.

After finishing the concerto, in order to overcome the problem of the score, Balada asked the first percussionist of the Pittsburgh Orchestra to record the soloist part (for Wood Blocks and five Temple Blocks) with a view to sending the tape to Lucero de Tena.[13] The full premiere took place on August 28, 1980 with the London Philharmonic Orchestra conducted by Andrew Davis at the XXIX International Musical Festival in Santander.

The performer's natural tendency to improvise was taken into consideration by Balada from the premiere and something was maintained in subsequent performances of the work, as in Madrid, January 10, 1981.[14] *Three Anecdotes* was often played by the *castañuela* star with renowned orchestras

---

12   Lucero Tena (1938) was born in Mexico City, although she lived in Spain from the age of twenty and became one the country's favorite musical ambassadors internationally. Initially, a flamenco dancer, her control of castanets was more powerful than her control of her feet and she decided to explore the potential of an instrument which she made available to contemporary composers.

13   This recording was made on November 8, 1978, at Indiana University in Pennsylvania. This version rarely has been performed.

14   Although we find mention of *Three Anecdotes* in 1976, when Lucero Tena reviews the composers who are writing for her in a press conference in London, the work's full premiere was performed in Santander, though the newspapers also review the full premiere by the RTVE Symphony Orchestra, conducted by Luis Antonio García Navarro. Both critics and audience were seduced by the soloist's electric playing and the excellence of the score. Enrique Franco in *El País* emphasised the piece's lighthearted nature and Fernández Cid in *ABC* judged the work to be a real find.

and conductors like Frühbeck de Burgos, Andrew Davis or even Mistlav Rostropovich. It has also been performed in its other form with solo wood percussion, and that will surely be the most viable version in the future given the unrepeatable nature of Lucero de Tena. Surprisingly, *Three Anecdotes*, divided into three short movements, is quite atonal, starts very abstractly with Balada recovering the textural pulse of the orchestra as the main driving force alongside the soloist.

Lucero Tena and Mistlav Rostropovitch
rehearsing *Three Anecdotes*

22.
The More I Hate You, the More I Need You

"Falling is allowed, getting back on your feet is a must," says a Russian refrain. Leonardo Balada had to apply a similar philosophy in 1976, when his marriage to Monica completely broke down after too much strife. Time had simply passed at different speeds for both of them and they no longer shared the same dreams and aims. But fortunately as life is no afternoon soap, Balada met the woman who would light his way and offer unceasing support to the present day. Joan Balada is undoubtedly the most powerful drive behind Leonardo's creativity. Her endeavors as a marketer in the Mellon Bank Leasing Department in Pittsburgh over several years were

Joan and Leonard in Aspen at the end of the '70s

clear proof of her professional abilities and use of a sixth sense to judge people, as well her firm grip on any vertigo she felt when working on a top floor in a city skyscraper. With Joan by his side, Leonardo had for the first time found a priceless collaborator in every imaginable way. Joan's work in Washington meant they left unfurnished the house Leonardo had bought in 1977 in a pretty residential area of Pittsburgh close to Carnegie Mellon University. Joan and Leonardo married in the country's capital on July 28, 1979. Both brought children to the marriage, three from her side and one from Leonardo's, and a plethora of shared hopes for the future.

Social life in Washington was so intense it brought to mind the old times in New York. Leonardo traveled to Pittsburgh to give his classes and returned home in a constant to-and-fro. The presence of the Spanish Embassy and the city's privileged cultural status with a musical complex like the John F. Kennedy Center, where the world's best musicians played, rekindled the old feeling of being located at the top of the world. Washington was particularly important professionally because it enabled him to rediscover opera as a genre that in the end fitted his style. The lyric genre had seemed far removed from the horizons of contemporary composers since it meant paying tribute to a nineteenth-century form of musical theater, with all its conventions, egos and group work. An operatic project directly encompassed an endless number of individuals who were all involved to the maximum and yet the final outcome was willy-nilly— always the direct responsibility of the composer. It was a huge undertaking where flexibility over objectives had to be the order of the day if one wanted to be successful. That clashed full on with the individualism of any other form of creativity, where the artist controlled the whole process.

However, once one overcame this working conflict in terms of trust and sharing of responsibilities, another factor existed without parallel in the rest of the world of performance: an almost complete dearth of singers equipped with the technical abilities necessary for the new atonal languages, and the fact that it was unlikely there would be audiences prepared to pay huge sums of money to come to a spectacle that wasn't of a piece with the well-honed, popular repertoire. And that was hardly surprising. A public that supported seasons at big opera theaters didn't want to take any risks as long as the usual repertoire kept it happy and fed its longings as an audience. From the 1940s a circular universe had been built where the music was eclipsed by the performances and subtle shades of this or that singer. Purely musical factors had been relegated to the background since the work was already considered to be a masterpiece in and of itself. This vicious circle had destroyed one of the constants in the history of opera, the hunger and enthusiasm for innovation. The unsuspected trajectory of works in the eighteenth and nineteenth centuries had first given rise to a focus on singers and now to a focus on staging. Contrary to appearances, both are irrevocably doomed. However, all these precedents weighed heavily on composer and theater when the writing of a new opera was on the agenda.

At the level of language, the aesthetic change wrought by Balada in his *Homages* had opened a straight road to melody as a useful, expressive element in his music. Eminently theatrical blood coursed through the veins of a composer whose father had exposed him from childhood to those passionate performances at the Liceu. External factors inevitably converged with these personal experiences. The moment seemed opportune to tackle the suicidal project of an opera. In the seventies there was a curious revival of the genre in the United States with leading figures prepared to invigorate seasons with new titles. Thus, composers like Giancarlo Menotti, Philip Glass or Alberto Ginastera, whom Balada already knew from his time in New York after interviewing him for *La Vanguardia*, embraced the challenge of opera. Washington became the flagship for that new kind of opera, although its aesthetic usually had to yield to the demands of nineteenth-century audiences in the final quarter of the twentieth. Ginastera was undoubtedly one of the standard-bearers for the new opera, even though he kept his style intact. Ginastera and Balada often met in the Capital District since both lived there with their wives and enjoyed a close friendship. Balada didn't lack arguments or motivation to take on the challenge of an opera and he was ready to bite the apple that might kill him but that inevitably gave him life.

Madrid. The summer of 1976. Enrique Franco. Spanish National Radio. This public body wanted to boost the repertoire for their radio orchestra, and suggested to a number of Spanish composers that they should create works for studio premieres without an audience. For some time Balada had been toying with the idea of an opera with the central theme of the Spanish Inquisition. When the proposal arrived from Enrique Franco, Balada decided that that might be an avenue to enable him to develop his style for the genre. The work would be a cantata for a few instruments and soloists, with one eye firmly on the stage. The first thorny step was the text. His previous experiences might have been fruitful at a human level, but it had required a massive effort to rethink his own ideas and adapt to someone else's. On this occasion Balada was ready to write his own text and prepare material to fit his own structures of sound. He began to recover his writing habits by penning articles for various Washington magazines and that sharpened his hand. He was ready to take the plunge and began researching historical documentation to shape his libretto for the cantata. At the National Library in Madrid he delved into the quite unpleasant *General Instructions of the Spanish Inquisition* dictated by Tomás de Torquemada between 1484 and 1488. Torquemada, the sinister arm of the most fanatical church in the Middle Ages, would be his antihero and the real engine driving his new conscious approach to the techniques of opera. Even though *Torquemada* wasn't technically an opera, it provided what Balada needed to test himself in order to make a confident entry into the universe of opera.

The structure's focus begins with an impossible dialogue with judgmental overtones between the fifteenth and twentieth centuries. Balada posed that dichotomy at textual and musical levels, where the pre-Renaissance element isn't resolved by a pastiche full of musicological references, but via an attempt to imitate the textures of that era from the prism of the contemporary. In short, the framework of *Torquemada* presents the lunacy of the inquisition in the eyes of twentieth-century society.[1] The inquisitor and his followers[2] are the past, while the chorus *en bloc* represents the contemporary audience's Greek conscience. This permanent dialogue is embedded in the structure of the music since Balada choses a process of accelerating interventions that finally dovetail the ideas of both sides.

The work was a great success, even though the radio premiere left very little in its wake since it was the closest you could reach to a premiere of electronic music. In any case, the main find to come from the project was that Balada's style could adapt perfectly to lyric and, consequently, operatic genres. Regrettably the idea of an opera about the Inquisition stayed stuck in limbo, like so many others, but there is no doubt that the attempt was a success and a first step towards grander projects with greater visibility.

The next commission soon arrived and was purely theatrical. The

---

1 *Torquemada* had its radio premiere with José Ramón Encinar conducting the RTVE Choir and sections of the RTVE Orchestra. Later the work broke the silence on radio with a performance in Pittsburgh by the Carnegie Mellon University chorus and instrumental players conducted by Robert Page. The score was premiered in Spain in the nineties conducted by Donald Wilkins, who toured the cantata in the summer to various Spanish cities.

2 They are performed by a baritone (Torquemada) and an "antique-style" quartet comprising soprano, contra-tenor, tenor and bass.

Catalan Composers' Association, which Leonardo had belonged to practically from its inception,[3] sent him a call from the brand-new Generalitat
of Catalonia, with a view to financing operas by Catalan composers. As
noted, opera wasn't a genre that appealed to active composers, so that
call/competition was a first step aimed at reviving the laurels of the country's lyrical genre. As usual with state administrations, the time from call
to deadline was minimal, but Leonardo had libretto and score ready in
record time to initiate his opera catalogue. The idea was inspired by a song
from the American West that told of the trials and tribulations of a man
sentenced to be hanged. That crux was transformed into a kind of exaggerated, acerbic cartoon drama in which the rule of money and its ability
to corrupt were laid bare.[4] The tradition of black comedy was familiar in
Spanish literature with wonderful examples from the nineteen-twenties
thanks to writers like Enrique Jardiel Poncela or Miguel Mihura. The
work *Hangman, Hangman!* was awarded the prize of a premiere in the next
International Festival in Barcelona. The strangest feature of the opera is its
text, written in three different languages,
Catalan (*Botxí! Botxí!*), Spanish (*Verdugo!*
Verdugo!) and in English,[5] a strategy followed in order to maximize the opportu-
nities for performance. *Hangman!, Hang-*
man! is dedicated to Joan Balada, who was
by now the composer's wife and corrector
of the English version. This is the most
performed version and the one recorded
on the Naxos label. The new opera fitted
the rubric of the call for entries: a one-

Joan and Leonardo Balada
in Washington

act chamber opera, under six soloist singers, a small chamber orchestral
ensemble and choir. Although after its first performance several critics
found similarities with the best work by the Kurt Weill-Bertold Brecht
duo, they have nothing aesthetically in common, and the composer never
intended there to be any. This opera is a brilliant attempt to combine
musical theater with singing numbers and a contemporary stage setting,

---

3　It is worth noting that, from its foundation in 1974, the Association only accepted composers
from the area of Catalonia. This fact essentially prevented Balada from participating in the project
of the Association of Spanish Symphony Composers, chaired by Ramón Barce and active from 1976.
4　This concept, referred to in the score, relates to the cartoons that appeared in the United States
at the end of the 1930s in which situations were as hilarious as they were extreme.
5　Both versions exist, though the Spanish translation has never been premiered.

222

and its genesis was complicated. The main problem, resolved in *Torquemada* thanks to the use of melodies with few inflections and pauses, was the establishing of an individual operatic style for Leonardo Balada. This approach is about sustaining a melodic composition without making huge demands on tonal levels for singers, while the instrumental weft elaborates more complex textures but always maintains an auditory point of support for the soloist. However, that prop, essential to sustaining the melodic line, isn't a trivial continuo, since Balada gives it a breath that appears and disappears across several instruments and avoids creating a sense of an excessive polarity of tone in the final outcome.

The work was premiered October 10, 1982 by the Chamber Opera of Catalonia, produced by Josep Maria Espada and conducted by the composer. Despite the audience's lack of familiarity with the stage references, the work was well received, but, as usual, hardly ecstatically. The theme was harsh and complex and the music brilliant, accessible and personal, but it clearly

Rehearsing *Hangman, Hangman!* at Carnegie Mellon University

needed a second or third performance to realize its full potential. The American premiere in the following year was a great improvement. On October 8, 1983 *Hangman, Hangman!*, in what might be called the original version, was performed in Pittsburgh in Akram Midani's production with the massed ranks of Carnegie Mellon University[6] under the orders of

6   For the reader who has no idea of the American network of university orchestras, we should note that despite the inevitable difficulties presented by the inevitable coming and going of students on their courses, the orchestras of the country's best universities play at an extremely high level and sustain programs, audiences and recordings of an equally high quality.

Werner Torkanowsky,[7] who by that time had been appointed conductor of the university orchestra.

Balada initiated his opera career with Johnny's sorrowful story creating a style of his own for a genre that was hard to break into. From the start the composer didn't hide his formal preferences; he was convinced contemporary music had much to offer even within the classical parameters of opera. But also whether because of limitations of time or means, or because it followed the fashion of the "baddies" winning, *Hangman, Hangman!* didn't come with an edifying end to please honest-to-God American families. Villains and corruption win out, and this happens in an environment that is so preoccupied by the need to be exemplary that the plot becomes something quite politically incorrect. Balada took several years to deal with that problem, fourteen to be exact, and a bunch of operas to boot. In 1997, with a text by Balada himself, nourished by Akram Midani's ideas, *The Town of Greed* was conceived and concluded, sequel and end to the story of Johnny, a horse thief transformed into a corrupt oil tycoon, an icon of big fortunes made overnight, the puppet and caricature of powerful people who gave him money and then got so tired of him that they sent him back to the noose. More bitter than the first part, harsher and more direct, less classical formally, *The Town of Greed* was recorded before its official premiere that took place in September 2007 in Madrid's Teatro de la Zarzuela with the resident orchestra and choir conducted by José Ramón Encinar.

The challenge of applying individual avant-garde style to the genre of opera was most unusual in Spanish musical life and Balada is surely the most successful at doing so in his generation. Entry to the genre by composers of the New Music Generation, wrongly dubbed the 51 Generation, also came late in the day, as happened with Balada, and they were possibly less flexible in terms of the classical concept of musical theater. Nonetheless, the big unfinished business remains the same for everybody: how to keep a work on stage, how to ensure the necessary further productions. That's why this opera duo, with their chamber tones and grotesque cartoon style,

7   The miraculous presence of a prestigious conductor like Torkanowsky as the head of a university orchestra stemmed in large measure from Balada insisting he be appointed. The German conductor had made the New Orleans Orchestra one of the country's best and then gone to Detroit as deputy and future replacement of Antal Dorati. That succession didn't take place and Torkanowsky accepted a post as conductor in a second-rank orchestra in Maine. When Balada put his name forward to be conductor of the student orchestra, pianist Harry Franklyn, the then head of the Music section, thought it would be impossible to attract such a distinguished individual to Carnegie Mellon. Fortunately, that wasn't the case and Torkanowsky went on to make the Carnegie Mellon University orchestra one of the country's finest university orchestras.

could certainly be performed more often and in productions that are less costly and more imaginative than those that tend to hog the budgets of the world's greatest opera venues. This is possibly one of the great unknowns in terms of the viability or not of the genre itself, something Tomás Marco has been trying to explore for years with his concept of Musical Theater.

Undoubtedly opera has been and is a genre capable of engulfing the unwary who venture near and if *Hangman* came up heads, *Zapata* came down tails: an executioner gave it life and a revolutionary killed it. The story of *Zapata* is plagued by dark moments and corrosive setbacks in which the protagonists, who should in principle have been helping the music along, stuck out like rocks across its path. The truth is that *Zapata*, a great opera in two acts commissioned by San Diego Opera has yet to be premiered though it was finished in 1984.

Zapata was to be conducted by Theo Alcántara in the San Diego Opera 1975 season, though in the event it was never premiered. He came to the post with the helping hand of another great name from the American opera scene, Tito Capobianco,[8] who took over the reins of the theater in 1976, defending and even extending its status as an outstanding venue for opera in the United States. The stars of opera constantly performed there, including all the great Hispanic singers of the time. Alcántara had been present at the premiere of *María Sabina* in Carnegie Hall and its score had made a lasting impression, so he soon met Balada to plan a collaboration. The conductor from El Alcarria was always committed to Balada's music and his work conducting Balada's scores is notable. Capobianco was an artistic director and producer cursed with a pile-driver personality and in the opinion of some, rather dictatorial in his manner. When the moment came to celebrate the first twenty years of San Diego Opera as an independent theater—its curtain went up for the first time in 1965—they started scouring the field to find the composer best fitted to create a first-rate premiere to bring energy and modernity to their theater. This substantial project slowly cranked into action in 1981. The list of candidates was headed by Giancarlo Menotti, whose relationship with Capobianco and Californian

---

8   Tito Capobianco (1931) was born in La Plata, Argentina, and for many years worked as stage and artistic director in various theaters like the Colón in Buenos Aires, San Diego, Cincinnati or Pittsburgh. He made his debut in 1953 in his city of birth with *Aida*, and has since directed in the world's most important theaters. In 1965 he premiered his production of *Les contes d'Hoffman* with the New York City Opera and in 1978 in the Metropolitan Opera House. His relationship with Balada was initially one of mutual respect but it all ended badly because of the director's excessive, destructive ego and Balada's unwillingness to compromise.

theater went back years. That initial idea foundered on the bad relationship between the Italian-American composer and the producer. Alberto Ginastera was also in the running, a compatriot of Capobianco and a composer experienced in the opera field, but his sudden death in Geneva in 1983, at the age sixty-seven, put a stop to that. Another candidate was Carles Suriñach, a renowned survivor of a generation in decline, who enjoyed a good reputation in the United States. But it was the impact of *María Sabina* that catapulted Balada towards that commission in San Diego. Capobianco listened to the recording of the cantata and part of Balada's music before the big interview that decided the future of that great opera. They were all convinced he was the best option and then began to erect hurdles on the way forward. The work would be molded for the great American baritone Sherrill Milnes, then at the height of his career. His special Verdi baritone timbre with its brilliant high notes would condition the voice of the main character. Conversely, Balada was expressly asked to ensure, given the baritone's strengths, that the line of song wasn't as complex as in the works of his they had listened to, that, in fact, he should resort to a tonal rather than atonal melodic concept. This huge commission and chance to write a big opera meant that Balada threw himself into a suicidal theatrical adventure without a life jacket. It wasn't the first time the composer had had to tailor the suit to a performer, but it was equally true that had previously happened when Balada wasn't a composer with such a reputation. To what extent he could safeguard his aesthetic status and fulfill the conditions of the commission he had no doubt thought through before accepting the proposal.

Plot was one of the complex areas where that adventure had to start. Balada's previous catalogue was full of work whose idiosyncratic themes spoke to their author's personality. On this occasion, the purely operatic work involved many other people, many points of view and a range of sensibilities that had to be accommodated. The chosen subject was the life and struggles of Emiliano Zapata,[9] leading Mexican revolutionary and defender of the rights of the poor in the south of the country. California's relationship with Mexican history and the future commemoration of the sixty-fifth anniversary of his assassination melded with the ineffable attrac-

---

9   No doubt Balada found the anarchist star of Zapata highly attractive. He saw in that Mexican's life a drama fit for the world's greatest stages and all the ingredients to make a fine opera. Emiliano Zapata (1879-1919) was the military leader of the Mexican Revolution and his daring and ideas about redistributing the land to those who worked it resisted all the bribes and siren songs from the powers that be. He invented the famous saying: "It's better to die standing than live life forever on your knees," taken up later by Dolores Ibarruri and Ernesto "Che" Guevara.

tion exercised over Leonardo Balada by a character like Emiliano Zapata, who was so committed and so subversive in the eyes of the political establishment. It was a promising cocktail and a real incentive for him to get started on the project, a feeling shared by those programming the theater's season, who gave their go-ahead right away. The team was so united that Capobianco himself collaborated in the writing of the libretto, that was put together with Gabriela Roepke, and written in English. The creation of the libretto was no simple matter. A text was required that had been penned with an ear to the music—it was a far cry from Cela and his María Sabina—with features directly related to staging and choreography. The text had to serve the music and avoid the risk of steering it away from its operatic, lyrical nature. The Zapata text went through a good number of revisions that enabled it to evolve from huge initial budgets to others that were more realistic.

The two-act opera enjoyed the financial support of the National Endowment for the Arts, as well as the theater's, which guaranteed payment in an advance and after delivery of the score. The presence of a voice like Milne's with great powers of projection ensured that Balada could write for an orchestra he knew perfectly, with all its strengths, chiaroscuros and fine control of rhythm, something that hadn't been his experience with *Hangman, Hangman!* What wasn't in his favor was the warning he couldn't move freely along melodic lines, because that could easily lead him to a neotonal style like Menotti's and he didn't want to fall under his yoke. To escape that fatal magnetic pull, he shielded himself in the orchestra's dissonant textures, making life difficult for the singers, though never taking it too far.

The work was on course for its premiere in 1985 when Capobianco became involved in a vicious conflict with the theater management and slammed the door behind him in San Diego, provoking an outcry in the media that was heard throughout the country. The stage director was leaving San Diego, and so were Balada and his *Zapata*, with nowhere specific to go. As soon as the shouting died down, Capobianco, Alcántara and *Zapata* turned up in Pittsburgh to attempt a transplant to the Pittsburgh Opera. For Balada, who would thus avoid trips to California, a possible presence in Pittsburgh must have seemed like great news, but there were a number of unknowns. Whether the commission was still on course, who would sing the role of Zapata, and who would pay for the work were unanswered questions. With many a grand gesture and total silence on the details, Capobianco assured him the project would go ahead, commissioned by Pittsburgh. When asked about Milnes or another singer of his stature, all he heard in response was the sound of the flowing waters of the three rivers. It was no minor issue, because Balada had designed a bespoke role for a singer with almost unique gifts. Once the score was signed off, they carried out the necessary revisions, and Capobianco then caused a great stir in the media by announcing that *Zapata* would be premiered in his first season in Pittsburgh. But when the time came to reveal the program there was no sign of *Zapata*. The wheel began to turn, and they said it would be in the next season, but the next season came and it wasn't. Once again they killed off *Zapata* at the last minute. As the guerrilla fighter's pistols were loaded, Leonardo produced a suite from his waistcoat pocket with motifs from the opera entitled *Zapata Images for Orchestra*. Torkanowsky also recorded scenes from the opera with Carnegie Mellon musicians and performed almost half the opera, but it has never been performed in its entirety. After listening to the symphonic version one might jump to the conclusion that the entire opera plays with tonal melodies that crowd out the work's contemporary features. The most popular melodies in the Mexican subconscious crop up in the suite, which is a reference point for the remainder of the opera, but *Zapata* is a work that clings to the spine of the purest Balada style.

The vicissitudes of *Zapata* continue to be a thorn piercing the heart. Almost all the commissions Balada has received for the composition of a new opera have first had to reject a premiere for *Zapata*. That doesn't mean the opera comes with a black legend: rather it shows clearly that people in the world of music prefer to premiere a work that is completely new.

And in the midst of all this dross, the dream commission arrived from Spain.

23.
The Columbus Catharsis

Catharsis:

For the ancient Greeks, the ritual purification of individuals or
things affected by some kind of impurity.

The effect that tragedy has on the spectator as it arouses and purifies
compassion, fear or horror and other emotions.

Inner purification, liberation or transformation aroused by a deep,
vital experience.

Elimination of memories that unsettle conscience or nervous
equilibrium.

Biol. The spontaneous or induced expulsion from the organism of
harmful substances.[1]

For years Balada has preferred to keep to a Spanish timetable in Pittsburgh. Those extra six hours would become three or four hours of intense
work before leaving for the university and momentarily hanging up his
composer's habit. He effortlessly keeps to that routine and sits at his crowded
desk from four in the morning. Any negotiation or call he had to make
to Spain would have been unthinkable without embracing his "jet-lag;"
notoriously, in the bull-hide that is Spain's shape the end of office hours is
about the only sacred thing left.

Balada was expecting an important call, the commission of the century,
as some had dubbed the proposal to write an opera for the celebrations of
the Fifth Centenary Anniversary of the Discovery of South America. A

---

1 Different definitions of "catharsis" that are all valid and illuminating for this chapter: *Diccionario de la Lengua Española*: Real Academia Española, 2000, 20ᵗʰ edition (first, 1992)

government body had recently been set up, pompously named "The State Fifth Centenary Company" that was summoned to proclaim, celebrate and rewrite, to the extent that it was possible, the history of the discovery of the New Continent by Europeans and vice versa. Aquiles García Tuero, activist, agitator and cultural promotor on behalf of Spanish and Hispanic cultures in the United States, had been appointed to lead the campaign, and found he was as soon at the top as at the bottom of a little world that was far too quick to forget. On May 20, 1987, on the eve of the great Columbine premiere in Barcelona, Alfonso Armada penned a splendid description of García Tuero in *El País*:

"An extinguished cigar between his fingers can last him over an hour. Braces over his jersey and hair like lank wool. His casual appearance contrasts starkly with the importance assigned to him, his high-level contacts and the money at his fingertips. Proud of his birth certificate, proof of his birth forty-four years ago in Quintueles, near Gijón, he is *the* promotor of Spanish culture in the United States. He has embarked on a huge project: the premiere of the opera *Columbus* in Barcelona and the re-creation of the admiral's journey in an ocean liner."

The call came at a classically untimely hour and woke up Joan once again, who was peacefully sleeping according to her American routine. As with any act involving public subsidies, a general call had gone out for pro-

With Jesús López Cobos at the beginning of the '80s

posals for the writing of what would be the event to launch those celebrations. Balada's proposal came with the backing of García Tuero and Jesús López Cobos, and was finally awarded "the commission of the century." It was 1984, another key year in his professional life that started off on a surprising note. Many proposals had been laid on the table, signed and endorsed by distinguished composers from all over the world, but on this occasion the one that stood was by Leonardo Balada Ibáñez. The stage for all the outrageous in-fighting was littered by a host of fine corpses, too many, no doubt; on the one hand, that showed the healthy state of Spanish composing and, on the other, the final choice ignited a feverish escalation of the national sport of envy, that proved especially emphatic in the world of music, encompassing musicians, critics and musicologists.

Balada could rely on several winning aces in that game. He was at the height of his creative powers, he had experience in the genre with two operas in his catalogue, and an array of works with a stage presence—something that wasn't the case with his Spanish colleagues in Spain at the time—as well as the fact that he didn't belong to any of the Madrid or Barcelona cliques; his aesthetic reflected a multicultural worldview that was a priority and he was an indefatigable worker. The reality of his dual nationality, assumed in 1981 as a consequence of his marriage and labor situation,[2] shouldn't have been an argument to carry any weight, but it was certainly a factor that marked him out. That telephone call from Aquiles García Tuero represented a watershed in Balada's career.

The commission to write an opera about Christopher Columbus didn't catch Balada in any offside trap. His interest in the Golden Age and experience with *Ponce de León* had already prepared him to construct a musical adventure from the myth and history of Christopher Columbus. Eight months before the commission, he had read a news report about Columbus's possible birth in Tortosa, a place that was very close to his heart. That story, one of so many on the subject of the admiral's mysterious birth, stirred strange butterflies in the composer's stomach and a ravenous hunger to compose an opera about that character and his feats. Less than a year later, that telephone call reverberated round the Mediterranean-style whitewashed walls of his Pittsburgh home. He had to travel immediately to Madrid to discuss the conditions for the commission and sign the contract.

The same envelope with the commission also contained a series of commitments entered into by the State Fifth Centenary Company: the opera's title would be *Christopher Columbus*, it would be sung by great names from Spanish and Spanish American opera, it would be promoted as

2   Leonardo Balada became a U.S. citizen in 1981, which meant the end to his annoying annual trips to the embassy as a foreigner with a U.S. residency card. That situation deprived him of his Spanish nationality for a brief time, which many of his Catalanist friends interpreted as an ideological move. When the bureaucratic misunderstanding was sorted out—which upset Balada no end—he immediately asked for his original nationality to be renewed.

much as possible on the mass media, and an advisory committee would be established to appoint the librettist, musical director and stage director to ensure the project's success. Part of that discussion included deciding lead and secondary roles, the theaters where the opera would be performed, and those who would control and manage the finances. No loose ends were left, and there was no shortage of money—there was a lot. It was to be the first big cultural project of Spain's first socialist government since the death of Franco, one that was destined to begin the modernization of a country that shortly would be first-rank internationally. Alfonso Guerra's famous words about changing the country were to be prophetic. The political source of a commission is always a double-edged weapon in a modern democracy like Spain, that is used to surrendering its sovereignty to a handful of motley individuals that end up turning the country into a backwoods ranch full of incompetent chancers. The polarization within Spanish society in the mid-eighties was a phenomenon that could be checked out in various attempted coups and conspiracies, not to mention the partisan nature of the media. All that directly implicated Balada, who now went from being an independent composer living in America to a participant from the very start in an ambitious project aligned to a political party. All these conditioning factors shaped the climate in which the opera would develop from day one and, above all, the boomerang effect Cainite detractors hoped for on the day of the premiere.

But such siren songs in the form of cash registers ringing or desperate bellowing in sour meetings were not to the liking of Balada who already bore a number of scars produced by similar backstabbing. Conversely, he was really enthused—and how!—by the tour planned for the work. *Christopher Columbus* would receive its premiere in Barcelona in 1987 and then visit the world's leading opera houses (Paris, Brussels, London, Milan, Rome, Berlin, Munich, Moscow, Tokyo, Buenos Aires, Mexico, Los Angeles, San Francisco . . .) and would finally reach New York on October 12, 1992 to inaugurate the season at the Met. Additionally, a commercial recording of the opera had been agreed with Sony, not to mention the television broadcast of the world premiere coordinated by Spanish Television and the sale of rights to the rest of the world. Could one hope for anything more?

The marathon task of selecting, finding and rejecting fellow travelers began. Naturally, one of the first items on the agenda was the libretto. Balada suggested Camilo José Cela, a long-standing collaborator, and Fernando Arrabal, with whom he had yet to work though he had had dealings with him over a failed project of an opera about *La Pasionaria* that went back two years. That project had led him to interview Dolores Ibarruri in person to test out her views about the idea. But the advisory committee reviewed all the suggestions, and awarded the commission to Antonio Gala. Balada wasn't at all surprised—Balada had got an inkling, although he lived so far away—and warmly welcomed the choice, since Gala is one of the great names in contemporary Spanish literature and also possibly the most important name in the theater over the last twenty-five years. There was no dispute over potential singers, as everybody agreed on the two great stars to head the project: Montserrat Caballé and Josep Carreras. The music would be the responsibility of Jesús López Cobos, but what about the production? There were lots of proposals but the idea began to gain momentum that it should be somebody from the other side of the pond.

On Sunday, December 30, 1984 those responsible for the project sat down at a press conference in the Saló del Tinell in Barcelona. Leonardo and Antonio Gala were the most visible, but alongside were Luis Yáñez, president of the Institute for Ibero-American Cooperation; Pasqual Maragall, mayor of Barcelona; Jordi Maluquer, overall director of Music, Theater and Cinema; and Aquiles García Tuero himself. The presentation was a great media success and, as usually happens in those parts, bells began to ring out joyfully. García Tuero referred that adventure back to 1980, when *Evita* was the big hit on Broadway, and somebody had suggested to him the idea of a musical about the life of Christopher Columbus. That idea would now be transformed into an opera and premiered in the spring of 1987 before setting sail to New York and Buenos Aires as definite ports of call. It was a weighty project, and weighed in heavily.

After all the preliminary hue and cry the question of stage director was still up for grabs. Balada was intending to back Tito Capobianco as his candidate since the latter was in full swing trying to sort out the premiere of *Zapata* after his departure from San Diego, and he thought it might help spur on that process, although it looked to be turning sour. Conversely, his wife Joan thought that was a mistake—Capobianco would influence the whole production and it wouldn't impact on the premier of the previous opera because there must be other hurdles only he knew about. Balada persuaded his wife and the advisory committee, and Tito Capobianco was given the post of stage director.

The first phase on the discovery of this Columbus was the creation of a text. Balada agreed to a week of working sessions with Gala in Madrid.

The composer came to the first day thinking he would be mounting a work closer to the style of *Ponce de León* or *María Sabina* than *Zapata*. He knew that an opera in America wasn't the same as an opera in Europe. Audiences' aesthetic background and appreciation were very different on each continent and he knew he must suggest something powerful, direct, contemporary and challenging for Barcelona. That line of thought had been his main argument when he recommended Arrabal, a dense, avant-garde dramatist, but one who was undoubtedly less poetic than Gala. That was the first reverse his overall conception of *Christopher Columbus* suffered. The opera began to assume signs of being a grand opera in nineteenth-century mode, and that added layers of extra difficulty which Balada now had to confront.

In any case, the sessions with Antonio Gala were extraordinary. Their collaboration was careful, precise and fruitful to such an extent that both maestros felt enriched. Leonardo and Joan arrived in Antonio Gala's house early in the morning and while the men got on with their writing, Joan strolled through that Madrid she liked so much. They all ate together and then the second session of the day started immediately. The libretto was completed in five days to everybody's satisfaction. Balada was aware the text was poetic rather than theatrical and, consequently, that would shape his approach to the music, but he had no regrets; there was only a job to be done.

The second phase was the necessary previous contact with the singers. Collaborating with Caballé, Carreras, or any other international *divo* or *diva* from the world of repertoire opera meant molding one's style and tailoring the sound. The relationship of renowned singers with contemporary musical languages has always been fraught. Working successfully in repertoire means singers have a status to maintain that is constantly threatened by a fall by the wayside, and that was a very powerful pressure. It was as if those great performers, who needed to keep the passion of audiences for the repertoire intact, came to contemporary music with lots to lose. It made them suspicious of new languages that obliged them to change their routine techniques, the formulas they had learned over the years, not to mention the extra time spent on preparation. Given those tensions, Balada assumed the responsibility of adapting his style to the virtues of those musicians. He admitted as much in an interview carried out by José Luis Téllez for Spanish Television on the occasion of the broadcasting of *Christopher Columbus*, "You couldn't possibly waste the melodic and tonal qualities of those singers." Not exploiting their quality would be like taking to the trapeze without a safety net. If you wanted those singers, you had to design clothes that would be a good fit.

That was why the composer went to New York to work specifically with the soprano on the nuances of her voice profile. After a brief, passionate speech in which Balada rehearsed his general idea and preferred aesthetic, the singer glanced at her husband, Bernabé Martí, and got down to work.

Balada started to cut that cloth to fit Caballé. Who would have thought to tell Pepito? Nardo was finally going to be a tailor, a sui generis one, for sure, but a tailor at the end of the day. Where there were dissonant breaks, they should be less dissonant (that is, not dissonant at all); complex leaps of sevenths that would be closer to octaves and

With Monserrat Caballé during a previous meeting

above all lots of *filato*, for that was what her style was famous for. And what about Carreras? That wasn't a problem. The bespoke musical suit for Caballé also conditioned the parts for Carreras, but that damned pair sang so well! Over time and as a result of the singers' continuous professional movements, Balada became a Caballé and Carreras groupie, and met them in the most surprising places, Vienna, Berlin, London, New York.

Three years of work, two acts, two hours plus of music. The day-to-day struggle with the score had been enough to convince Balada. The opera would be melodic, even Puccini-like, if its melodies were sung in isolation, but in-between, the orchestra became Baladan, with aleatory episodes, *sprechsgesang* in the choir, electronic, aleatory sections, atonal, beautifully lyrical melodies and, of course, an ethnic edge, that had become lost under the flashing neon-lights of grand opera and was now reborn between the soloists' interventions. *Christopher Columbus* would resonate with Andalusian, Catalan and South American Indian popular music, though they too would be cut as only Balada could cut them. Only the orchestral éclosion in the final act, when the Indians were present on stage culturally and musically, was the most explicit and no doubt that was the why it was one of the main sources of conflict with the press and a sector of the audience.

After *Zapata*, Balada noticed that G. Schirmer publishers, who had been responsible for publishing and distributing his scores for over a decade, had been curiously siphoning off income in the form of new undeclared editions. During the process of creating *Christopher Columbus*, Balada spoke calmly to his agent about this worrying development and, given the serious doubts they shared, he decided to tear up his contract, anticipating the dangers that might come from the poor handling of an opera which was about to enjoy such a high profile throughout the world. That was when Joan and Leonardo began to discuss the idea of creating their own press that would allow them to manage materials with his agent in a more direct, quicker way than with a big multinational company. Soon afterwards *Beteca Music* was born, the Baladas' own label, under which most of his scores have been subsequently published.

With the opera written, soloists on track, orchestra and choirs in full rehearsal and the poster of the season proudly displaying the prodigal's name at the Gran Teatre del Liceu, they received the worst possible news. Sad headlines issued from press agencies through-out the world: tenor Josep Carreras had leukemia. That treacherous illness, that slashed like the sword of Damocles, though never enough to alarm us, struck at the very heart of the music. The friendship and work over those years with Car-reras relegated *Christopher Columbus* to the background. People stood by their friend rather than the professional.

With Josep Carreras years after Christopher Columbus

Before they had time to react, a communiqué was issued suspending the opera *sine die*. *Christopher Columbus* would wait for Carreras, because he *was* Christopher Columbus. In the following next months, contradictory news appeared as the tenor fought tenaciously for his life. Plácido Domingo and then Luciano Pavarotti offered to premiere *Christopher Columbus* with Caballé, but Carreras rejected their offers: that opera would be his motivation, an icon against adversity, the buoy enabling him to cling on to his professional life. Inevitably, the 1989 press conference was momentous, Josep Carreras had recovered and survived an illness that claimed thousands of victims throughout the world; he would continue to sing for them, and would start with *Christopher Columbus*.

That unfortunate interregnum gave Balada no respite. *Christopher Columbus* had focused his attention for two long years, but a backlog of calls on his creativity was now building up and fighting to emerge in several directions. Between 1987 and 1988 his catalogue was expanded with four works that inaugurated the new publishing house, although in reality *Alegrías* was the second movement of *Reflejos* (*Reflections*). It glanced in the direction of a different texture: a string instrument with flute with the specificity that there was to be no soloist. With *Reflejos*, Balada pursued his idea of generating flexible works; there was a version for string orchestra and for quintet, which was the one finally premiered with the Atlanta Virtuosi.[3] Divided into two movements, *Penas y Alegrías* (*Sorrows and Happiness*) comprises an exercise in compact, not soloist, textures, in which the working of textures and chromatics isn't so different from what happens in *Christopher Columbus*. It can be said that *Reflejos* is the nonvocal part that predominates in the opera and that usually goes unremarked alongside the power of attraction of the melody that predominates in the musical theater. *Penas* represents a work of shifting textures against spurts of melody, a constant in Balada's compositions when he works for small ensembles. The lines of melody unfurl around extreme chromatics very similar to the pleas and lamentations in *Christopher Columbus*. *Alegrías* is located in a more descriptive area where melodic and rhythmic effect tends to gain space from the textural, and nourish itself on the same essences as the opera.

Fantasías sonoras, a commission from the Benedum Center in Pittsburgh and premiered by the Pittsburgh Symphony Orchestra, equally doesn't represent a break with the coherence of the Columbine moment. The prism of the fantasy located in the opera is captured within this symphonic poem, where the orchestra zigzags in patches flecked with color that revisit the

---

3   The work was a multiple commission from the Atlanta Virtuosi, the New England Quintette and The Cambridge Players, and received financial support from the National Endowment for the Arts Composers Commissioning Programme.

climate of incessant movement found in *Christopher Columbus*. Only his frustration over *Zapata* led Balada to create a suite from the opera as a way of promoting and airing a score that in 1987 already seemed sentenced to years of silence.

Carreras's pride kept *Christopher Columbus* alive, but the change of date brought a few adjustments. The most important was the departure of Jesús López Cobos from the program, who had previous commitments he couldn't drop, and was replaced by Theo Alcántara. At the time Balada welcomed Alcántara's appointment, because the conductor from El Alcarria was familiar with his music, but he didn't anticipate the darker side to this narrative: it gave Tito Capobianco more power over the production. A new date was finally fixed for the premiere, September 24, 1989, when the curtain of Barcelona's Liceu would rise for the world premiere of Leonardo Balada's *Christopher Columbus*.

What happened next is an account worthy of the best thriller by Francisco González Ledesma:[4]

Barcelona. The end of a hot, humid August in 1989. A composer arrives from the United States on the eve of a premiere so he can attend rehearsals for his latest opera with piano and soloists. A taxi stops by the theater door. Tourists are making so much noise on La Rambla that the sepulchral silence inside seems like a bad joke played by the devil, as González Ledesma's Inspector Méndes would have said. The composer's footsteps echo down the cool corridors of the spectators' area by the main auditorium, when he is suddenly stopped by a head of production.

"Maestro, we weren't expecting you so soon. I'm so sorry . . . but there's no rehearsal today, it was canceled at the last minute, I thought someone would have told you."

"Wonderful. Many thanks for letting me know in such good time."

"We are very sorry. And there's something else you should know before tomorrow's rehearsal. It's been decided to make a series of vital cuts."

"What do you mean "vital? Has someone died? Has someone threatened a bomb attack? Has something fallen apart at the last minute?"

"That's a decision taken by the stage director."

"What you are actually saying," said the composer, as he nervously

---

4   González Ledesma (1927-2015) was a prize-winning writer of comics, Westerns and noir. Many of his noir novels are located in the Raval, Barcelona's old red-light district or *barrio chino*, where he was born and lived. The Liceu stands in La Rambla on the fringe of this area.

scratched his chin, "is that the score has been cut without the composer's permission."

In a blind fury, exhausted by several hours of jet lag, the composer headed towards the nearby hotel where the opera's musical director was staying. The hotel lobby, that was not as cool as the theater, displayed all the shabby trappings of a hotel undergoing a refurbishment. He asked for the director, and was informed he had gone out. His fury rocketed even more when he asked for notepaper to scribble a message and his pen wouldn't work. He leant on the counter, reined in his temper, grabbed a pencil and wrote: "Theo, I've just heard cuts have been made without my agreement. Tell Tito that *Zapata* was his opera, but *Columbus* is *mine . . .*"

He immediately walked to the Plaça de Catalunya and jumped into a taxi to go home and wait for a response. His wife was still working in Pittsburgh, so the wait seemed endless. When they returned to their hotel, the musical director and stage director were waiting for their keys when they saw the note that the composer had left in Theo Alcántara's pigeonhole.

"You take it and tell me what it says, Tito, I'm going out to buy a newspaper."

The fact that the note was read by the individual it wasn't meant for provoked an angry response from the stage director, who began to bellow out all manner of insults that were no doubt echoed by the composer in his room who was cursing everything that moved. A telephone call put a stop to all that unleashed rage. He was wanted in Madrid to settle final details relating to the relaying of the opera on radio and television. The composer was back on an airplane moving away for a while from a problem that was sure to explode sooner or later. In the composer's view, the two days in Madrid were a pretext to ensure he wasn't present at the mutilated rehearsals. The stage director had threatened to abandon the production a month from its premiere if the composer put in an appearance. But that only served to gain a few days, an elastoplast holding back the surge of water into the *Titanic.* Two days later a crisis meeting was called with the singers and entire staff of the production. You could have cut the tension with a razor. That dawn gathering turned into a kangaroo trial of the composer in a modern version of the Inquisition. Musical and stage directors supported the cuts made to the score while the singers waited to see what happened. Forced into a corner, the composer accepted the cuts made to the tenor's role since his condition, after his recent illness, meant he couldn't reach any note sharper than a G-5. But he saw the cuts to the end of the opera as an attack on his artistic integrity. Furious, he put a spanner in the works and withdrew his score. The premiere was canceled.

It was a major disaster. Thousands of millions of pesetas tied to a public subsidy were about to go down the pan, not to mention a premiere to be attended by the king and queen, television channels and journalists from over half the planet, as well as the enormous expectation at the return to the stage of one of the great names in modern opera and the performances planned in the world's most prestigious opera houses. No doubt, Balada had taken a radical decision, but it was necessary to maintain his dignity. The composer kept firm for the whole afternoon and evening, allowing himself to be courted, until he finally agreed to let rehearsals go ahead late into the night. His pain at witnessing cuts to his score were exacerbated by other more trivial problems, like the librettist who wanted to have the same font size on the poster as the composer and to give separate interviews to the media. The heavens seemed to have opened! When the composer's wife arrived, she found him prostrate in bed with a sciatica attack of biblical proportions, feeling that all his hopes and dreams had been dashed. The big day of the premiere was approaching and he could hardly move. Emotional tension that had been building up over five weeks and had ravaged him physically.

D–Day arrived. The red carpet was laid out in front of the theater for all the pillars of society who had signed up for the premiere. Facing them, a special contingent of police held at bay two separate demonstrations: One by Catalan republican *independentistas*—including colleagues of the composer—and another by indigenous peoples against the pomp and ceremony of a discovery of America that had led to the extermination of a civilization—towards whom the composer also felt favorably disposed. Leonardo and his wife arrived at a moment of maximum aggression between the pickets and the forces of public order.

"Hey, where do you think you're going? You can't come in here."

"Why? I've got to."

"Please, cross over and walk down the opposite sidewalk. This is an official act attended by the royal household."

"You're quite wrong, this is the premiere of an opera."

"I couldn't care less what you think, sir, you can't come this way. If you persist in your attitude, I will have no choice but to detain you and take you to the police station."

"But none of this can start without me."

"So, I suppose you're the composer."

"Absolutely, I am Leonardo Balada."

"Proof of identity, please," and the composer showed his identity card. The policeman compared the name registered there several times to what he could see on the poster.

"You may go in, sir."

The performance started late as was to be expected for what was a political rather than an artistic act. As music took over the theater, the cuts sent blood rushing to the composer's head and his back felt it was being whiplashed. The much-feared finale came, the Indians had been deprived of their five minutes of glory, and the curtain fell. Applause all round, faint jeers for the text and huge ovations for the performers. A success, a failure? Hard to decide. The next day's reviews were equally divided. Locals mercilessly attacked the score and the text, national reviewers gave the work a favorable write-up, and internationally it was described as a big success and a masterpiece.

Scene from the first act of the premiere in the Gran Teatre del Liceu, Barcelona

The composer could hardly get up from his seat in the remaining performances and consequently didn't go on stage at the end of the work. The final curtain saw the composer appear as if in retreat from a battle front, walking stick in tow, suffering from the aftermath of over a month of endless tension and bad feeling. But the story didn't end there; gangsters and threats were yet to come. For the moment the return home was short-lived. The International Olympic Committee summoned the composer to an interview. Juan Antonio Samaranch wanted to commission that composer in the headlines to write the music for the upcoming Olympic Games that would take place in Barcelona in 1992 when the Fifth Centenary celebrations reached their climax with a Universal Exhibition in Sevilla and the American premiere and conclusion to *Christopher Columbus*'s tour at the Met. He couldn't have held a better calling card. The fruit's ripe and ready to be plucked, thought the composer, who was reasonably happy and hopeful for the future. Lausanne and Samaranch had only received the bad reviews from Barcelona, and none of the good ones, so the interview ended on a polite "we'll be in touch," a headscarf for Joan, a resurgence of sciatica and, as they left Switzerland, news came that the commission for the music for Barcelona '92 had gone to Mikis Theodorakis.

And while *Christopher Columbus* failed to disembark in South America, *Zapata* plunged out of sight amid other future commissions. Divorce was reached with the stage director Capobianco's clan and a proposal came from Ian Campbell, now director of San Diego Opera: they wanted to premiere an opera about Columbus in 1992. Balada's agent suggested the opera that was already written, but the organizers didn't want anything to do with that stage director, who was a heavy-weight ballast. Given the news that the Argentinian would no longer be involved with the opera, hopes were renewed of a landing in America. That was the moment a sinister call from the other side of the Atlantic threatened the composer with a court case over his appropriation of the opera. It had all become a parody of a gangster film. As the opera was a public commission, the intellectual property was Balada's, but the possible shifting of the score from the schedule initially agreed upon might be treated as breaking the contract.

But the blackest episode in this biography still has few stings left in its tail. Balada prepared a suite, as he had done with *Zapata*, to keep the score in the news and alive for the 1992 anniversary. More legal threats ensued, more out of ignorance than conviction, since they forgot that the musical notes belonged to Balada, and when he transferred them to an orchestral suite, they ceased to be subject to any contract, and belonged to the area of intellectual property. Of course, one has the right to wonder how an undiluted *Christopher Columbus* might sound, with its every note and section, which is reason enough to call for a proper premiere.

It is also true enough that the work was born with an artistic burden that acted as a breeding ground for harsh reviews from certain sectors of the press. Some of these critiques would hardly pass any guidelines for professional ethics, because they attacked *Christopher Columbus* as a politically motivated work and didn't bother to adopt a modicum of objectivity and judge the work's artistic content from a musical perspective. These reviews barely considered the risks implicit in the adjustments Balada had had to make before, during and after creating the opera, even though none were totally obligatory. Balada tried to defend his neomelodic turn as the result of changing times, anticipating the aesthetic resurgence of a level of neoromanticism one can certainly detect today, if not so much in Balada's own work. That artistic danger—imposed rather than really sought or justified—was intelligently identified by Antonio Fernández Cid in his double review in *ABC*.[5] Local and national reception was generally negative, though there was a justified lack of knowledge of the circumstances of the premiere and the score. Antonio Gala's text was attacked and Balada was accused of simplistic eclecticism, but these reviews were nearly all superficial and swayed by political rather than aesthetic attitudes. In any case there was no point in making excuses, nor could it be concluded that *Christopher Columbus* was a failed project. It was simply an opera that didn't fulfill the exacting expectations it had generated. What ought *Christopher Columbus* to have been like if it were to be considered a truly historic event? As a product directly initiated under political auspices, the idea was born, like all political initiatives with a sell-by date linked to the longevity of the politician of the day. What can be said about the decisions Balada took in respect of his musical language? Was Balada faithful to his style? At the time Balada was still immersed in his period of subjective ethnicity. It is true that the opera had taken up time over ten years, and, that by its very nature, didn't bring any great freedom or scope, but it is equally true that one could already intuit that change: that experience over a decade served to reassess and further consolidate the road to follow. Would a hundred per cent avant-garde opera have triumphed throughout the world? Such

---

5   Antonio Fernández devoted two pages to *Christopher Columbus*, one in advance on September 21 and the second afterwards in September 28, 1989 in *ABC*, and both are insightful and intelligent.

Scene from the first act of *Christopher Columbus*

an extreme project would probably not have attracted Caballé or Carreras to the stage, and it would have been less fertile ground for Antonio Gala's text. Over the last thirty years, fewer than ten operas have received general acclaim and fewer than five have been honored by being transferred to several productions. One should never forget that it was an opera called upon to sell Spain to the world, and not to a tiny group of intellectuals, but to a mass public quite ignorant of contemporary musical trends. No doubt, Balada's aesthetic take, with a different text and staging and, above all, with a complete and accurate reading of the work, would give us another view of *Christopher Columbus.*

The opera can now be judged more dispassionately after the salvaging and publishing of the original master recording by Sony published by Naxos. After years in a desk drawer waiting for the signatures of one or other of its protagonists, one can now reenter the Liceu to evaluate an opera which has worn the passage of time well, with orchestral color and performances that have the sound of a great musical soirée. Machiavelli said: "A prince must always allow himself to be advised, but when he wants, and never when other people deem fit . . ."[6]

Around 1992, the fortunes of *Christopher Columbus* were revived with the composition of the second part of the opera, *The Death of Columbus,*

---

6   Nicolas Machiavelli, *The Prince*, (1513).

which enjoyed financial support from the National Endowment for the Arts and Caja Madrid. It was finished in 1996 and premiered in Pittsburgh with teachers and students from Carnegie Mellon University. On this occasion, Balada wrote the text, with Professor Ángel Alcalá as consultant, and it was recorded in its entirety by Naxos.

The best musical performance of the real *Christopher Columbus* Balada had originally conceived, now sounding free and, naturally, entirely Baladan, could be heard. Complex melodies, fewer leitmotifs, greater incisiveness in terms of intertextual issues, rich orchestration, in a word, music that lives, a perfect frame for a more melodious, formally classic style, that had died in the heart of its creator.

Deep into a fertile period of composition, Balada made another turn in his creative consciousness and started out on a journey towards a personal surrealism, though never jettisoning features from his previous periods. Once again the character of Columbus reappears in his artistic odyssey with *The Resurrection of Columbus*, a work he composed in 2011, but the 2013 premiere, part of the commemoration of the composer's eightieth birthday, was

cancelled because Robert Page, former choral director at CMU, passed away. Balada resurrected the myth, and his text reflected his experience with Fernando Arrabal, *Faust-bal*, in 2009, visible in the display of brilliant images and style. The character of Christopher Columbus becomes an alter ego for the composer himself who participates in his own aesthetic journey, on a quest for the perfect opera, an opera by Leonardo Balada.

During the time when *Christopher Columbus* was being performed in Barcelona. Photo: Carles Fontserè

24.
Twelve Ways to Look at an Orchestra

A huge contradiction surfaced a few days before Ramón Barce tried to persuade the politicians driving the transition to democracy of the vital need for a national composers' union. Agustín González Acilu, Miguel Alonso, Carlos Cruz de Castro, Claudio Prieto, Miguel Ángel Coria, Jesús Villa-Rojo and Barce himself reached a curious agreement at the end of what was an amicable encounter: Spain's first composers' union would be called the Union of Spanish Composers of Symphonies. But it was questioned how many symphonies had been written in Spain over the last fifty years, and how many symphonic orchestras there were in the country. It was a disconcerting detail, apart from the two national orchestras, the rest could be counted on the fingers of one hand with fingers to spare. What on earth did the composers think they were doing?

Many recycled their language putting "full orchestra" instead of "chamber orchestra" or "heterogeneous ensemble"; conversely, others had a good relationship with the orchestras that did exist and worked exclusively for them and, finally, the most audacious were compelled to leave the country, even go to other side of the ocean to seek their fortunes. An audacious exile like Balada had been compensated by links he made with a range of first-rate orchestras as well as formations based in universities. The number of orchestras in the United States is as great as the number of symphonic composers fighting a thousand and one battles, and over recent decades, most of the latter have been frustrated in their attempts to get their work performed.

In Leonardo Balada's case, if we review his catalogue, we see that compositions for orchestra represent the largest, most successful part of his career. Leonardo Balada's favorite instrument is undoubtedly the orchestra with all its fierce and violent, concentrated and flexible potential, that can encompass every possible drama, every possible dream. However, it is no less true that he had always taken the greatest risks and tested himself to the full in the voracious field of chamber music. We can affirm that Balada's chamber music output is the hidden pearl within his repertoire and the most recent pieces are among the most effective, beautiful works written today. In any case his great wagers in composition were exercises in risk taking over many years, with an uncertain life beyond what was written on the blank paper. Orchestras were too busy filling programs with great works from their repertoire and tended to leave living composers out in the cold. Fortunately, coinciding with the premiere of *Guernica* (1966), Balada found an elegant, comfortable vehicle, the best imaginable to give shape to his dreams of sound: the orchestra. The 1980s had swung him towards that fascination for the stage we have already mentioned, but the transition from the twentieth to the twenty-first century was fruitful in terms of time and output in explorations of the infinite mysteries of the orchestra. The vicissitudes, frustrations and difficulties in the field of opera gave way to peaceful adventures in symphonic concert halls where conflicts had more to do with the fears of programmers than jeers from audiences who were much more intelligent than they were generally given credit for.

The great challenge of a symphonic score has always been the quest for music with a coherent style and aesthetic that avoid traditional structures distinguished by the eternal interplay between climax and anticlimax. That kind of writing had never interested Balada; his symphonic textures tend to flow as a whole and at no point do they simply turn their backs on what happens at the beginning. Every well-made work of art is as simple or as complex as life itself, and can't be grasped without its beginning, but at the same time it changes, transmutes and is perhaps transformed to attain something much more remote in an attempt to satisfy the natural need to communicate within a time span. It is up to the listener to find the coherence embedded in dissonant chords and melodies that weave in and out, that live and die. Balada's symphonic compositions contain a series of options that mark out the composer's unequivocal stance. The beginning of each work is frequently textural, tense and often dramatic, closer to the purest avant-garde than to any other individual style, but with the first snap in the listener's attention, it changes within the range of harmonies, later in the tensions between rhythms and only when the work or context demands it, do melodic features develop. That is the only way it can respond to a need to halt and gather that mysterious moment of emotional intensity when the listener is reduced to breathlessness. We can only take a deep breath when the work has penetrated beneath our skin, when final harmonies have faded into taut echoes in the concert hall and fused with an outburst of applause. Balada mentally structures his symphonic creations. There is no text, program or outside resource that condition the message; he is free to do and undo at will and all is unpredictable within a perfect plan. That's why his music sounds so fresh, and ready to whisper what the listener wants to hear. Balada tries to create dilemmas, counterpoints and conflicts that forge a personal language unfettered by aesthetic bars or corsets. There is no need to look back to the past if one's mind is turned to the future.

After the *via crucis* of *Christopher Columbus*, Balada emerged strengthened in his convictions and ready to devote himself to concert halls without ever losing sight of the stage. In 1991 he was commissioned to adapt *Divertimentos for a String Orchestra*, an atonal work commissioned by the Center for the Diffusion of Contemporary Music and premiered by the string section of London's Royal College of Music. The work is a minefield where the composer experiments with different *creative* textures and lines preparing a path back to the big symphony orchestra. In 1992 he completed that process of regaining the sensations and chiaroscuros of an orchestra with *Canción y danza*, a work composed for a symphony band complimented by harp, amplified harpsichord and a soprano who intervenes in the opening section. There are evident echoes of Mompou in what was a homage on the occasion of the centenary of his birth. Now Leonardo Balada had recovered his feel for the sound of orchestral instruments after his journey through the world of opera, and he threw himself into orchestral composition with renewed energy and ideas.

Almost all the symphonic works written by Balada from 1992 were the result of commissions; some were quite specific, and others were the result of knocking on one door after another; some were paid, others weren't, but all were marked by a similar sense of very human disbelief. This detail is worth special emphasis, since the universe of commissions implies visibility for the individual selected, but the reverse side is a series of stipulations as regards performers, length and even themes that many find unacceptable. Balada decided to look at the orchestra through a pane of polymorphous glass, and gradually created airs suffused with a different coloration, trying out forms and occasionally adding inspirations from reality itself. Sixteen years of creativity concentrated in twelve ways to look at an orchestra.

Look one: The improvised orchestra

1992 was an emblematic year. The Millennium Concerts held to celebrate the thousand years of the existence of major Catalan institutions had led to huge commissions for composers currently on the radar. It was 1992 when a commission fell to Leonardo Balada and it wasn't connected to Olympic festivities or the discovery of America. The commission was inspired by one individual, Antoni Sabat, the visible source of the invitation after his experience with *Hangman, Hangman!* in Catalan in the 1980s. Predictably, the commission followed quite surrealist paths. After a first firm proposal, with a date and public go-ahead, the entire project quickly faded into obliv-

Balada conducting the premiere of *Celebració*

ion. In the meanwhile, the sumptuous year of the Fifth Centenary sent the Balada family off on a packed round of activities. The composer was called upon to give lectures in the most important ports on Columbus's voyage on the pretext of a talk about the opera. Everything was ready—suitcases, sunscreens, passports and the turquoise waters promised by the luxury liner, and when they all seemed set for a quiet vacation, life metamorphosed into an infernal race against the clock.

A fresh call from Sabat reinstated the Millennium commission thanks to a last-minute financial input. The stressful side to the affair was that they were about to go on their long voyage and the deadline for the submission of materials was thirty days. The orchestra commissioned for the premiere was the Prague Symphony Orchestra and rehearsals would be held in the Czech capital before the august concert in the Liceu.

As Balada had already admitted in several interviews, he found holidays quite boring, so the score of *Celebració* was ready for the agreed dates and places. Weaving it with a golden thread, he returned to preexisting material, concretely *Reflejos* (1987), for nonsoloist flute and string orchestra, and generated a different beginning to illuminate the millennial birth of Catalonia, thanks to a surreptitious amplified clavichord,[1] a double bass and violoncello in the guise of a primitive *basso continuo* that was more idyllic than real. Embedded in a texture out of which reflections of the inspirational piece arise, surrealist mutation takes the helm and leads into a throbbing, rhythmic finale that gives a sense of modern life. It was one of the first glimpses of that new surrealist mode he had begun to weave into some later works and that will even appear in operatic form in 2009.

Look two: The inertia of the predictable

Why compose a symphony? How does one define this form in music today? Ought we to find a new name for present-day symphonies? *Krljavestica*,[2] for example, or even *Xixu*, the name of my parakeet. The truth is that definitions belong to another era and are no longer apposite or valid, whether in their initial sense, or the image they literally evoke. Balada says that perhaps all symphonies should be called symphonic poems or be given a more or less meaningful title, that the word "symphony" seems to retain an aristocratic spirit, and offer something more symbolic than real.

1992 was the fiftieth year of the Lausanne Chamber Orchestra and Jesús López Cobos, then its conductor, commissioned Balada to write a celebratory piece. That spurred Balada on to take a fresh look at the orchestra. The work opens timidly amid the cold mists of the Swiss city. As usual, the composer assigns minutes to each section, and decided there would

1 As mentioned previously, Balada had just experimented with an amplified harpsichord in *Canción* in that same year of 1992.
2 *Krljavestica* is a Serbian term that defines a kind of initiatory rite with ancestral roots which acts to keep at bay evil spirits, vampires and witches in rural enclaves. A recent work, premiered by a student of Leonardo Balada, Christian Kriegeskotte, has that title; it was premiered at Carnegie Mellon University in April 2008.

be two; the first would be slower, more textural and dissonant, gradually reaching out to the city's nearby lake and assuming more complex sounds and rhythms. The five minutes of the first section are carefully drafted, but the second section was seven minutes long. When Leonardo came to concretize them on staves, he realized he had only just begun the battle. He then cast his prejudices to the wind and prepared to change the initial structure by transforming the work into a symphony that lasted almost twenty minutes. The problem was a question of language, and how he could sustain the tension for a further six minutes. That was when he began to seek out popular Swiss melodies and, when he found the right one, he grasped and reshaped it. But there was a danger: he couldn't lose sight of the initial section. If the center of gravity disappeared, the work would falter and become unbalanced. How could he solve that? By tirelessly rethinking and creating. Inertia can have that impact on creativity; it occasionally forces one to re-knot a tie in order to look better in the photo.

Look three: The prince and the pauper

It was ready to go. The cava was in the fridge, with a press conference to launch the new season while the score of *No-res* rewarmed in the oven. Then in the heat of battle André Previn announced that he was going, and he up and left the Pittsburgh Symphony Orchestra. Once again hopes were dashed and it was time to pick up the pieces and begin a mission to salvage self-esteem. When Maazel assumed the leadership of the orchestra in 1988, Balada explained the problem of the premiere of *No-res* that had been agreed. The orchestra management and Maazel justified taking the work out of the season's program because of the recent failure of a work by William Schumann. As long as the orchestra was financed by private donors, the program had to respect their taste and interests. Nonetheless, Maazel wanted to position the orchestra among the top rank of American orchestras. Following the path marked out by Steinberg, the orchestra should call on outstanding soloists in order to avoid apathy and routine. This objective led him to commission a series of concertos from a number of renowned composers to be performed by his orchestra. The idea was to allow a relaxed, very direct collaboration between soloist and composer, and ensure quality and strong empathy between audiences and orchestra.

However, at the time an oboe was playing in Balada's head. Maazel had brought with him some of the leading soloists he had heard play in the world's most distinguished orchestras. These included Andrés Cárdenes on the concertino violin or Cynthia de Almeida, one of the best oboists in the world and also the oboist of the PSO. Commissions went to prestigious composers like Benjamin Lees, Ellen Zwilich or Rodion Schedrin, with Leonardo Balada and David Stock, the only ones based in Pittsburgh. Balada's commission was for 1993 and was a concerto for oboe. *Music for Oboe and Orchestra. Lament for the Cradle of the Earth* responded to an ethical and formal stance that let Balada discover yet another different role. From his fascination with the aurora borealis in *Auroris* (1973) to his identification with *No-res*, Balada's interest in and quest for the goddess Nature had become exponential. The growing deterioration suffered by nature had become a raucous cry for help in the composer's mind. Nature, strength and light, beauty and its consequences. Thus *No-res, Christopher Columbus* and Union of the Oceans (1993)[3] or *Dawn* (1994)[4] are examples of the way nature was influencing the Mediterranean composer's thinking about sound.

But this *Lament for the Cradle of the Earth* conceals a very specific view of the relationship between soloist and orchestra

With Cynthia de Almeida and Lorin Maazel at the premiere of *Music for Oboe and Orchestra* in 1993

and one that becomes the driving force for the composition. It isn't a conventional concerto with a dialogue between soloist and *tutti*, but rather a fight staged between two characters who are perfectly delineated. News of the destruction of the Amazonian forests hurt Balada so deeply he decided, in a very personal way, to put that doomed struggle into music.

It is a work that is mid-way between a concerto and a symphonic

---

3   A work for symphony band, commissioned for the inauguration of the Museum in Anclas de Salinas, Asturias, conceived by Philippe Cousteau and realized by the architect Luis Castillo. The inauguration took place on September 30, 1993 in the presence of King Juan Carlos I and the premiere of the work was conducted by Balada himself.
4   A work for flute and orchestra premiered in 1994 by Julius Baker and the CMU Symphony Orchestra in Washington D.C.

poem. *Lament* doesn't try to illustrate any text or preestablished image, but to encompass an ethically ecological belief and stance in relation to the world. Throughout its twenty minutes plus, the oboe reflects the actions of humanity, while the orchestra represents cyclopean, unshackled nature. The struggle, or what amounts to the same, the music, harbors multiple processes and a variety of compositional solutions where the most avant-garde features mercilessly engulf any ethnic coloring, until, at a given moment, humanity/oboe vanish in unintelligible echoes, immersed in the sounds of the forest.

Look four: Ethnic internationalism

Far from running out of energy, the personal, subjectively ethnic musical internationalism Balada creates and explores in the mid-seventies was strengthened and deepened over the years. At a dinner, the American composer and conductor, Michael Tilson-Thomas, affirmed that Balada's music held the key to the most genuine avant-garde of the moment. A mixture of contemporary techniques and ethnic references that spoke straight to the collective subconscious without being predictable or simplistic.

That was praise indeed, but independently of its impact on Balada's ego, for the first time he grasped that his originality was a response to creative need rather than to any intellectual or aesthetic positioning. He didn't have recourse to melodies as a source of color or a concession to audiences; he used them because he felt they were at once an engine, challenge and creative axis. Hitherto, similar movements in twentieth-century music had simply tried to draw attention to the harmonic, rhythmic or melodic features contained in this or that popular melody, whereas Balada brought other horizons to those songs of the earth. His vision was to extract pure, human essences from those traditional songs by eliminating all that was local from their sinews and attaining a universal sensibility without consideration of race, place or prejudice. Balada used those ingredients, hewed and adapted them to his individual style and language, and thus resolved a difficult, complex equation around originality.

The climax of this style as applied to the orchestra is the strange, polymorphous triduum entitled *Folk Dreams*, completed in 1998, but begun independently in 1995. It encompasses three works that respond to three commissions linked to an individual or an orchestra. The first ethnic crack of the whip was prompted by a commission from the Cincinnati Symphony Orchestra. In 1995 it was celebrating the hundredth year of its existence, which all coincided with the presence of Jesús López Cobos as conductor. The orchestra management decided to commission short works from all the living composers who had premiered a work with the orchestra in the course of those hundred years. The dark side was that there would be no payment: long live labors of love! Paradoxically, Balada gifted them *Shadows* which included a Catalan melody among a collection of harmonies and themes that were in the air.

The second act of *Folk Dreams* took place soon afterwards, when Mariss Jansons, the new conductor of the city orchestra, arrived at Pittsburgh International Airport. To celebrate his arrival, Balada was commissioned to create a small-scale work that would be performed as a kind of welcome to the conductor. Balada turned to sources in Lithuanian folklore as he realized that Jansons came from that Baltic country. *Line and Thunder* was composed in 1996, although the score was only performed two years later.[5] More melodic than its big sister, the work begins immediately with a central melody from the violin that then reaches out to different colors within the whole orchestra. The formal structure becomes three-part with a more rhythmic middle section before returning to, and concluding on, a more lyrical note.

And finally a third commission that came from the beloved land of Ireland was set to complete the ethnic cycle. Colman Pearce, the Irish composer and conductor, and a longstanding friend, put the extraordinary National Orchestra of Ireland at the disposition of Balada, promising to premiere the whole cycle including the third with the Irish focus. It premiered in 1998 with the name of *Echoes*. In the definitive version, *Line and Thunder* became the first movement, while *Shadows*, by virtue of its rather more self-absorbed nature, is the central movement. Three samples of internationalism that in a way represent the beginning of the end for the turn to the ethnic, since the pretexts behind the melodies will take on different features in the twenty-first century.

Look five: Pure magic

When strolling through the streets of Granada, one understands the meaning of the word "*duende*." The courses and Festival of Granada lie behind that fascination. Balada took out his pencil and began to work on a musical terrain he had yet to explore in any depth: flamenco. It was a music born in

---

5   The premiere was performed February 20, 1998, with the PSO conducted by Mariss Jansons its dedicatee.

Balada with Joan and Colman Pearce in 1990

the magical triangle midway between Sevilla, Málaga and Cádiz, enjoying open house in the cave dwellings of the Albaicín, and it could only be a question of time before Balada came to take look inside. Given that Balada's style now involved intense explorations of the ethnic, it is strange he hadn't yet beaten new musical paths with the *cante jondo*. A joint commission from the Cincinnati and Hartford Symphony Orchestras in 1997 lit the fuse to enable flamenco and avant-garde techniques to marry.[6] It is a highly significant work, because Balada finally penetrates the inner workings of the most gypsy, most Spanish of styles, launching an unannounced cycle of compositions that investigate specific features of the Spanish sensibility, a cycle that concludes with the aesthetically parallel *Concerto for Piano and Orchestra no. 3*, *Passacaglia* and *Caprichos no. 3*.

In essence it isn't a radical new mix, since the *duende* had intrigued composers from all over since the nineteenth century, who had applied it to their respective avant-garde. But perhaps the pure essence of *cante jondo*, beyond local color and stereotypes, was a subject yet to be tackled. The most successful pieces within this complex world of adaptations or reread-

---

6   The work was premiered March 13, 1998 by Ángel Romero and the Cincinnati Symphony Orchestra conducted by Jesús López Cobos and is recorded for the Naxos label with Eliot Fisk, the American guitarist resident in Granada accompanying the Barcelona and National Symphonic Orchestra of Catalonia, conducted by José Serebrier.

ing of flamenco in contemporary music have come from interpretations for solo instruments, whether in works for the piano by Tomás Marco or Joan Guinjoan, or Mauricio Sotelo's brilliant, idiomatic response.

The idea of composing a concerto for guitar and orchestra under the creative rubric of Balada's ethnic internationalism ran into an obstacle that was fortunately soon overcome. The demise of Narciso Yepes had created a huge gap in the world of guitar playing and for Balada in particular. But the sudden, timely emergence of Ángel Romero heralded a new cascade of light. In the great tradition of Spanish guitarists, Romero is a virtuoso of the old school and a brilliant, intense performer. The score by Balada—who still boasts that he barely knows how to pick up a guitar despite the amount of music he has written for it—is much more than a concerto. Although the instrument dominates and leads the work, the orchestra's presence is no bit player and almost threatens to become the star of the show. As happens in the parallel concerto for piano—the third in the catalogue—purely Andalusian inspiration, devoid of folkloric features, permeates the coloration of the orchestra. Balada endows the textures with roles that don't follow the usual pattern for a concerto. Now and then he strengthens the changing harmonies that verge on traditional timbres, or else starts to urge on the soloist with a magnificent burst of clapping that has a purely rhythmic function. The hovering shadow of a concerto

Balada with Ángel Romero and Jesús López Cobos

with its star soloist, together with the nature of the commission and audience, surely condition proximity to, or distance from, more or less melodic themes, but in Balada, the essence is never lost.

The division of the concerto into three classical movements, each with a meaningful title, is symptomatic of the concerto's opening out to a public with which it wishes to communicate. *Sun, Moon and Duende* for a *Concierto*

Mágico. Balada's deep sense of Andalusian folklore lurks anonymously in the first two movements as is always the case in classic *cante jondo*, but he uses the third to pay a double homage, a glance to the past and to the future inspired by the Catalan composer's work. On the one hand, the rhythmic impulse, a *zapateado* that has already appeared and will reappear in later works; on the other, a nod to Federico García Lorca with the final reference to *Anda, jaleo!*, which will be the sole protagonist of *Caprichos No1* (2003).

Balada's *flamenco* gaze towards the orchestra betrays an array of intentions. The massive use of the orchestra's range of sound is standard in his work, but the guitar's distinct resonances point to a general repositioning of his music. Balada initiates a more chamber-like treatment of the orchestra, one that is more individualized in its use of tone, with a return to a specific tempo for the percussion that had remained a melodic resource and barrier in previous phases. The orchestra is now more colorist, less harmonic and more horizontal; Balada reinvents himself yet again as few know how. In a word, he gazes magically towards the horizon.

Look six: An alternative

"You know, I want to play a concerto for piano and Spanish orchestra, do you see, but I don't want to have recourse to the *Nights in the Gardens of Spain*, or the romantic concertos of Albéniz, Rodolfo Halffter or Xavier Montsalvatge . . . I mean . . . they are slightly odd."

Two possible responses:

Glad I don't know you, goodbye.

Are you aware of Leonardo Balada's *Concerto for Piano no. 3*?

Rafael Frühbeck de Burgos, a dear friend of Balada and well acquainted with his music, suggested he should compose a concerto for piano and orchestra. It would be in the grand style for a major concert hall, commissioned by Radio Berlin's Symphonic Orchestra, except in one respect: there was no budget. Balada searched every nook and cranny to pay for the work such an ambitious project would involve, until he remembered that as a tenure-track professor at Carnegie Mellon University, he had the right to apply for a grant for this kind of creative endeavor, one that hadn't been activated for many years. He checked that the money from that source was still available and then devoted all his time and energy to the composition. A big concerto that, like the previous piece for the guitar, would be fully in Balada's new style; he hadn't revisited that particular musical terrain since his 1974 masterly, but now distant, *Second Concerto for Piano, Percussion and Band.* The work was dedicated to Rafael Frühbeck de Burgos, who was expecting Alicia de Larrocha to be the soloist. She turned down the offer and the hot potato fell to Rosa Torres Pardo who assumed the challenge of plunging herself into a new, complex concerto. Soloist and composer met in Washington, and their views began to coalesce around the idea of a concerto that could easily travel, with Spanish airs and more than a dash of modernity in order to add to the limited contemporary concerto repertoire.[7] Composed between October 11, 1998 and February 22, 1999,[8] the work was premiered in the Berlin Konzerthaus February 12 with the aforementioned conductor and soloist.

Balada with Rafael Frühbeck de Burgos and Rosa Torres Pardo

The Spanish, or rather Andalusian, motifs driving the work are evident, although the gaze of the orchestra, guided by the piano's more resonant presence, invites a different, if no less colorist, approach. The concerto is almost an exercise in aesthetic meditation drawing the listener into a more ethnic avant-garde universe to witness an unleashing of techniques more akin to the surrealism Balada had previously explored in *Diary of Dreams* (1995) for violin, cello and piano trio, and developed in later work. The concerto's first movement is one of the wittiest in the contemporary repertoire. A *pasodoble* gradually disintegrates under attack from dissonant knife thrusts redolent of the universe of Erik Satie. Conversely, the

---

7   Pianists often make this complaint, but we should bear in mind that many excellent concertos for piano and orchestra written by Spanish composers do exist.

8   After the premiere Balada made a few adjustments to the score after the premiere and the concerto was recorded a few months later by Rosa Torres Pardo with José Serebier conducting the Barcelona and National Symphony Orchestra of Catalonia July 10-13, 2000. The first revisions were made to solve recording problems in March 2000, while the opening and final movements were revised for a second time in November 2000.

second movement is more intense, profound and concentrated, a display of orchestration and development based simply on a study of the typical appoggiatura found in medieval Andalusian music, in striking contrast to the complex, understanding tribute to the Aragonese *jota* that brings the work to a conclusion with a flourish.

Look seven: The orchestra listens; he who listens finds

On occasion music springs up where you least expect it. Making the most of a series of recordings of his work for the Naxos label, Balada had an opportunity to deepen the roles of soloists and orchestra within that aesthetic phase of ethnic internationalism. They were busy recording the *Piano Concerto No3* and *Concierto Mágico for Guitar*, but the record risked being on the short side. Once again Carnegie Mellon University came to the rescue and commissioned a concerto-style work and Balada set to work as intensely as ever. *Music for Flute and Orchestra* is unlike its sister pieces. Composed in 2000, it concludes the trilogy for flute that began with *Reflejos* (1978) and was followed by *Dawn* (1994), but *Music for Flute and Orchestra* went off on another tangent as it left Leonardo's head.

The usual concept of a concerto with soloist and *tutti* and the traditional formula of counterpoint and dialogue is quite absent from this piece. Balada had warned from the start that this wasn't a concerto, it was rather a new project close to the spirit of *Reflejos*—although here it involved a string quintet or chamber orchestra—or of *Dawn*. There was the consideration that perhaps the flute's sonorous presence wasn't strong enough to take on the challenge of being virtuoso solo. It is certainly true the ancient wind instrument had been a source of unrivaled fascination among contemporary composers who have used its exquisite timbre as a means and as an end. However, its pure, inevitably melodic lines can be a trap for the contemporary composer. Balada recognizes the flute as the absolute protagonist in his work, so much so that the orchestra is forced to do something extraordinary; it must simply listen. In *Music for Flute and Orchestra* the flute introduces and develops its content from melodies salvaged from Catalan farmsteads, although that is no reason to see it as an ethnic work in the Baladan meaning of that term since the material—that goes back in some cases to Mompou's *Songs and Dances*—is so profound and original that it goes beyond previous boundaries and expands outwards to re-create a more complex universe of sound verging on the surreal. *Music for Flute and Orchestra* yields an orchestra that is intrigued by the soloist's melodic line that never erupts in an obvious material form, but tends to soar, avoiding tonal octaves and fifths. The orchestra listens and tries to imitate using the cluster, but now and then increasingly well-defined lines surface that recreate sounds from Catalan folkloric ensembles. It is a process that shall be described as musical surrealism, where structures of musical sound evolve from one recognizable subject to another that is radically different, but equally definable.

Music for Flute and Orchestra is a completely new reading of the role the orchestra plays in relation to the soloist; at times it listens rather than accompanies, at others it imitates rather than develops and invites an exploration of the fourth aesthetic way of Surrealism from the aesthetic site of the third.

Look eight: The fourth way

The fourth way is that place where materials aspiring to live and travel are transformed by a Mediterranean surrealist light which metamorphoses within itself as it searches for its own elemental roots and flowers with another face and form. The fourth way makes it possible for a baroque *passacaglia* to transmute into a Spanish *pasacalles*, an old man into a young boy, sadness into happiness, while life is to be always life.

A surrealist path with Dalinian flourishes and Baladan depth had been a constant from the late '90s. The first steps, biochemical experiments in the fourth way, were gradually engineered from the hospitable terrain of ethnic internationalism. It was 2000, and, in the heat of the computer revolution, the Cadaqués Competition Committee commissioned Leonardo Balada to compose a work. The rubrics in such cases are usually clear enough. It was a test piece for a prestigious prize, and should contain a high level of technical difficulty, but at the same time clear lines from which the jury could unequivocally identify the good and bad features of participants. Few orchestral works in history can have enjoyed so many, diverse readings on the occasion of its virtual premiere, as *Passacaglia* did.

In brief, it is a work that directly explores and exploits the concept of transformation implicit in the concept of musical surrealism Balada wants to introduce. Using the structural simplicity of a *pasacalles*, centered on fixed rhythmic beat and the continuous reemergence of a single theme— specifically with three notes—he develops an intense instrumental work over little more than ten minutes. The pretext is the *pasacalles*, a traditional form used in Spanish public fiestas that, as a result of the avant-garde fondness for the folkloric within European Baroque, was imitated and transformed by musicians of that period. For reasons to do with simple orchestral brilliance, Balada gives us a reverse transformation, from baroque *passacaglia* to Spanish *pasacalles*. But we must be aware of clichés, the work is considerably more complex than might be deduced from this clumsy, inadequate description, since, although Balada alerts us to his recourse to a "straight and simple" Spanish *pasacalles*, it is nothing of the sort. It would be wrong to think that Balada is an orchestrator pursuing a popular song, since there are always compelling personal feelings that bring a personal, subtle touch. The work was premiered outside the competition by the Orchestra of Cadaqués conducted by Sir Neville Marriner.

Years later, in 2003, the promising fourth way—summoned to give a whole opera in 2009—would beget *Prague Sinfonietta*. Its scant, astonishing ten minutes allows one to hear the how, when and why of Mozart's famous Prague Symphony's magical metamorphosis into a lady dancing the *sardana*, white skirts and hose included. This Mozartian *sardana* adventure stemmed from a commission by the Torroella de Montgrí International Music Festival and was performed by the Czech Sinfonietta conducted by Charles Olivieri-Munroe in August 2004. The rapid process of composition meant it overlapped with the fifth symphony, and Balada tried to engage all the actors involved in the commission with his own personal artistic needs: Prague, Catalonia, symphony, sardana, Mozart, Vicenç Bou,[9] chamber orchestra and Balada. A surrealist journey on a supersonic plane from a high point in the Age of Enlightenment with a stop-off and tavern on the Costa Brava . . . while Dalí watched askance.

Look nine: Joan's favorite work

Transformation, fusion, communication, revision . . . the Baladan view of orchestras in the twentieth-first century inhales all these "ions" and the clear intent to make music an exercise in emotional and human intensity. The million-dollar question was inevitably asked during a dinner at the Balada household: what was the composer's wife's favorite work? An equivocal answer was expected, but her response was clear and surprising. For Joan Balada, Leonardo's wife and beacon, the *Concerto for Cello and*

---

9 Vicenç Bou, a composer of *sardanas* from Torroella de Montgrí, is the pretext for the *sardana* motif that Balada picks up in this work.

Orchestra no. 2 is her favorite work. Curiously the cello was the instrument that had yet to appear in the ethnic style, but, perhaps it had to make a late appearance on the scene, because purity of style was seriously threatened by the surrealist fourth way. Ever since 1968 when he finished the *Concerto for Cello and Nine Players*, commissioned but never premiered by Gaspar Cassadó, Balada owed this instrument a great concerto.

Leonardo with Joan in Vienna

Its composition took up a good part of 2001 and, while a spiritual melody and jazz rhythm emerged with unusual energy, an obvious second title emerged for the concerto: *New Orleans*. The work was premiered on March 9, 2002 in Berlin by the Berlin Radio Symphony Orchestra, with Michael Sanderling playing the cello and Rafael Frühbeck de Burgos conducting. The choice of the cello was driven by this string instrument's closeness to the male voice in its timbres. Sometimes, when Balada is asked which instrument he feels most motivated to write for, his reply will focus on the guitar or cello. Thanks to *glissando* and fourths, the song of the cello develops and suggests a really invigorating human feel, occasionally a humanity that is overexposed as a result of the emotion contained in its twisting intervals. It is the image in sound of a human being. For its part, the guitar presents a different kind of component that is no longer purely musical—where its ductile qualities and range of timbres or the sensual song-line are valued—but the elemental spirit embedded between its strings.

The *Concerto for Cello and Orchestra no. 2* is based on a Negro spiritual that Balada takes as his starting point, enabling him to begin the intense process of developing the two sections of the original melody. The key to the harmony resides in the use of the perfect fourth as an essential element in the subsequent development, thanks to which one feels close to the soloist who launches on a fantastic journey. It is a mixture of melodic elements springing from popular roots and processes from avant-garde techniques of composition; Balada sustains the identity of the main melody which he extends and develops it without ever forgetting its essence. The roots of the sound's culture remain pure in the composer's creative concept that extracts it from its natural location and transplants it into more dynamic, complex universes of sound.

Once again it is a concerto structured in two movements, slow and quick, with the significant titles of *Lament* and *Swing*, where the orchestra is revealed as the center of power and real transmitter of elements of counterpoint with the soloist. One doesn't expect a simple adaptation of jazz features to a concerto, but a fresh, living reading of the essence that breathes within the soul of black music. Balada gives an orchestra that accompanies and cohabits in the same space as the soloist, thus consolidating a way to use the orchestra in a concerto that is firmly established in a contemporary aesthetic perspective.

Look ten: Solutions for one or several voices

The first year of the twenty-first century. The old questions asked by children of the civil war, now grandparents, as to who were the "goodies" and who were the "baddies" in Spain's social and political life now seemed old hat. The sad gazes of those who lost the wretched war had gradually transmuted as they gratefully watched victory being returned to them over time. One morning, the telephone at the house of friends rang: Odón Alonso was at the other end of the line. Confused words echoed along the cables at a hellish speed: Festival, Commission, Autumn, Soria, Dionisio, Emilio, Ridruejo, Ruiz and month. At the other end that staccato nonsense fell into a recognizable structure: it was a commission from the Autumn Festival in Soria that was directed at the time by Odón himself. Emilio Ruiz the writer and he were enthusiastically suggesting he compose a work based on texts by Dionisio Ridruejo. But the problem, which came as no surprise, was that he had only a month to write the score. On the other hand, the selection of texts had been made and all that was needed was Balada's go-ahead for the adventure to start.

The text, being by Ridruejo, might have a Falangist drag that would be difficult for a republican like himself to justify. Leonardo had to grin and bear it. He put himself to work, although the prepared text was so long there was no way it could humanly mesh with a composition for solo singer, choir and orchestra, which was what the commission required. Balada rethought the work structurally with a narrator declaiming Ridrue-jo's texts, a choir commenting on the writer's words through the prism of Emilio Ruiz's lines and a huge orchestra. It was the return of the Balada of the "tragiphonies," of his attempts to change the nature of opera, of a creator who wanted to adapt his innate need to tell stories to contemporary musical language. The text wasn't finished, by a long shot, and it kept pouring out from emails or faxes, whatever the time of day or night, and it was like assembling a work in the style of the best of films when the protagonists don't know how the story will end. As Cavour said, when you have an assignment for somebody, find a person who doesn't have the time, as the individual with time on his hands never does or will do anything. Balada arrived in the Castilian provincial capital at the end of spring with the work completed before his deadline.

Regarding the premiere, the orchestra that would perform the closely woven score with its dense, packed bars, was an orchestra assembled on a temporary basis, a Philharmonic Orchestra created and conducted by Pascual Osa, though he wouldn't be there for the premiere. Alonso wasn't prepared to risk erecting such a building in so short a time, and an unexpected surprise lay in store for Balada. The composer looked in his suitcase to check he had brought a baton and took responsibility for the premiere. The surprise was the choir that was programmed to come, the National Choir, that had already sung at the festival, had been forced to withdraw because of a strange confusion over dates. The replacement was a choir of keen, optimistic amateurs, backed up by a handful of professionals. It was a fearful challenge, since Balada, who had been expecting a professional choir that had weathered a thousand contemporary storms, had conceived a complex work full of special effects. *Dionisio: In memoriam* was premiered on time and was modestly successful. But it was the second premiere that gave proper visibility to this important work. The Community of Madrid Orchestra and Choir, with Carlos Hipólito as narrator and José Ramón Encinar as conductor, were responsible for the recording on the Naxos label.

Dionisio poses a classic problem for contemporary composers: a combination of orchestra and voices in conflict over vying timbres and dynamics. When a voice appears on stage, it inevitably takes possession of the space, because of its meanings rather than its musicality. The intelligibility of texts conditions composer and orchestra so the latter tends to sacrifice textures and movements on behalf of the words. On this occasion, Balada was taking on a specific text, of undoubted literary value, which brought with it a parallel narrative, the fact that Ridruejo belonged to the political apparatus that had emerged from the victorious side in the civil war.[10] And, of course, Balada uses this to suggest what the texts don't say through sound. From the start, the orchestra introduces blasts of melody from the *Cara al Sol* hymn, which, in the composer's words, is a score with lots of potential, independent of its ideological content. This material fuses and develops with melodies from the folklore of Soria. Balada resolves the problem of voice and orchestra by having recourse to questions, answers and an imitation of motifs. That option enables him to remain faithful to the basic text, without sacrificing his own universe of timbres. Moreover, *Dionisio* sets a precedent in the fashioning of material in works that were immediately to follow and that based their themes on the human drama of the civil war.

A similar problem was posed by the composition of *Ebony Fantasies* (2003), but in this case there was the additional issue of the material that had to be elaborated. Four Negro spirituals act as a prompt to develop another example of Balada's orchestral writing in the context of large ensembles and ranges of sound. The four movements of this American fantasy are aesthetically coherent with the rest of the Catalan composer's output. His study and work essentially focuses on the handling of the tensions between sounds, and the melodic component remains a thematic concession endowing the piece with soul and a degree of intelligible stylistic unity, an element the composer regarded as vital if he was to communicate with his audiences. It is worth underlining that the two examples that comprise this tenth look contain work more related to sound than text (which the narrator deals with in *Dionisio*), and focuses on the singing component. The use of voices, random interpellations, clusters and above all divisive rhythms, engender a peculiar fusion of pure choral sound and orchestral sound. *Ebony Fantasies*

---

10   It is worth remembering that Dionisio Ridruejo, from Burgo de Osma in the province of Soria, is the author of two lines that are part of *Cara al Sol*, the Francoist anthem par excellence, written by Juan Tellería. Before the civil war, Ridruejo had become involved in the intellectual movement José Antonio Primo de Rivera had tried to establish. The idea of a group of violent activists, like the S.S. or the Italian Blackshirts, didn't appeal to a figure like José Antonio who was more of an ideologue than a violent activist. Ridruejo took on the responsibility of generating an intellectual spirit close to the Falange, that after José Antonio's death and the rise of Franco clashed with the more barrack-room perspectives and sank in a morass of disenchantment. After his return from the front and the Blue Division in Russia, Dionisio Ridruejo extricated himself from Francoism and was even imprisoned later when he joined a revolutionary movement.

was composed in Pittsburgh in 2003 and premiered on February 17, 2004 in Madrid's National Auditorium by the Community of Madrid Orchestra and Choir conducted by Lorenzo Ramos.

Look eleven: Polyhedral sound

Undoubtedly the sorrow and sense of defenselessness provoked by the collapse of the Twin Towers in New York, September 11, 2001, is a memory that will mark generations. The fallout from seeing and feeling that horror and its short- and long-term consequences was soon to permeate artistic creation across the world. That morning Leonardo Balada relived the bitterness and agonizing tensions that Nardo the child had felt in the bombing raids during the civil war, and was deeply moved by the tragedy in New York. When he was invited to write a symphonic work for the Pittsburgh Symphony Orchestra a few months later, in April 2002, the eleventh look, a look that bore a sense of recapitulation, began to take shape. Balada took the opportunity to give a new reading of orchestral textures in a polyhedral look which embraced all the turns, aesthetics and cruxes he had offered to that point. Financed by the Heinz Endowment Creative Artist Residency Program together with Carnegie Mellon University, the work was premiered on October 30, 2003, conducted by Hans Graf. Meanwhile, eleven months of composition ensued when Balada looked at himself in the mirror long and hard, was embarrassed and horrified by what he saw, then warmly welcomed what he saw and revisited his entire career and aesthetic in a kind of affirmative autobiography of musical sound. His human material was an impressive symphony orchestra, but he wanted to add a new element, a new focus, a new turn to change his mode of expression, including electronic music in a symphony for the first time and granting it prominence. On this occasion it wouldn't be a prerecorded contribution of resonances, as previously; his thinking now required live recording and live modification of orchestral textures.

The work develops in three movements that are arranged according to aesthetic rather than temporal criteria, but aesthetic elements, as the composer comments in the score's prologue, can be performed independently, like separate symphonic poems. There is definitely a common thematic thread that isn't textual, textural or ideological, but purely linguistic, since the element that unifies the whole work is simply a polymorphous interval in a minor third. The first movement is an abstract, *pointilliste*, deeply felt

Opening of score of *Symphony no. 5*

memory inspired by the tragedy of September 11. Many people think that *9/11: In Memoriam* is one of the most important symphonic works of this century. There are no glimpses of melody except for a brief, expressionist three-note motif alongside the minor third. The work evolves with an unremitting violence that is only checked in order to unleash itself once again in the final pages towards an unbridled finale. Conversely, the second movement, *Reflection*, displays a beautiful, recognizable, felt universe, using the beginning of a Negro spiritual as its basic sound, a piece that is connected to *Concerto for Cello and Orchestra no. 2*, and signals a desire to mark out the essence of what it is to be American. Finally the third movement, the third episode, the third journey into the depths of Balada's polyhedric soul, *Square Dance*, is a positive, surrealist, at times surface vision musically based on a very American partying melody. Despite these a priori elements, the addition of electronic music brings a more complex, more profound patina, though, without that, it still sounds sparky and even amusing, in evident counterbalance to the first movement. The three movements, unified by the intervals and harmonies in minor third, were eventually entitled *Symphony no. 5, American*.[11]

Balada was extremely exercised by the problems generated by the electronic section on the day of the Pittsburgh premiere; he wasn't at all happy with the resulting sound. Given these doubts, he decided not to use the version with electronic music for the performance recorded on the Naxos label, and retained only the live, natural version. Though both scores survive, that final outcome has meant that the analogical version of the symphony has prevailed. Even so, this work comprises a range of highly interesting, multiple readings, both in the aesthetic contribution of electronic music and the separate performance of each of its movements as independent works. In this spirit, the first movement can have a dramatic impact on all kinds of audiences.

Look 12: Behind yourself

Pedro Salinas had already said it: "I look for you behind yourself,"[12] and it is this look that seeks out what is beyond the instrument, between dermis and epidermis, to the miracle that sends a shiver down the spine. Artistic maturity is tangible when the themes of artists are able to transcend the boundaries of their work, the frames of their pictures, the restraints of the printed page, and come to reside in that place that is behind ourselves, the one that best defines us.

---

11 Balada's agent assigned the titles of the movements and even the addition of "American" to the symphony.
12 Salinas, Pedro, *La voz a ti debida*, Editorial Castalia, Madrid 1989.

Two commissions, two works, two orchestras, a theme and a profound sentiment. A commission from the Barcelona and National Symphony Orchestras of Catalonia; a commission from cellist Michael Sanderling. *Symphony no. 6 "Symphony of Sorrows"* (2005); *Concerto for Three Cellos and Orchestra* (2006). A homage to those who fought for their ideas. To remember and understand.

When the wells of artistic creation reach the shifting terrain of emotion, the dangers of over-emphasis can undermine the final outcome. Balada set out to erect the edifice of his sixth symphony, when the seventieth anniversary of the start of the horrific Spanish Civil War was on the horizon. That fact didn't influence its genesis at all, since Balada had long been searching within himself for answers to questions that could only be asked recently and that can't find responses even in the here and now. The dedication to the Sixth Symphony is clear enough: "Dedicated to the Innocent Victims of the Spanish Civil War." Not to some, not to others, simply to the Innocent Victims, both capitalized, both belonging to a single side, the side of those who lost everything. Fights between brothers and sisters never yield victors, only losers. Political ideas become mere pretexts enabling the depraved to justify the unjustifiable and claim it is right to order the killing of enemies who yesterday were neighbors. Time has turned all those in the first category into losers, and everyone else, into victims.

Balada conceived this symphony with a single movement in the form of a struggle, fusion, development and shock outcome between two standard musical tunes from either side. Balada strips bare and dissects the two anthems to show that there was only music beneath their tunes. A deep meditation on the use of ideas—music being merely an idea that can transcend the limits of what is objective—like projectiles launched to creates rivers of hatred between people. The rebel anthem, *Cara al Sol*, opens the skirmish, an opulent, martial tune, that, without the sourness of the text, simply becomes a versatile exercise in sound, pirouetting in search of resolutions in time. It is set against the *Himno de Riego*, the old anthem to freedom, against broken dreams that appear and reappear, evoking times past. Balada believes that though he was attempting to be neutral,—hearts are moved before brains—and it is only then that one realizes where they are located and which way the arrow is pointing. An obsessive interval in a minor second, vacillating and common to both anthems, suggests the bitter portrait of a tragedy that still hurts in people's gazes. At a given moment, the interval and anthems develop in a funereal, paradigmatic "*dies irae*" that acts as a prelude to the tragedy seeking out each one of us behind our own selves.

Dedicated to cellists Michael Sanderling, Wolfgang Emmanuel Schmidt, Hansjakob Eschenburg and the Berlin Radio Symphony Orchestra, the *Concerto for Three Cellos* breathes a similar air, an air of struggle and tragedy in respect of the freedom of the individual. On this occasion the work uses as its main motif the famous German song "Die Moorsoldaten," written in 1933 by an anonymous political prisoner in a German concentration camp. The song was later taken to Spain by the German volunteers who fought the forces of Francoism as members of the International Brigades. It wasn't the first time that Balada had had recourse to this impressive element from the history of resistance. In his 2005 *Caprichos*, the third in the cycle, dedicated to the International Brigades, that melody resonates from the violin. Once again the musical loan involves the listener emotionally over and above the abstract purity of sound and helps fashion an extraordinary construct where the orchestra flows alongside the soloists, in dense resonances that become increasingly diaphanous from the abstract, textural beginning that characterized Leonardo Balada's penultimate focus on the orchestra. The artist possesses a tireless creative spirit, and his work embraces that category of the penultimate.

25.
Balada in the Classroom

Upon reaching Carnegie Mellon University, one always feels a blast of fresh air and sees the sculpture of a few individuals climbing uphill, an allegory of the ascending path taken by all members of that institution. Paths of concrete score a great swathe of green where some play, others stroll and a few think. Almost everybody seems to be in a rush. Few individuals share a laugh; most stare at the ground. If it rains or snows, the huge cloisters of two parallel buildings give shelter to those in flight. There are no arches or curves, only a straight line. In contrast the College of Fine Arts aspires to be ancient, though it has existed for barely a century. Its English-style structure, like some timeless shrine to knowledge, is quite a kitsch mix of the exuberant neoclassical with the typically American. First, the T-shaped structure of the central and perpendicular naves looms large; both are high and impressive, with external friezes and paintings that display a collection of great figures from the history of art. The perpendic-

Carnegie Mellon University now, with the College of Fine Arts in the background

ular nave, that acts as the main entrance, houses two concert halls, the older and more solemn, Kresge Recital Hall, and the more modern and diaphanous, adaptable, multiuse space known as the Alumni Recital Hall. As we climb the worn stairs that look to the north, guided by the location of the bathrooms, we reach a dark, dismal spot opposite a heavy, dark wooden door where lack of light makes it difficult to read: Leonardo

Balada. The office is a small, motley space less than eight yards square. The door cannot fully open because it would hit a Steinway upright piano (all the pianos there are Steinways). The office has its separate entrance to the classroom where Balada gives most of his classes and is furnished by two cupboards full of books and scores that reduce even further the space and wedge in a table littered with the letters and packages that arrive under his name. Not that they all reach him. They are often returned to sender because there is nobody there by the name of Leonardo Balada Ibáñez. Miraculously, there is room for a small shabby blue couch and a coatrack with several hangers. An air conditioner is embedded in the window, the box kind that is always working, whether it's summer or winter, because when the central heating is switched on, the temperature is Saharan and when it's summer, it is Amazonian.

The classroom can accommodate some twenty-five students seated on moveable chair desks and features a rather battered Steinway grand, a television, a stereo and two blackboards—one blank and one lined. When classes are combined, as happens in the so-called Composers' Forum[1] that occurs every Friday, Balada calls out the register with the patience of an old-fashioned schoolmaster. He reads out over the piano the multiethnic names of a dozen plus future composers who greet each other amicably. Balada likes to teach. Talking, listening and correcting music is an exercise that keeps him young and active. He follows the same ritual in individual classes: he listens to his student and assesses the motivation, inspiration and challenges that have filled a week devoted to composition; he places the score on the stand and starts to edit with a pencil that is at hand. He is especially interested in formal structures, how, when and where the climax comes, the preparatory or closing interlude, the compensating elements introduced at some moment in the work, and he often quotes himself as an example of the many errors made or possible solutions found. He under-lines the importance of reworking schema that have been preestablished formally or temporarily. This doesn't mean a previously written outline has to be produced, but that there must be some mental consideration of the directions a work in progress should take. He also favors work with tim-

---

1 Balada has created a series of activities at Carnegie Mellon University inspired by similar ones he had benefitted from elsewhere. One such is the Composers' Forum, a weekly event when students and teachers are given time to talk about and analyze their own music in brainstorming sessions where everyone is equal and everybody learns from everyone. His second great innovation was the Contemporary Ensemble, a heterogeneous group formed by students who devote themselves to performing specifically contemporary music.

Balada in class

bres and constantly frets about enabling performers and audience through the use of technical recourses that must necessarily be clear and simple. Working materials deserve a chapter apart: he frequently gives them the nod, knowing how important final outcomes are: the completed work and the composer's reaction at the premiere.

This is one of the fortes of the pedagogy espoused by Balada. A composer is a composer because he makes music, because the music is performed and finally because that music is heard and is subject to criticism. That is why the Composers' Forum is so successful and can count on the support of all students affiliated to the composition department.[2] Every work composed will be performed and later on each student, equipped with a recording and score, will defend his work in front of his or her colleagues. Balada or another member of the department will regularly bring along composer colleagues who in turn describe one of their works or even their career to the students. This experience, born from Balada's early years at university, is a seminar that has made Carnegie Mellon chair in composition one of the country's best.

---

2   The composition department at Carnegie Mellon University usually admits 25 students per year.

The composer is incisive and direct in the classroom; he likes to ask questions because nothing should be left to chance in musical creation. The justification of the slightest change in harmonies can give substance to the work being written. However, he also takes an interest in his students' personal situation. One cannot compose if one's mind is elsewhere; that is why he demands intensity and dedication, modesty and hard work, and, above all, lots of enthusiasm and high expectations. Experience has taught him that a few lines are sufficient to evaluate the abilities of a budding composer. On the other hand, he is cautious and supportive towards his own colleagues. He can't stand empty-headed notions, lack of professionality and coldness or absence of judgment in relationship to anything in life. He is a humanist composer, who believes in the emotional impulse and the all-powerful drive of an idea, who believes in tireless work and is of the opinion that there are no mathematical formulas that guarantee good work, which isn't at all the same as correctly written work.

No doubt there are multiple variants in measuring the quality of a teacher in any subject. Arousing interest, creating good professionals, being a model and guide, having followers and/or those who applaud the actions of the maestro are indicators of a successful instructor. When Leonardo Balada teaches, it is easy to see how the mysterious business of translating and communicating knowledge to others is something that fulfills him as an individual. Balada enjoys teaching classes and communicates a passion

Balada at a Course on Composition in Madrid in 1991. Photo: Ricky Dávila

for this activity. A long time ago he observed that watching where students go isn't as important as being aware that one has given one's all. It would be easy to select from the host of students he has taught in his thirty-eight years at Carnegie Mellon University, together and his years as a high school teacher in New York, the big names who are today's respected composers and enjoy an international reputation for their creativity. His students from these years can be counted in their hundreds, and one must now add the growing internationalism of his class: alongside his American students, there are those from Asia, China, South America and Europe, not to mention his power of attraction for budding Spanish composers keen on making the leap to the United States.

The Contemporary Music Festival in Málaga devoted a whole cycle to Leonardo Balada in January 2012, which included a piano concert where former students were asked to contribute a short piece. The response was so great it can serve as a gauge to measure Balada's human and professional qualities as a teacher. Composers from all over the world, from the United States to Japan, Argentina, Taiwan or Korea, as well as Spain, offered and also agreed to write original pieces in homage to their former teacher. And they weren't only old students from Carnegie Mellon, but also from his summer courses in Spain or previous teaching in New York.

And what is the music of Balada's students like? Are they worse or better than he? Here is one key to his pedagogy. Balada teaches and describes the systematic elements within musical composition, but, as far as the purely creative pulse goes, he simply advises with a smile or critical comment depending on the occasion, and always from the perspective that you cannot modify the interests, motivation or problems each composer hopes to resolve as regards to his or her score. That is the essence and the secret. Perhaps teaching activity rejuvenates Balada, perhaps he likes to look into the mirror and see in the reflections of his students a solution to a compositional problem he has experienced or is wrestling with at that very moment. Be that as it may, teaching has a special magic that keeps any practitioner active and energized, with all the heartaches and upsets that accompany the need to communicate a message that can be arid and frustrating, but that involves the excitement aroused by the knowledge that, in one way or another, something flows out of the actions of each of those who have learned alongside you.

26.
The Rebellion of Symbols[1]

Balada—*Faust-bal*—Arrabal. An illustrious trio of names that started work on an operatic project at the beginning of 2004 at the poetic time of 5 p.m. on the dot. Balada's natural attraction to musical theater, together with an idea that had been buzzing around his head for years, launched him into one of the most media-visible projects of his career—the creation of the universe of *Faust-bal*. It is a story with tastes and aromas that seemingly belong to centuries-old tomes, but that opened Balada's path to a well-defined operatic project, with a guaranteed premiere, with no hiccups along the way, generating a new sonorous space in his oeuvre. *Faust-bal* is a place where symbols mutate and aesthetic concepts fuse to produce a genuine musical drama with surrealist glitter from reflections that are only too real.

Arrabal and Balada had been fated to come together for some time. Their lives had followed parallel paths and gazes from afar: France, the United States; fascinations in common, personal styles, dramatic arts; their works circulated internationally for the greater glory of both and to the envy of so many. For Balada, after the brilliant, incisive finales to his operatic diptychs, *The Death of Columbus* (1996)—the continuation but not conclusion to *Christopher Columbus* (1986) and *The Town of Greed* (1997)— an incisive, acerbic coda to *Hangman! Hangman!*(1982)—the attractions of musical theater brought on an insatiable thirst to commit to another operatic challenge that would disrupt and send into crisis a well-honed personal style. After two stage projects that amounted to mere flashes in the pan—a sung *Guernica* and an opera focusing on the central character of Dolores Ibárruri, *La Pasionaria*—Balada and Arrabal met in New York

---

1   This chapter is based on an article with the same title published by *Intermezzo*, summer 2008, the Teatro Real Season 2008-2009, by de Dios Hernández, J.F., "La rebelión de los símbolos," 76-78.

with a view to reviving on stage that brilliant Dalí, who had so fascinated the musician and with whom he created that event and film in New York. Their rendezvous took place in that same hotel lobby where both Arrabal and Balada had met the eccentric painter thirty years before, and the idea for the opera they so wanted began to gel as a vague, cosmic, theatrical hour. Perelada was the place chosen to perform that dazzling crash of malleable trains, but, third setback, the idea never came to anything. Luis Antonio García Navarro sent them off to the Teatro Real in Madrid. While the project was still hot, the tragic course of destiny shut the door on that hapless *Dalí*. Balada's penultimate masterpiece, *Zapata* (1984), still slumbered in the hope of being staged. He began to shake the dust off and believe there was life, but there was a fourth setback. An original title and universe was needed to land Madrid's Teatro Real.

The year 2004. A meeting in the Teatro Real. Jesús López Cobos, Emilio Sagi and Leonardo are waiting for Fernando Arrabal. The writer arrives at another theatrical hour, approximately ten thirty-six, with a folder under his arm. On the front page, a title: *Faust-bal*. Much to the surprise of Balada, who had been nurturing the idea of a new *Guernica*, Arrabal proposes his rebellion of the symbols, his rereading of the myth of Faustus, the decline in the male reading of the world, an Arrabalesque original served up for Balada. As the story flowed from the dramatist's lips, the musician was already composing the music, *Faust-bal*, Arrabal, Balada.

It was to be a feverish process of creation for the composer, a common situation when intellectual passion is harnessed to such an attractive aesthetic. The amalgam of old setbacks connects inexorably. The hungry aesthete sharpens his teeth: *Faust-bal* will be the culmination to the Mediterranean surrealism Balada had been unraveling ever since their frustrated *Dalí* and which he had woven again into his masterly *Diary of Dreams* (1995). An intense period of work followed from March 2004 to April 2007, from first outlines with protracted dialogues and huge cast to final libretto with five main characters and one supporting role. The work is barely ninety minutes long. It will have one act, two parts—eight and five scenes, respectively—and will be commissioned by the Fundación Teatro Lírico for the Teatro Real.

What is *Faust-bal*? *Faust-bal* is an open, apocalyptic reflection on the pragmatic, violent realpolitik of present-day society, and is packed with last-minute realities though it never delves too deep. Arrabal's revision of the Faustian myth assumes the colors of an ancestral war and never loses

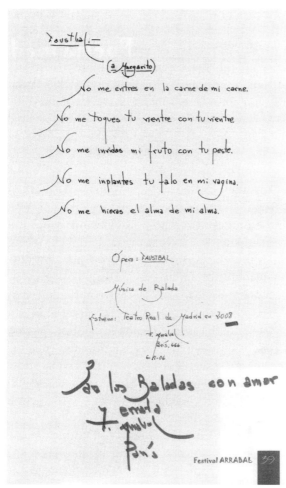

A poem by Fernando Arrabal dedicated to Joan and Leonardo Balada and published in Festival Arrabal

sight of *Pánico*.[2] The exhaustion of a failed patriarchal society, destroyed by war, carrion for a selfish conqueror, with verbal and physical violence as the only valid language or the corruption of natural virtues, drives the symbols to rebel. Faust will be Faust-bal, Marguerite will be Margarito, Mephistopheles and God will lay bets on the boundaries of good and evil and love will destroy not redeem. Woman in Arrabal and Balada is the symbol of perfection over and above the intransigency of human beings and their desire to undermine change. An excess of virtue and success, say Balada-Mephistoles-Arrabal, can only be satisfied by evil. Conversely Arrabal-God-Balada retort that lunatic, perfect talent can only lead to good.[3]

2 The *Movimiento Pánico* was founded in 1962 by Fernando Arrabal, Alejandro Jodorowsky and Roland Topor. The name comes from the god Pan and fits within the post-surrealist and neo-Dadaist tendencies that began to appear in Paris at the end of the Fifties. A mixture of humor, terror and randomness are the main features of a movement that brings theoretical content to the development of *Faust-bal*.

3 Arrabal's poem: "Don't enter into the flesh of my flesh. / Don't touch your belly with your belly / don't invade my fruit with your plague. / Don't implant your phallus in my vagina. / Don't

Real musical drama, a dense flow of theatricality that only achieves movement thanks to the live music, is nourished by the desire to communicate. The weight of Arrabal's icons is sharpened in Balada's musical imagination that seeks out a truth where the symbols are more than guests of honor and its structure, inevitable measure of the intensity, unfurls all the potential tragic beauty of decline. Balada sets out from a series of unavoidable compositional premises: clarity of exposition, the encapsulation and balancing of emotional and musical tensions, the use of the entire arsenal of technical recourses offered by the history of music and, above all, skill in creating profound spaces of musical sound in which the sonorous is located above the purely textual. The edifice of *Faust-bal* is thus built via a modern orchestra with contemporary textures and techniques and the emotive, evocative power of the sound transcends vacuous number-punching and worn-out restrictive "isms." Well-defined melodies that can be sung spring from this foundation and are always supported by an instrument within the orchestral weft, since the need to understand the soloist is always a priority. This is undoubtedly one of Balada's battle fronts in terms of musical theater: the total intelligibility of everything that happens.[4] In relation to *Christopher Columbus*, writing for the voice in musical theater is complex because the plot plays a role that cannot be ignored. This is a problem endemic to contemporary opera, where the difficult equation of the avoidance of nineteenth-century elements can often lead to the elimination of the plot line and that transforms the opera into a meditative cantata where action isn't organic but an extra. Tone and timbre are fashioned by the writer who composes directly for the orchestra, who defines and nurtures every sound and breath. The work also involves a very precise formal, structural treatment, suited to innovations that come with a particular surrealism of sound that *Faust-bal* exploits and takes to the highest level.

The opera's leading protagonist is, without a doubt, the orchestra. It is exuberant in Balada's hands: woodwind duos and brass trios, a significant role for the piano and four percussionists that, alongside strings and

wound my soul with your soul. Opera: *Faustbal*. Music by Balada. Premiere: Teatro Real in Madrid 2008. F. Arrabal, Bos, 666. 6.11.06 To the Baladas with love and errata. Arrabal. Paris." Published in *Festival Arrabal*.

4   This has been no peripheral problem for contemporary aesthetics. Great composers and musicologists have conscientiously analyzed the problem. In the words of a foremost Spanish writer of opera, Luis de Pablo, who, in the review *A tempo* (Bulletin of the Madrid Association of Composers No 0, October 2011), interviewed by Juan José Talavera, bluntly states that in many contemporary operas: ". . . Nobody can understand the texts, and when they are understandable, it is because someone is reading them. Well, isn't that great! That's a terrific solution."

electronic elements, makes for an animated orchestral pit. The dramatic control wielded by the orchestra's interventions plays a role that is unusual in contemporary opera. Excess had led to a mistaken conception of musical theater, forcing the limits of what can happen on stage. On this occasion, the orchestra constitutes a character in itself: always active, owning a complex, changing ethos, accompanying with its concentrated gaze, the soloist, as it is the only source of truth. It is summoned to give color to the identities of the characters and a touch of fury that, in the manner of Michelangelo, will spur the work into life.

Faust-bal, symbol of perfection and hope for an apocalyptic humanity, is evoked texturally thanks to the strings, and melodically suggests the *Cant dels Ocells* that can always be intuited, but only becomes clear at the end of the drama. Her singing is extended, lyrical, moving, a feminine character with the poise of a great stage heroine and the role of a lyric soprano. For his part, Margarito, with a brilliant tenor's air, is drawn beneath the orchestral sound and savage violence of the bombs. Threatening brass drills the subconscious: disturbing, aggressive singing with big intervallic leaps, precise chiaroscuros that, like siren songs, are never cheerful, are always poisonous and turbid. Mephistopheles rises on minor 7th chords and flies with the color of a lyrical baritone. Balada severs this chord from the

Ana Ibarra, protagonist of *Faust-bal*

old tonal system making it contemporary and effective in the creation of movement. God always appears with choirs of children who scatter harmonious chords that come together in typically Baladan clusters, a feature of all his compositions. These heavenly choirs contrast with a deeply bass God who resonates cavernously. Amazona, Faust-bal's lover, introduces a beautiful, atonal lyricism. She isn't hostile, but her mezzosoprano voice brings balance to the duets with her beloved. Each character captures part of the choir—that is far removed from the Greek concept of the chorus; a function served by the orchestra—that concentrates the motifs coloring each character. In this way the Choir of Angels, Choir of Amazons or Choir of Warriors are vehicles for each leitmotif. Balada tries to go beyond the Wagnerian concept of leitmotif, using the recourse to bring psychological rather than simply personal consequences. Some secondary characters who appear on stage aren't central, though they are important for the plot, like

Escena I-1

(Dios, Mefistófeles, Angeles,Coro Femenino. Coro Masculino)

-1-

First page of *Faust-bal* published by Beteca Music

the Judge (bass baritone), the cloned girl (Faust-bal's daughter, a nonsinging role) or the curious, fleeting Choir of Spectators.

The work marks a new aesthetic turn in Balada's output. These turns, that went from the neobaroque of the '50s via the extreme avant-garde of the '60s to a highly individual, subjective, ethnic internationalism that today puts the seal on Leonardo Balada's unique style have always been additional consequences arising from an extremely individual reading of aesthetic positions. Balada never disowns, rather he assimilates all he can use from each period, as otherwise he would be in permanent self-denial. The aesthetic magic of *Faust-bal* is that it draws on all that went before and elaborates a new, much more personal style, if that is possible: a *Mediterranean Surrealism* that brings a Dalinian aesthetic to his score. Only in *El Cant dels Ocells*, evoked by Faust-bal's singing, is there a close link to his use of folklore, a stylistic feature that is still very much part of Balada's orchestral writing. Fruit of a transition that incorporates rather than discards, Balada reaches new artistic heights in a distinctive surrealism of sound that arises from a combination of what has gone before and what is driven by impulses from Arrabal's text.

Balada's surrealism in *Faust-bal* is based on the idea that materials are in a state of permanent transformation until they turn into something completely different thanks to a long labor of transitions. Light and lean in terms of its length, Arrabal's text allows Balada to develop this concept with surgical precision. Each scene merges seamlessly with the next, in a continuous cinematic fade that supports the process of transition. It can be observed how elements of a subsequent scene begin to surface in a previous one in a continuous emotional tug-of-war that allows the music to intersperse and deepen the psychological dimension of the leitmotif. It is here that the orchestra performs its role as protagonist, like a furious, unleashed subterranean river, where human wretchedness and goodness coexist as in real life. Paradoxically, *Faust-bal*, an opera of symbols, ethics and abstract interpretations, never loses its balance as if on a circus tightrope, thanks to a natural, and all too human structure, a counterweight that allows it to breathe with us.

Madrid's Teatro Real dressed up in style on February 13, 2009 for the world premiere: the splendor of an event transcended the purely musical. After the dress rehearsal with the public, a reception filled one of the rooms adjacent to the theater with people from the world of music, stage and media. The presence of cast and creators held everyone's attention.

Balada talked nonstop and was congratulated by everyone who had seen the performance, while Arrabal ruminated by himself in one corner with a group of admirers from France who conversed among themselves about the import of the work, though never with its author. The situation was the exact opposite of what happened on the day of the public premiere and, above all, in press commentaries. Media noise generated by an opera is always scant; it's not like a pop concert, the premiere of a film or the launch of a new car. The presence of Arrabal on the program, and to a lesser degree, of Els Comediants headed by Jaume Font, focused press and television interest. It was strange to read articles that didn't even mention the name of the score's composer. Once again the interstices of the Spanish music world broke down when evaluating a work as complex as an opera. Reviews greeted the score favorably, and obviously they were the ones that named the composer of the opera's music, and audience reaction was unusually enthusiastic, which was also surprising given the nature of audiences at the Teatro Real. Some media, mainly television, interviewed those peculiar people who come to a contemporary opera and then sweep angrily out of the theater after a quarter of an hour complaining it wasn't an opera *comme il faut* with tasty canapés in the interval, glasses of cava at the beginning, and ladies smelling of naphthalene and wearing big necklaces and accompanied by husbands who are financial advisers to banks.

Faust-bal was launched with a double cast for nine performances and was broadcast live on the radio, and widely reported on television and in the press. Everyone in the musical world expressed an opinion on the work, and that was unusual given the sad reality of the late-night nature of premieres in Spain and the malice aforethought that greets them.[5] *Faust-bal* was a success from every point of view.

Another kind of public recognition took place between rehearsals and performances. The Cardinal Cisneros Secondary School in Alcalá de Henares held a homage to Balada when its music room was secularly baptised with the composer's name. Balada's meeting with those youngsters, for whom music was pure entertainment, and a composer a man with a

---

5   A revealing anecdote: After the publication in *El País* of a letter from a conductor entitled "The problem with music" which criticized the absence of references to the composer of an opera, while column inches were devoted to librettist and set-designer, a large part of the world of contemporary music had gathered at a concert celebrating the eightieth birthday of Agustín González Acilu at Madrid's Royal Conservatoire of Music. Many of those present—composers, instrumentalists, musicologists and music lovers—complained bitterly about what had been a revealing example of the lack of musical culture in the Spanish media.

big curly wig and over a hundred years old, was much more fruitful than many of those shallow articles. The event culminated in a piano concert in the university's musical auditorium when Pablo Amorós performed music by the composer.

That February in 2009 was Leonardo Balada's penultimate leap on Olympus. It was a time when one of his operas benefited from the logic and atmosphere of an era when many new ideas were beginning to flow: it was a time for proper recognition. At that age he was still like a young man looking forward to every premiere, who dreams of music and can still be surprised, something that only those who see beyond the immediate can enjoy. Leonardo isn't someone enamored of great pomp and ceremony. In the previous year he received one of the most prestigious awards given in the United States, the Music Prize of the American Academy of Arts and Letters. Nobody noticed in his country of birth. It wasn't the first prize he had received. One of the strangest awards deserves a special mention—the one he received by the name of Master Prize 1980 granted by the Equestrian Circle of Barcelona in 1981, together with Luigi Dallapiccola in the music section. In any case the previous award was the first to recognize his career as a composer, a tireless life of creativity, a mind that invented a genuine world of musical sound. But Balada *is* unusual, an American from

Joan and Leonardo Balada at the event to award the American Society Prize in 2007

Barcelona with a transatlantic heart and an Iberian soul. One can't expect official recognition when those in charge don't know or don't want to know who Leonardo Balada is. However, it is sad to see how awards ceremonies are full of friends patting themselves on the back. He is an uncomfortable figure, not because he is fond of polemics, but because he works hard and committed the sin of lèse-humanity in his country: he owes nobody any favors. He represents what many would like to have achieved and couldn't or didn't dare.

There is no better recognition than to endure indelibly in the memories of music lovers.

27.
The Orchestra in a Piano

Leonardo Balada's ceaseless activity over the last ten years has healed several wounds that had been open for years. The career of a composer brought up on the piano had left glaring omissions in his catalogue as regards this instrument. Although computers have extended the range of instruments for initial composition, the versatile piano has traditionally been the one most used by composers. That explains the abundance of writing for piano rather than any other instrument during most of the eighteenth, nineteenth and, of course, twentieth centuries. And that is why the dearth of material for the instrument is striking when taking a first glance at Balada's catalogue. Today there are seven works in Balada's select catalogue for the piano, almost all composed in bursts within short periods of time, bound by forays that attempt to put the entire sound of an orchestra inside the piano that also functioned as an escape valve for a style that was often channeled within straitjacketed lines. When it comes to his most recent creations a proper space should be dedicated to the piano. Thanks to these works, one can follow the evolution of a composer who moves naturally in the language for the piano with a great sparseness of line and texture bringing new color and depth as few have done in the recent history of composition. Balada's writing for the piano infuses the keys with elements that are more akin to the orchestra, with fluid movements of great beauty imbricated by clusters of sensuous sound, thus achieving a crucible of communication that never loses sight of the specificities of a markedly contemporary language. If Balada's work over the last thirty years has been flecked with pretextual content, establishing an aesthetic of subjective ethnicity, the same cannot be said of his writing for the piano. The latter is characterized right from the beginning by work that is more atonal and dissonant allowing glimpses

Balada comnposing on the piano in
Carnegie Mellon, in the 1970s

of references sometimes to Chopin, at others to minimalism, and always Baladan. This tendency is confirmed by works he has composed since 2000.

Balada's catalogue for piano hinges on three distinct phases in his output. Close to the dissonant, decidedly atonal neoclassicism that enjoyed such preeminence in the United States at the end of the '50s, the first led to Balada's initial success in New York and was his point of reference when he returned to Europe. At the end of the '70s, the second was more avantgarde, complex and personal, a denser, more powerful set of compositions within the cycle of masterpieces, *Transparency of the First Ballade by Chopin, Preludis obstinants* and *Persistencies*. There is a line of discourse in all these that is distinguished by harmonic tensions and a sense of tempo linked to a structural use of melodic and thematic elements. The formal planning of these works displays Balada's knowledge and control of purely musical tensions: he is traveling on paths leading to the recovery of the melodic element as the engine for structure and emotional content. Balada's aesthetic is already fully personal in that phase of composition, an almost impossible combination in his generous use of timbres from post-Darmstadt music (closer to Randomness than American Minimalism), that never loses sight of precise lines of basic intelligibility.

But it is the present third phase, the one generated in the twenty-first century, that reveals a composer fully focused on his mature style and attention to the sounds he desires to create. From pure expressive necessity, Balada seeks external props to give his work a well-defined communicability. If the path of subjective ethnicity is put aside, something far removed from the piano's musical identity and tradition, Balada's writing for the instrument today is extremely demanding, at a musical rather than technical level, at an expressive rather than épatant level. It includes, with its emotional density, one of the great undiscovered treasures in the Catalan composer's catalogue: *Contrastes, Alairving Variation* and *Mini-miniatures.* The first two were commissioned by the City of Jaén International Piano Competition and Carnegie Mellon University together with the third, dedicated to pianist Pablo Amorós, comprise this third approach to the piano. The dichotomy of an artist completely at one with European music of his time yet complemented by an American Balada integrated in the aesthetic currents of his adoptive country. The composer thus functions as a hinge, a vital connection between two universes of sound that seem so remote from each other. The Europeanizing music where Balada explores the tension and relaxation between atonal and extreme clefs finds its counterpoint in *Alairving Variation,* where recourse to swing and the harmonies of swing acts as a pretext to develop a complex web of counterpoint rich in shades and agogic accents.

The cycle makes such technical demands that it requires the most complex, challenging virtuoso playing. It is no project for any ordinary pianist; the scores require distilled technique and a high level of formal control. Alicia de Larrocha, Jonathan Sack, Rosa Torres Pardo and Anthony di Bonaventura, among others, have performed these works, but always separately or incompletely.

Balada's first work to reclaim the solo piano in the twenty-first century is *Contrastes* (2004). The work was the result of a commission by the 57th City of Jaén International Piano Competition in 2005. This piano composition stems from two conflicting ideas. Introduced by the opening bar, the first is lyrical in character, while the second appears with the second bar. It is in an opposed vein and develops into a virtuoso, rather dramatic piece of writing. The two ideas constantly alternate and chords appear throughout the work marked "*sostenuto*" for the pedal, with resonances that go from tone clusters to traditional chords, thus shaping the harmony of the composition in general. It is a complex work with a rhapsodic structure that is technically very demanding with a complicated formal weft. Sequences of intense atonal lyricism alternate with rapid sections that prioritize the control of resonances.

As was observed with *Persistencies,* it wasn't the first time that Balada had written a piece for a piano competition, and that experience led him to conceive a complex, much denser work than his previous efforts. *Contrastes* requires the listener to listen carefully, but above all requires the pianist to assimilate the work and squeeze every last drop of expressive content from the performance.

Alairving Variation (2006), in its genesis and later life, is quite different. It is a short piece linked to Carnegie Mellon University and fiftieth birthday of Alan Fletcher, then head of the College of Fine Arts music department, and a musicologist and composer. That act of homage brought together several composer friends of Alan Fletcher, and each agreed to contribute to his birthday present via the composition or performance of a series of works realized *ad hoc* and without great technical or aesthetic demands. The final product is a delicious musical box, a real find for those seeking rare treasures and for all the unredeemed opponents of live music. The work barely lasts three minutes, evolving from a slow tempo, which is hard to resolve technically, as the thirty-second notes, the unit structuring the work, act as the vehicle for the first notes of the central melody. Polyphonic textures intensify thanks to a concentration of lines, where Balada returns, in its brief development, to his present-day, idiosyncratic concept of musical surrealism based on the abstract plasticity of complex themes. The structural material is a song from swing that is given a harmonic rather than melodic treatment to initiate a swift variation. In that process the song moves completely away from the initial motif in a few bars. Finally, in an eloquent final coda, Balada returns to his jazz source and brings a smile to the faces of his audience.

For the moment, Leonardo Balada's catalogue for the piano ends with *Mini-miniatures*, a work composed in April 2010 and dedicated to pianist Pablo Amorós. It is a sequence of eight brief pieces that last from the thirty seconds of the first to the two minutes of the fifth. The lyrical alternates with virtuoso and are undeveloped. There are small snatches that generate personal universes that overlap when tempi are slow or quick. Balada's conception of these brief pieces presents performers with a new challenge, since he retains a space for the pianist to participate in that expressive journey according to the best tradition of the randomness of the avant-garde of the '50s. The pure abstraction implied by the title, and an absence of external factors that in some way condition the work, allow this particular aleatory or rather purely pianistic vision to open out, and the performer is compelled to fashion the frame into a seamless composition defined by its communicative intent.

The rapid, jagged first piece creates fragments of textures with notes and chords that seem disconnected but then come together thanks to a macro-rhythmic vision, where speed generates evident intensity. Conversely, the second piece conveys an almost tonal lunar lyricism interrupted by increasingly dissonant chords that darken the repeated melody whose steady pace is energized by emerging dissonance. The third miniature comes back to the first and its structure in a series of great staccato leaps. It develops quickly and subtly and repetitions are conspicuously absent. The fourth returns to a slow tempo and a theme where chromatics and light syncopation drive complimentary strands. The composition involves a rich dynamic freighted with changes that force the performer to activate a lucid plan of attack. The fifth is the slowest in the sequence and possibly the most complex musically, since it is the freest and sparest. Its practical lack of movement and absence of definite lines create the space for a complex progression. With the sixth the nature of the breaks becomes an element driving the dynamic *forte* and the piano to an extreme. The seventh evolves along a clearer, more defined line of composition where frills appear in the form of trills that are deconstructed in the simple, static final piece, offering the pianist scope to show lots of expressivity.

Consequently, this is a work that delineates a more abstract Balada who ignores previous insights or inspirations, and navigates a course that belongs to the musical surrealism that had appeared in *Faust-bal*. Balada interprets that aesthetic stance personally, in function of the infinite transformations the work can undergo—in this case two are tangible: one that has infrequent intervals and another that is more melodic and extended—though that transformation could hardly be described as a variation or development.

For Balada, the piano surges in distinct waves, but its importance in his repertoire is clear enough. Recorded in December 2010 and edited in 2011, Naxos will publish the first complete recording of Balada's compositions for piano with Pablo Amorós, a musician who began collaborating with the composer in 2009 and who stands out as the main specialist in his work. It is worth noting that 2010 witnessed the first concert devoted wholly to Balada's compositions for piano with a reception and success the composer didn't anticipate when the idea was bruited. That orchestra within the piano is like the hidden face of the moon: nobody can see it, but everyone feels its presence.

28.
Caprichos and Other Venial Sins

The new millennium found Balada hard at work in a whirlwind of activity. His already impressive catalogue as a composer increased by thirty works from 2001, making the first years of this century among his most productive. Although as an artist he is associated with the writing of large-scale symphonies and operas, Balada has most recently begun to write again for smaller ensembles thus diversifying and expanding his catalogue. Fruit of a timeless journey that has led him to research the most varied subjects and themes, Balada's aesthetics today enjoys a richness hewn by thought and freedom. It is a coveted state of grace, the realm of artists who owe debts to nothing and nobody and can generate new artistic spaces supported by firmness of conviction, aesthetic history and genuine integrity. Such an assertion isn't based exclusively on audience reception of his work, which is no guarantee of anything at all, but—and this is the most complex reason—on respect and demand from the performers themselves who see their paths converge on Balada.

Although creative maturity is usually linked to a process of artistic refinement, it also is usually consonant with a much-reduced output. Balada's case is exceptional since his artistic vigor is matched by an unusual volume of compositions. It may be true that musicology (like any other historical science) tends to reduce the driving force behind composition to simplified, reductionist causes, but it would be a category error to conclude that Balada is currently experiencing a phase of a quest for identity. Music in the United States, habitually preoccupied by that complex quest, tends to treat artists like separate compartments. While society demands creative music that is more akin to entertainment, composers explore their terrain according to the format that lies in their own sights. In other words, writing an opera for the Met is not the same as writing for a heterogeneous instrumental ensemble, a specific soloist or a contemporary music festival. Languages tend to be cut according to the cloth from which a garment is being made. This idea surfaces frequently in the area of hats, an example the composer often uses to explain his artistic lines of work. Balada has reached a point when these considerations don't exist because they blur the final goal of an individual communication of sound. There is no hesitation about what to say, and no regrets or *pentimenti*, because some artists, at a given moment in their career, can ignore vogues and chitchat.

The creation of his subjective ethnic focus has evolved from complex gazes that turned on different prisms of human identities in their infinite variety. Specific recourse to certain melodies or timbres, usually linked to a country, cultural or ethnic group, serve as a pretext to lay bare essences that, without losing their initial inspiration, go beyond what one expects of them. In this way Balada can go beyond the currents channeled by nineteenth-century nationalists and penetrate features related to the subconscious, feeling, memory or the intention underlying all those pretexts without ever losing sight of the elemental source. The crux isn't the introduction and development of a central motif, but the musical consolidation of an increasingly philosophical, at times ideological, impulse. That is the way he communicates with audiences, without grandiose gestures. Such an approach might risk embracing contemporary neo-Expressionism or a limited politically committed art. However, Balada lucidly sidesteps those traps by creating such a personal universe that an objective historical perspective is needed, and an aesthetic point of view, to be able to judge him as he deserves.

Over recent years, Balada has been involved in a series of freely inspired projects he has composed for a variety of reasons for heterogeneous ensembles. Diverse circumstances has driven this increasing activity. It shouldn't be forgotten that Balada has grown exponentially as a fully independent composer, and distanced himself from schools, power bases or media concerns. This hugely enhances him as an artist and human being. Conversely, he should be seen as a consummate professional whose status leads to a range of commissions that will definitely come to fruition and guarantee visibility. The composer's international nature, that in another era might have been an obstacle in terms of receiving official commissions, homages or prizes, is nowadays simply a detail, an extra factor that guarantees success.

As this Gordian knot is unraveled, one comes to the reason for the composer's creative moment. Most of Balada's works over the last ten years are concertos for soloists and ensemble, whether that is an orchestra, a heterogeneous or chamber group, alongside a series of astonishing solo productions that usually spring from ideas inspired by one of these concertos. This new creative phase found its perfect vehicle in the cycle of *Caprichos*, which, as the very name indicates, don't respond to any preestablished formal criteria but are driven by a special concern with specific issues. He wrote thirteen *Caprichos* from 2003 to 2005, led by a range of motivations: from a homage to García Lorca for guitar and orchestra or string quartet to an investigation of the double bass's concerto potential in *Quasi Jazz*.[1] In the meantime, *Caprichos no. 2* and *no. 3* for violin and chamber orchestra were inspired by different parameters and "programs."[2] The third was based on tunes hummed by the International Brigades during the Spanish civil war, and the second, with a harp, on the most outstanding contributions of Spanish America to world music. 2009, a year when Spain commemorated Albéniz, was the motivation for two works, the fifth (2008) and the eighth (2010) in the series of *Caprichos*,[3] a revamp of the popular song *La Tarara* in the seventh (2009) and an impossible mix of Japanese and Canadian folklores in the ninth (2011). However, *Caprichos no. 6* is probably the densest and most complex, and the closest to the fresh look at Mediterranean Surrealism, favored by Balada ever since his *Diario de sueños* (1955), and the *Capricho*'s secondary title, *Human Psychic Reactions*, suggests a Freudian rather than an elemental theme for the music. Different visions, different solutions for diverse problems that challenge the composer, that evolve, are laid bare and explored with unusual freedom. The second decade of the twenty-first century has led to four works that seek out their themes in Spanish music. In 2013 Balada immersed himself in the popular Catalan tune *La pastoreta* working to give it a chamber-music texture, an element that continues to predominate in the cycle, without ever becoming overbearing. In this

---

1   We shouldn't forget that in the 1980s Balada almost made a subgenre from the *quasis* with *Quasi un Pasodoble* in 1981 and *Quasi Adelita* in 1982.

2   It would be tempting to raise the idea of program for some *Caprichos*, but the musicological nature of the term would only muddy the waters. Balada isn't attempting to tell anything and, even less, to describe anything—these compositions arise rather from pretexts and motifs that act as an external axis around which materials are previously ordered.

3   In this case the term "transparency" is also reclaimed. *Capricho no. 8, Abstracciones de Albéniz*, recovers this particular tool that, like a look through a mirror, allows us to glimpse various elements that inspire fleeting leitmotifs triggered by a given theme, in this case, works from *Suite Iberia*. Balada rescues this particular structure from *Three Transparencies of a Bach Prelude* (1976) and *Transparency of Chopin's First Ballade* (1977).

case, violin, cello and piano regales listeners to a free, complex work that transforms textures and melodies.

Adam Levin is the dedicatee and spur for Balada's return to the textures of the guitar. The *Caprichos* series focused on this instrument in successive years, 2014 and 2015, the unifying thread being two composers, Enrique Granados in the eleventh, *Abstracciones de Granada*, and in the twelfth, Manuel de Falla and *El amor brujo*. Both invoke great virtuoso material and are divided into five and four small sections, respectively, in which Balada elaborates themes or aspects of themes while maintaining the aesthetic keys to his most recent repertoire. They have attracted international premieres and enhanced Balada's long-standing international profile, even with an instrument as idiosyncratic as the guitar.

The last of the *Caprichos, no. 13*, also written in 2015, goes back to transparencies, another structure of sound that defines Balada's art. Ever since the early 1970s his concept of a transparency has essentially remained the same. It isn't a process of variation, but work in layers of sound where the previous melody is foreshortened or appears as a distant echo or pretext; classical techniques of composition aren't used, rather there is a process of permanent, surrealist metamophorsis towards another well-defined, but distant, space of sound. Fruit of a commission from the Quantum Ensemble, guitar, violin, clarinet and piano, *Capricho no. 13* has a secondary title, *Transparencies from Spain*. The division into three parts probably denotes the three places that have influenced the composer at a biographical or musical level. The first launches off from Andalusia, while the middle piece visits Catalonia and the third ends the journey in Castile.

Each *Capricho* represents a challenge, a twist, another turn of the screw that helps one quickly construct a Baladan aesthetic in the deepest sense of the term. After analyzing this collection that one cannot assume is concluded, a few clues can be found that connect the *Caprichos* aesthetically and linguistically. From an aesthetic point of view, one can divide the series according two clear pretextual concepts. On the one hand, there is the latent presence of Spanish music generating material, a feature that is an idiomatic constant in a large part of Balada's music. The *Caprichos* corresponding to uneven numbers: first (Homage to Federico García Lorca), third (Homage to the International Brigades), fifth (Homage to Isaac Albéniz) and seventh (Fantasies on "*La tarara*") finding inspiration for their aesthetic activity in Spanish music or derivatives thereof. From this point in time, the nature of the *Caprichos* has fused with the unique sequence of memories of sound

Balada has begun to compose over recent years. As a result of commissions or his own creative needs, the most recent items in the cycle are driven by Spain, its wealth of musical sound and the influence of past maestros on present-day composers. It isn't about signaling respect for composers from the past; Balada's historical perspective allows him to trace lines of contact between generations that were barely visible in his youth. It is a truism that each generation survives at the moment when it denies the dominance of its masters, not by dint of any qualitative criteria but from the mere idea of progress towards new work. The generation educated between the 1950s and 1960s had developed a complex relationship with the preceding one, simply because it was absent, and thus they were educated by their aesthetic grandparents, which meant that the act of rejection was even stronger. Out of a sense of coherence, Balada anticipates a day when it will be possible to establish lines of contact between all the generations in a twentieth century as brilliant as any in the best eras for Spanish music.

Conversely, the inspirations of the *Caprichos* from the perspective of actions and their consequences can be categorized, namely that a work becomes in turn a precedent of a later creation in a fruitful game of Russian dolls: a recourse found in contemporary art and the art of Leonardo Balada. The degree of penetration of a theme, whether it is artistic or worldly, casts out nets of creative impulses over shoals where several, not single, fish can be caught. Pretextual elements can prompt different gazes on the theme in question—subject matter from *Don Quijote* could be highlighted in contemporary Spanish music with works by Cristóbal Halffter, Tomás Marco or Zulema de la Cruz among others—but also based on purely musical criteria—as can be perceived in the work of Ramón Barce or Leonardo Balada. Indeed, pretextual and musical factors have prompted different complementary gazes from Balada. As well as the obvious references to Columbus or orchestral adaptations of his operas in the form of suites,[4] one can trace other subtler processes in works like the *Concerto for Cello and Orchestra no. 2 New Orleans* (2001) and its reference to Negro spirituals with *Spiritual* (2002), or his series on the Spanish civil war that inspired his *Sixth Symphony* and *Third Capricho* in 2005.

The sequence of the *Caprichos* gains a sense of unity through the iden-

---

4 It is noteworthy that the suites from his operas, particularly *Zapata* (1984) and his *Zapata: Images for Orchestra* (1987) and *Christopher Columbus* (1986) and *Columbus: Images for Orchestra* (1991), alongside extracts in the form of arias from the latter, are not presented as simple extrapolations, but as new approaches where the composer extracts features he judges to be the most symphonic.

tification of cycles like the one with the popular song *La tarara* as its source of inspiration. It is present in the first work in the cycle, in the seventh—a work built entirely around this tune—in the eighth, though on this occasion the reference is Albéniz's *Corpus Christi en Sevilla* in its abstract form and in the tenth and thirteenth. In an even subtler way, one also finds a sequential element between the sixth and seventh, the theme of which focuses on human reactions as indicated by the title of the sixth and its movements, thus distilling a clear artistic continuity that aligns this small cycle with a more surrealist current.

Finally, one significant factor in the cycle is undoubtedly purely linguistic. Conversely, what in principle stood as a series defined by the concerto (the first seven are)—although the relationship is never straightforwardly soloist-orchestra—but interactions with chamber orchestras or instrumental ensembles, and later ones, give way to compositions for soloists (no. 8 for guitar, no. 9 for violin and a return to the guitar in nos. 11 and 12). Musical issues with the guitar (nos. 1, 8, 13), violin (nos. 2, 3, 9) or clarinet (no. 6 with piano and no. 7 with instrumental ensemble), equally offer us fresh readings for this heterogeneous sequence of compositions.

The real-life context of these *Caprichos* is another element to take into account. The first of them that partially prompted the idiosyncratic title, was the result of a commission from the Austin Classical Guitar Society. The work was premiered in 2006 by Eliot Fisk and the Miró Quartet. The guitar has always been a perfect instrument for Balada's musical language, especially when the focus arises from elements related to things Hispanic. Balada's guitar compositions tend to demand a high level of virtuosity based on that conversation he had with Narciso Yepes about it being better for him not to be too familiar with the techniques of the instrument. Most *Caprichos* share something in common: though the majority are a kind of concerto, there is no simple question-answer routine, but rather a dialogue based on thematic density and developments that are always unpredictable. The use of clusters, previously mentioned, is also another feature of the language for the guitar, that equally operates with rhythmic elements as its basic component (in the first, the beat of the *peteneras* has the stamp of García Lorca's original).

It should also be noted that *Caprichos no. 1* was the set work in the "Miquel Lobet" International Guitar Competition in Barcelona held in November 2011. The finalists had to choose between Leonardo Balada's *Caprichos no. 1* and Leo Brower's *Quintet for Guitar and String Quartet*.

The violin is the main protagonist in the second and third in the series—in the second, as part of a string ensemble (quartet or orchestra) and in the third, a chamber orchestra.[5] Inspirations come from very different places and subjects. In the second, Latin America is clearly the source, and its three movements are drawn from the three most important rhythms in twentieth-century Latin American music: samba, tango and jarabe (the Mexican contribution to the trio).

For its part, the third is a consequence of the first in the cycle. The influence of García Lorca, together with the period studying the civil war that marked out an episode in Balada's compositions for the *Sixth Symphony* (2005) provides the grounding for the third in the series which draws on songs and popular tunes the International Brigades carried with them during the conflict. There are five movements: the odd numbers relate to Spanish songs and dances, while the second is inspired by a German melody and the fourth, a lament, by an Irish song. In *La plaza del pueblo*, the first movement, is an adaptation of the popular song *El café de Chinitas*, that is very well known because of the harmonies composed by Federico García Lorca, and which had not been included in *Capricho no. 1*. The movement begins with a rhythmic *ostinato* that generates a dramatic, electric atmosphere. Only the first semiphrase of the motif is developed which soon melds into a previous chordal motif. Use of preexisting material is always free and references are mostly light touches. In the second movement, *In memoriam*, Balada pays his first homage to the international nature of the brigades. To this end, he reconnects with a melody that originally sprang from resistance to the Nazis—*Die Moorsoldaten (The Soldiers from the Marshes)*, written and premiered in the Börgermoor concentration camp in Germany in August 1933. It is characterized by its harmonic progression, with a permanent beat of semiquavers in a continuous crescendo from a C 3rd to a C 6th (the numerical paradox of 36). In *Si me quieres escribir, (If you want to write to me)*, an uneven meter adapted to fit the famous tune, begins the movement and, unusually, is played by part of the orchestra. Unlike the previous movement, the descending element is foregrounded, adding an evident reference to the theory of Greek ethos or the effects of the Camerata de' Bardi.[6] With *Lament*, the homage creates an atmosphere of extreme nostalgia thanks to an Irish melody, *The Bantry Girl's Lament*.

---

5   The version for violin and piano of *Caprichos no. 3* was premiered at the Juan March Foundation in Madrid, May 29, 2007.

6   At the end of the sixteenth century, a group of intellectulals led by Count Bardi began to try to find musical theater as it had existed in ancient Greece, in which specific musical devices responded

This extremely popular tune has enjoyed a long life and many titles. Its history in the civil war was linked to the 15th International Brigade, the Lincoln Batallion, and the remains of a defeated Irish battalion it incorporated. The original song became *Jarama Valley* and Balada transmutes it into pure emotion. Finally a *Jota* concludes the work. This represents a fresh approach by Balada to the rhythm and melodic structure of the form, in a sinuous, virtuoso composition where the violin evolves in dialogue with the orchestra in a brilliant, diaphanous finale. The work was premiered and dedicated to the American violinist of Cuban origins, Andrés Cárdenes. The original version was premiered on November 15, 2005 by Cárdenes and the Pittsburgh Symphony Chamber Orchestra.

Balada didn't have to wait long to find a suitable pretext to shape the fourth *Capricho* in the cycle, written in 2006. The work was commissioned by the Pennsylvania Council for the Arts and premiered by Jeffrey Turner, a solo double bassist in the Pittsburgh Symphony Orchestra, and the Pittsburgh Symphony Chamber Orchestra conducted by Andrés Cárdenes on March 27, 2008 in New York's Carnegie Hall. The usual audiences in this concert hall fund the concert series that draw on the classical and romantic repertoire for chamber orchestras. Balada conceived for that milieu a work that was unusual from the outset, because the double bass isn't an instrument with an opulent sound, which increases the difficulty of counterpointing with an orchestral ensemble. If the strange nature of the group of musicians is added to an inspiration which isn't jazz, but a rhythm or rather a jazz tune, there are all the ingredients for a scandal. However, the work was very successful and soon recorded on the Naxos label. The four movements of *Caprichos no. 4* confront a double bass with a string orchestra with the jazzy additions of a clarinet and piano. The titles of the movements clearly show that Balada isn't developing the piece from parameters of jazz but from a concept of swing. The work starts off with a *Tan-ta, Tan-ta Ta*, seeking to imitate the most traditional jazz beat before moving on to the second movement with *Down, down, down*, and a slow, sad, meditative tempo closer to a pre-jazz spiritual. The third movement, *Funeral*, evolves a funeral march in suitable rhythmic keys that tend to flirt with the space and Doppler effect, approaching, arriving, then disappearing. The work ends on *Swing and Swing* in a a furious dance routine recreating that strange concept that is so difficult to define and which gave its name to a style of jazz.

---

to the theory of affects, namely, to provoke emotions in the listener. That signaled the birth of opera in 1596 with *Dafne* by Jacopo Peri and text by O. Rinuccini and in 1600 with *Euridice*.

In a dramatic change of focus, Balada returned to a Hispanic beat in the fifth *Capricho* in the series, that started off in 2008 in the run-up and culmination to the year commemorating the centenary of the death of Albéniz, the composer from Camprodón. The work was commissioned by the Spanish Music Festival of León and premiered in June 2009 by Aldo Mata and the Iberian Chamber Orchestra conducted by José Luis Temes. With Albéniz on his horizons, Balada turned to a process of composition he had developed at the end of the '70s, on that occasion launching the transparencies with Bach and Chopin. *Suite Iberia*, where he makes a lightning raid on *Suite Española op. 47*, was the motor for his fifth *Capricho* to create fresh transparencies, specifically from *Triana*, *Corpus Christi en Sevilla*, *Evocación*, *Sevilla* and *El Albaicín*. In each one, the cello plays with great freedom and virtuosity and, as in the fourth *Capricho*, hooks into Albéniz's rhythm and dense, emotional resonances. The order of the transparencies relates to a sense of theater at which Balada excels. Recognizing that the alternating tempi are essential to ensure a good reception for the piece, *Evocación* occupies the third movement in a slow, meditative mode. Balada doesn't just seek to pay homage to the maestro's work, but to use Albéniz as a vehicle that enables him to develop his own language.

As mentioned previously, *Capricho no. 6*, from 2009, is undoubtedly the freewheeling verse within this particular sequence. If the remaining eight drink from a specific musical well, the originating feature is now a study in sound of human psychical states. The tonal element also adds something new to the cycle, since piano and clarinet are charged with elaborating material that is clearly abstract in inspiration and beyond any recognizable musical referent. The keys to Balada's creation of these "four brief movements of human psychical reactions," as the composer's secondary title puts it, are to be found in reactions prompted by specific inner readings of his own during and after the premiere of *Faust-bal*. The level of the characters' psychological development in that opera produced particular problems of sound that Balada decided to tackle in a piece where he could feel freely inspired. In this regard the titles of the movements are highly significant: *1. Anger, 2. Tears, 3. Anguish, 4. Shivers*. The work is much shorter than previous ones—it is barely ten minutes long—and each human reaction possesses a corresponding melody or timbre. In the case of *Anger*, staccato introduces a jagged rhythm that is interrupted by the clarinet's *glissandi* and an interlude with a change to a longer *tempo*. For its part, *Tears* tries musically to reflect the tears streaming down, while *Anguish* evokes an obsessive

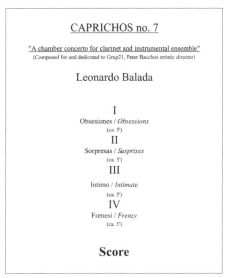

Caprichos no. 7

universe thanks to an insistent *ostinato*. Finally *Shivers* is the shortest of the movements and shares with the first a tense, suffocating atmosphere that seeks resolution in a brilliant finale thanks to a cluster of sound.

The outcomes of *Capricho no. 6* have clearly influenced the seventh, that continues the tonal line of the clarinet but on this occasion against a chamber orchestra, sustaining the movements inspired by the human psyche. *Capricho no. 7* returns to the impulse of an outside source. The well-established universality of the popular song *La tarara* enables Balada to conceive the *Capricho* he dubs *Fantasies*. Premiered in December 2009 in Barcelona, it was commissioned by CoNCA (The National Council for Culture and the Arts of the Generalitat of Catalunya) for Grup 21 conducted by Peter Bacchus. Unlike the other *Caprichos*, it was published by DINSIC Publicacions Musicals and not by Beteca Music. In Balada's words, *Capricho no. 7*: ". . . is like a surrealist canvas in which the material is transformed in a toing-and-froing from abstract to ethnic, from atonal to modal and vice versa . . ." The treatment in the score is more complex than in the previous pieces. Its four movements: I *Obsessions*; II *Surprises*; III *Intimate*; IV *Frenzy*, introduce a soloist who shapes a specific voice against two lines of tension that confront and complement each other from the previous material provided by *La tarara*. *Obsessions* reveals the percussion block (including the piano), against strings (violin and cello) and clarinet soloist in a complex, constantly evolving process of tensions subject to the moment and material. In *Surprises* Balada develops a different concept of harmonics. A sinuous, undulating motif evolves continuously in a tempo that gradually suffuses the rest of the ensemble. This radical contrast in dynamics exemplifies the desired surprise effect that the clarinet is charged to introduce. *Intimate* slips along a path of spare creativity that is typical of Balada's most recent compositions. The clarinet flows beautifully while the strings weave in and out with crystalline resonances that shear the pretextual song. Percussion makes a single entrance in a moment of bar 47. In *Frenzy*, the work recovers the feeling of anxiety and the clarinet's presence, spurred on by an injection from the popular tune, and generates an increasingly complex texture before disappearing in an evanescent whimper, like the frenzy in present-day society.

Caprichos no. 8, no. 9, no. 11 and *no. 12* tend to break with the harmonic continuities of the others and are com-

Capricho no. 8

posed for solo instruments. Written for American guitarist Adam Levin, they have been premiered in Spain, the United States and Peru. The return to Albéniz, Granados and de Falla as a source of inspiration and creation of a new concept beyond the transparencies and reaching *Abstraction* in the case of the first, highlight Balada's process of creative maturity in the present century. The divisions into four or five brief movements in this work are common in the *Caprichos* for guitar where Balada reflects profoundly on the innovative maestros of the twentieth century more in terms of aesthetic concepts rather than in any perceptible reference. If the cello and instrumental ensemble in the Fifth were charged with embodying that musical imprint from pieces in *Suite Iberia*, Balada now reclaims others in a more dissonant, complex fashion. They reiterate *Triana*, *Evocation*, *La tarara* (even though previously there was a quote from *Corpus Christi en Sevilla*) and

Sevilla and the addition of *Cadiz* in the fourth movement, like the previous one, an original part of *Suite Española op. 47*. The concept of the series as *Caprichos,* which are thus not tied to any formal, tonal or textual program of action, the new framework of abstractions stimulates Balada's irrevocable longing for the kind of avant-garde explorations he reserves for the guitar, an instrument he knows so well.

The genesis of *Capricho no. 9,* written for solo violin and made possible by the mediation of violinist and conductor Andrés Cárdenes, is very similar. This ninth *Capricho* is dedicated to Rebecca MacLeod, one of Balada's most brilliant students. The work was premiered on March 24, 2011 in the Kresge Recital Hall at Carnegie Mellon University. Following the thread of the previous *Capricho,* and immersed in a fresh operatic adventure, *Capricho no. 9* is a short work where the violin expands with almost diaphanous, atonal freedom. The "almost" responds to unrecognizable references to a French-Canadian melody and Japanese tune that are connected to the dedicatee.

Interspersed with the *Caprichos,* Balada composed other works that also tended to break his inertia in terms of big formats. Some concertos were commissions that always came with a premiere for the work in question. 2010 was a fruitful year for concertos, with the *Concerto for Viola,* an ambitious work commissioned by the Barcelona Municipal Band, which premiered the piece in May 2011 in the city's Auditorium with the British soloist Ashan Pillai playing the viola conducted by José R. Pascual Vilaplana. Balada arranged a version of the concerto for symphonic orchestra without strings. 2010 also saw the *Double Concerto for Oboe, Clarinet and Orchestra* commissioned by the Symphonic Orchestra of Querétaro, Mexico. The work was premiered in the orchestra's official concert hall on July 8, 2011 to great critical acclaim. The piece's secondary title is *Modern Fantasy on Two Folkloric Mexican Tunes.* The climax of this many-sided concerto features an array of guitars, but, all in all, it is great tonal challenge led by the woodwind instruments.

2010 also brought closure to a trilogy that began in 1972 with the Castilian *Voices no. 1.* In 2006 *Voices no. 2* renewed the vein with a piece for the composer's own mixed a capella choir. The Pamplona Choral Grouping had a change of name for the second in the series to the Pamplona Chamber Choir that premiered this work in June 2006, conducted by dedicatee David Guindano drawing on *Christopher Columbus.* One of the cuts reluctantly accepted by Balada, when he was warned of the possible sinking of the

opera at the Liceu, was the finale that developed themes from several popular South American Indian melodies. As a result of the request from Guindano and the Pamplona choir, this study was born, with complex rhythms
and melodies that explore a range of contemporary vocal techniques. Balada
avoids any hint of specific sources, as he does in the cycle's third piece, that
is resolved through onomatopoeias linked to these ancestral chants. It is a
work that is easier to listen to than to perform. The performers are always
stretched to the limit by the piece's technical demands.

The cycle finally closed in 2010 with *Voices no. 3* for the same choir,
though with quite a different complexion. Dedicated to musicologists Maria
Ángeles Ferrer Forés and Juan Francisco de Dios Hernández, it is a complex
work inspired by Mediterranean abstract surrealism informed by Palma de
Mallorca, where it was conceived. The only working text are the names of
both dedicatees. And the choir is called upon to display an array of technical
resources more from the field of contemporary writing for a single voice
than a purely choral effort. The work was premiered in February 2012 by
the Community of Madrid Choir conducted by Lorenzo Ramos.

Leonardo Balada's work in the present century has been unceasing and
original in every case. Far from reaching a peak and assuming a single way
of interpreting the creative act, Balada unleashes a torrent of unbridled
experimentation that leads him to thread his compositions together and
endow his latest music with striking new realities of sound.

As he moves into his eighties, Balada enjoys a degree of public recognition, if not recognition by audiences—a very different concept. Málaga
dedicated its 2012 Contemporary Music Festival to the figure and work of
the Barcelona composer anticipating other anniversaries and celebrations.
Many recordings are in the pipeline preparing to generate new universes
of sound and new pieces are already simmering in the artist's mind. A
tireless toiler, Balada rests when he creates. In recent years his catalogue
has increased exponentially, and that will fortunately make this biography
obsolete in next to no time. We are always interpreting the penultimate
work of a composer who hopes to be writing scores until he reaches his
hundredth birthday.

29.
Memories of Sound

The writing of a biography unleashes a continuous process of revisiting the past, checking and filtering all the elements that have marked the life of an individual. In Leonardo Balada's case, the genesis of this book coincided with a creative process[1] that initiated a sequence of memories in sound, an exercise of remembering that involved checking, revisiting and remaining faithful to individual memories. One should perhaps go back to *No-res* (1974) to identify this biographical tendency in Balada's output, an element that periodically returns as a motif or sound element. It is his *Sixth Symphony* that probably relaunches this process of autobiography and sound creation. Several generations experienced the Spanish Civil War as a wound that would not easily heal. Those who could or needed to express their feelings and experiences artistically have been compelled to revisit those sensations, places and emotions. The act of making memory is a natural part in the life of every human being who feels the need to analyze and understand him or herself in order to get on with the business of living. In the twenty-first century Balada decided, in a nonprogrammed way, to initiate the writing of memories in sound that would lead him to review his past. One finds in these memories real or induced memories, individual and collective outcomes, abstract assessments and real influences.

This kind of creative activity has two quite distinct profiles. In Leonardo Balada's case there is an unusual growth spurt in his artistic catalogue as a result both of new work and the reworking of previous compositions. A natural cycle probably exists that brings an noncritical gaze at the artist's early periods from the perspective of today. It is reasonable enough for

---

1   The process began in 2007 and concluded in 2010 with face-to-face interviews in the United States and Spain.

first works to be forgotten or undervalued as a result of a later aesthetic development. Works composed in the first phase of an artist's creativity[2] are usually conditioned by a learning framework that entails a complex bias prompted by a sense of influence and obligation that is contrary to pure creativity. This bias is quickly overcome after a composer has written his first professional works. Only the passage of time allows a serious, proper revision that generally doesn't imply rewriting. However, this is not the case with Balada who has recently revised several of the works that were shaped by his final student years at Juilliard. *Música tranquila* and *City*, composed in 1959, discussed in previous chapters, have expanded Balada's catalogue at the same time as they have benefited from a return to past memory. Something similar happened with *End and Beginning*, a work composed in New York in 1969 for a classical and rock music ensemble, which was published by General Music-Schirmer.

Conversely, there are the works that revisit the human, lived past, what would belong to the province of memories rather than revisions. A purely musical interest lies behind the choice of a preexisting text, one totally unconnected to this project, but there is another retrospective interest that marks out its choices in the terrain of lived feeling. The cycles dedicated to the civil war, in the form of symphonies and concertos and a group of *Caprichos*, clearly define a kind of induced memory that had been gestating over the years helped by reading and historical perspective. In this category we find *La Pasionaria: her Goodbye to the International Brigades*, a big-format work written in 2011 for choir, mezzosoprano and orchestra and inspired by the well-known farewell speech Dolores Ibárruri made on November 1, 1938 in Barcelona. The work was financed by the Catalan National Council for Culture and the Arts and finally concluded a saga that was first an opera project and finally coalesced in the semistaged cantata format that Balada has so often used. The figure of Dolores Ibárruri (1895-1989) *La Pasionaria*, had fired Balada's interest over the last few years. Her farewell speech to the International Brigades emerged in the course of his research for the stage project. The text's form and content attracted Balada because of their universal appeal, a feature ensuring the avoidance of a simplistic localism that might lead to a character circumscribed to Spain: it transposed her profile to an undeniably international context. *La Pasionaria* can be

---

2 In this case we aren't referring to pedagogic practice (exercises in harmonic progressions or formal essays such as attempts at sonatas or similar forms), but to creations already informed by a degree of musical baggage and creative maturity.

seen as a point of convergence of various lines of work that were driven by motifs from the civil war. The melody comes from songs the *brigadistas* sang during their participation in the struggle. This same work was the engine of *Caprichos no. 3* (2005) and tangentially the *Concerto for Three Cellos and Orchestra* (2006). *La Pasionaria* is a work that connects with the spirit of *María Sabina* (1969), *No-res* (1974), *Torquemada* (1980) and *Dionisio: in memoriam* (2001). Works for narrator or singer and mixed choir that interact in a kind of semistaged space, where the power of the words and their interaction with a large orchestra and percussion section, generate what is really an alternative genre to opera. The connections between the characters of María Sabina and La Pasionaria are obvious enough, although in this case the roles go from declamation in the first to sung sections in the second. This change reveals how closely the latter is linked to opera as a genre. The string introduction is redolent of the dramatic axis driving the piece. The vocal presence starts with an initial moving *Ay!* and the words *No pasarán* in *sprechgesang*. The text sung by the mezzosoprano remains faithful to the text of the historical speech and she uses mostly the notes of E and G to declaim her interventions. As in *María Sabina*, the choir participates in the manner of a Greek chorus, interacting without additional text, and is a vital element in the texture and tensions of the overall sound. Inevitably, the work gradually fades into silence as the choir hums with closed lips.

The complexity inherent in the structure of these works for narrator, choir and orchestra brings with it a growing number of issues for premieres and subsequent performances. Commissioned by the Càrmina Chorale of Barcelona, *La Pasionaria* received economic support from the National Council of Culture and the Arts in Catalonia, and has been awaiting its premiere ever since it was finished on December 29, 2011.

However, no doubt the most autobiographical work, and the start of a cycle must be *Memorias no. I*, written in 2012 with the secondary title: *Barcelona, 1938, Impressions from the Composer's Childhood during the Spanish Civil War*. Here there is the beginning of a biographical creative process in which Balada promises to explore his life from within palpable parameters of sound. Commission by Carnegie Mellon University to commemorate the first hundred years of the School of Music, it is a work for a large symphonic orchestra. Memories of the civil war and the final bombing raids on the city frame the creative process of a work that connects with the programmatic symphonic poems. In his introduction to the work, Balada outlines the features that suggested the work, contextualizing both the when and the whyfor. As happened with *La Pasionaria* (2011) and previous works, the melodic presence derives from melodies that come from the war itself, including tunes sung by the International Brigades. It dramatically highlights the gratuitous, terrifying aspect of the bombing of Barcelona and the impact that sound must have had on a child who was barely five years old. The orchestra comprises two woodwind, three French horns, two trumpets, a broad percussion and string section with violins *in divisi*. The work has a clear dramatic line fostered by the strings with special emphasis on bass tones at highly evocative moments. The work lasts less than ten minutes and was premiered as part of the activities to celebrate the centenary of Carnegie Mellon's School of Music in Pittsburgh's Carnegie Hall on September 16, 2012.

Both ways of reflecting on a creative past are synthesized in *Transparency on Chopin's Prelude no. 7*, composed in January 2015. A revision of *Transparency on Chopin's Ballade no. 1* (1977), this new transparency, nourished by the Baladan concept of the oneiric, filtered variations, is also written for solo piano, but is distinguished by its surrealist aesthetics. If the first of these transparencies emerged from creative protocols developing material, *Transparency on Prelude no. 7* seems more like a process of capturing the dynamic, rhythmic element within the respective Chopin prelude. A moderately slow tempo and dynamic piano develop into a vertical, chordal work like the original prelude.

Balada's repertoire for the human voice must be one of the largest in contemporary music. No doubt the text is the most complex phantom haunting compositions for voice. Balada has selected and created a variety of texts and many are completely unmarked by reflections on the musical sound. In every case, his work has survived, while the texts that have occasionally caused an uproar in the media, have usually been minor items in their author's oeuvre. Balada has never hesitated when he felt it necessary to develop his own texts, something he has done well and always with results much more suited to his own interests. *Cantata without Words* (2016) gives one solution Balada has explored in respect of the human voice, that is the nontext, namely, the vocalizing and gestures that go above and beyond the prosody that comes from words. In his cycle, *Voices*, Balada had already suggested a nontextual treatment for the choir, but it is probably *Cantata* that takes this line of approach to its fullest expression. The range of instruments involves a mixed choir and a symphonic orchestra, in the form of a dialogue between textures of sound that Balada likes a lot. The work was commissioned by the Community of Madrid Office for Tourism and Culture, and premiered by the Community of Madrid Chorus and Orchestra conducted by Maximiano Valdés.

Balada is still writing what must be one of the most structurally ambitious corpuses of sound in contemporary music. Reviewing one's life is one of the most complex exercises that any human can undertake. Every experience, every gesture, every disappointment, every success, every upset, all the hugs, glances, memories, smiles, mornings by the window, conversations, negotiations, a torrent of notes that became colors and challenges, projects and solutions. From Nardo Balada Ibáñez to Leonardo Balada, a life has been lived and continues to be lived in a realm of sound that has become the emotional inheritance of all who know him.

The constant allegory of Columbus, that character who had the ocean in his sights, who meditated, enslaved, and fought and dreamt of different worlds, journeys with all in the transatlantic gaze of Leonardo Balada.

Catalogue of Compositions

2016 Cantata Without Words (45') Choir and Symphonic Orchestra. Commissioned by the Office for Culture and Tourism of the Community of Madrid. Premiere: Orchestra and Choir of the Community of Madrid, Maximiano Valdés, conductor, Madrid, 2017. Publisher: Beteca Music, 1967, Madrid.

2015 Transparency of Chopin's Prelude no. 7 (1 min. 30') Piano. Short surrealist version of Chopin's work. Publisher: Beteca Music.

2015 Caprichos no. 13 - Transparencies from Spain (ca. 10 min.): **I Transparencies from Andalusia** (3'), **II Transparencies from Catalonia** (4'), **III Transparencies from Castile**(3') Guitar, violin, clarinet and piano. Commission and premiere the Quantum Ensemble, Tenerife, Canary Islands, February 2016. Publisher: Beteca Music.

2015 Caprichos no. 12 (Abstracciones de "El Amor Brujo" de Falla) (ca. 11') Guitar. Four short pieces based on de Falla's composition. Commission and premier Adam Levin, Miraflores, Lima, Perú, March 18, 2015. Publisher: Beteca Music.

2014 Caprichos no. 11 (Abstracciones de Granados) (ca. 11') Guitar. Five short pieces based on compositions by Enrique Granados. Commission and premiere Adam Levin, Instituto Cervantes in Chicago, September 20, 2014. Publisher: Beteca Music.

2013 Caprichos no. 10 (6') **for Violin, Cello and Piano**. Based on the popular Catalan melody "La pastoreta." Publisher: Beteca Music.

2013 Fantasía on a Concerto for Viola (ca. 5') Viola. Premiere: Ashan Pillai, Tres Cantos-Madrid 2013. Publisher: Beteca Music.

2012 The Resurrection of Columbus (50'). Opera in one act, sequel to **The Death of Columbus**. Premiere: Carnegie Mellon University. Published: Beteca Music.

2012 Memories no. 1 - Barcelona 1938 (7') (the composer's childhood impressions of the Spanish Civil War). Orchestra. Premiere: Carnegie Mellon Philarmonic Orchestra. Publisher: Beteca Music.

2011 La Pasionaria: Goodbye to the Internacional Brigades (2011) (30'). Mixed choir, mezzo-soprano and orchestra. Commissioned by "Concell Nacional de la Cultura i de les Arts," Barcelona. (Cantata that is a free interpretation of La Pasionaria's farewell speech to the International Brigades in Barcelona in 1938).

2011 Caprichos no. 9 (7'). Violin. Premiere: Rebecca MacLeod (violin), Carnegie Mellon University, Pittsburgh, March 2011. Publisher: Beteca Music.

2010 Voices no. 3 (Fantasia on the names of Maria Ángeles and Juan Francisco). A capella choir. Premiere: Madrid, Teatros del Canal, Madrid Community Choir, conducted by Lorenzo Ramos, February 2012. Recording label: Naxos.

2010 Mini-miniatures (ca. 8'). Piano. Colection of eight small pieces for the piano. Dedicated to Pablo Amorós. Premiere: Contemporary Musical Festival Málaga 2012, Pablo Amorós (piano). Publisher: Beteca Music. Recording label: Naxos.

2010 Double Concerto for Oboe, Clarinet and Orchestra. Modern Fantasia on two melodies from Mexican folklore. (17'). Commissioned by Symphony Orchestra of Querétaro, Mexico. Premiere: July 8, 2011, Querétaro, México. Publisher: Beteca Music.

2010 Viola Concerto. Viola and woodwind (17') (There is also a version for symphony orchestra without strings.) Commissioned by the Barcelona Municipal Banda. Premiere: May 8, 2011, Ashan Pillai (viola) Auditori de Música, Barcelona. Publisher: Beteca Music.

2010 Caprichos no. 8. Comissioned by Adam Levin. Premiere: Adam Levin. Publisher: Beteca Music.

2009 Caprichos no. 7 (20'). Chamber concerto for clarinet and instrumental ensemble (flute, percussion, piano, violin, cello). Comissioned by ConCA (the Generalitat of Catalonia's National Council for Culture and the Arts) for Grup 21, Peter Bacchus (artistic director). Premiere: December 2009, Barcelona. Publisher: DINSIC Publicacions Musicals.

2009 Caprichos no. 6 for Clarinet and Piano (10'). Four brief moments of human psychic reactions: I. Anger; II. Tears; III. Anguish; IV. Shivers. Publisher: Beteca Music.

2008 Caprichos no. 5 "Homage to Isaac Albéniz" (20'). Cello and string orchestra in four movements based on compositions for the piano by Albéniz: I-Transparencies of "Triana"; II- Transparencies of "Corpus en Sevilla"; III- Transparencies of "Evocación"; IV-Transparencias of "Sevilla" y "El Albaicín." Commissioned by the XXII Spanish Music Festival in León. Premiere: July 29, 2009, the Iberian Chamber Orchestra, Aldo Mata (cello), José Luis Temes (cond.) Publisher: Beteca Music.

2007 Faust-bal (80'). Opera in two acts. Libretto: Fernando Arrabal. Commission and premiere: Teatro Real in Madrid, Jesús López Cobos (cond.), February 2009. Publisher: Beteca Music.

2006 Alairving Variation (3'). Piano. Commissioned as a homage to Alan Fletcher. Premiere: Contemporary Music Festival Festival, Cordoba 2010, Pablo Amorós (piano) Publisher: Beteca Music. Recording label: Naxos.

2006 Voices no. 2 (8'). A cappella choir. Premiere: July 2006, Pamplona Chamber Choral, David Guindano (cond.). Publisher: Beteca Music.

2006 A Little Night Music in Harlem (12'). Commission and premiere: Hungarian Chamber Symphony Orchestra, Alberto Santana (cond). Recording label: Naxos. Publisher: Beteca Music.

2006 Concerto for Three Cellos and Orchestra, "German Concerto" (23'). Commission and premiere: Michael Sanderling (cello), Berlin Radio Symphony Orchestra. Publisher: Beteca Music.

2006 Caprichos no. 4 "Quasi Jazz" (22'). Solo double bass and chamber orchestra (Four modernist movements inspired by jazz). Commission: Pennsylvania Council on the Arts. Premiere: March 27, 2008 by Jeffrey Turner (double bass) and the Pittsburgh Symphony Chamber Orchestra, Andres Cárdenes (cond.) Publisher: Beteca Music.

2005 Symphony of Sorrows" (23'). Orchestra. Commission and premiere: Barcelona and the National Orchestra of Catalonia, February 2006, Salvador Mas Conde (cond.). Publisher: Beteca Music.

2005 Caprichos no. 3 (dedicated to the International Brigades) (23'). Violin and chamber orchestra. Premiere: Andrés Cárdenes and Pittsburgh Symphony Chamber Orchestra. Recording: Naxos. Edición: Beteca Music.

2004 Contrastes (6'). Piano. Commissioned by the 2005 City of Jaén International Piano Competition. Recording Label: Naxos. Publishers: Beteca Music.

2004 Caprichos no. 2 (14'). Violin and string orchestra or string quartet and harp. Publishers: Beteca Music.

2004 Adagio no. 2 (4'). Violin. Publishers: Beteca Music.

2003 Symphony no. 5 "American" (23'). Orchestra. Commission and premiere: Pittsburgh Symphony Orchestra. Hans Graf (cond.). Recording label: Naxos. Publisher: Beteca Music.

2003 Prague Sinfonietta (10'). Orchestra. Commission and premiere: Torroella International Festival, Czech Sinfonietta, Charles McMunroe (cond.). Recording label: Naxos. Publisher: Beteca Music.

2003 Ebony Fantasies (21'). Choir and orchestra. Premiere: Community of Madrid Orchestra and Choir, Lorenzo Ramos (cond.). Recording label: Naxos. Publishers: Beteca Music.

2003 Caprichos no. 1 (20'). Guitar and string orchestra or quartet. Commission: Austin Classical Guitar Society. Premiere: 2006, Eliot Fisk (guitar) y Miró Quartet. Publisher: Beteca Music.

2003 Adagio no. 1 (5'). Cello. Publisher: Beteca Music. There is also a version for violin, 2006.

2002 Spiritual (12'). Cello and piano. Premiere: Juan March Foundation, 2008.

2001 Irish Dreams (6'). Brass and percussion. Commission and premiere: The River City Brass Band, March 2002. Publisher: Beteca Music.

2001 Dionisio: in memoriam (30') Narrator, choir and orchestra. Text: Dionisio Ridruejo. Commission and premiere: Soria Autumn Festival. Publisher: Beteca Music.

2001 Concerto For Cello and Orchestra no. 2, "New Orleáns" (19') Premiere: Berlin Radio Symphony Orchestra, Michael Sanderling (cello), Rafael Frühbeck de Burgos (cond.), Berlin, 2002. Recording label: Naxos. Publisher: Beteca Music.

2000 Passacaglia (10'). Orchestra. Commission and premiere: International Conducting Competition - Orchestra of Cadaqués, Neville Marriner (cond.). Recording: Naxos. Publisher: Tritó S.L.

2000 Musica for Flute and Orchestra (21'). Recording label: Naxos. Publisher: Beteca Music.

1999 Concerto for Piano and Orchestra no. 3 (20'). Premiere: Rosa Torres Pardo (piano), Berlin Radio Symphony Orchestra, Rafael Frühbeck de Burgos (cond.), 2000. Recording label: Naxos. Publisher: Beteca Music.

1998 Folk Dreams (19'). Orchestral Suite in three movements: *Line and Thunder-Shadows-Echoes*. Premiere: National Symphony Orchestra of Ireland, Colman Pearce (dir.). Recording label: Naxos. Publisher: Beteca Music.

1998 Echoes (6'). Orchestra. Premiere: National Orchestra of Ireland, Colman Pearce (cond.). Recording label: Naxos. Later included in *Folk Dreams*.

1997 Concierto mágico (22'). Guitar and orchestra. Commission: Cincinnati Symphony Orchestra and the Hartford Symphony Orchestra. Premiere: Ángel Romero (guitar), Jesús López-Cobos (cond.). Recording: Naxos. Publisher: Beteca Music.

1997 The Town of Greed (35'). Tragi-comic "cartoon" opera for chamber orchestra, sequel to *Hangman, Hangman!* Libretto: L. Balada based on an idea of L. Balada and Akram Midani. Premiere: Teatro de la Zarzuela, Madrid, 2007. Recording: Naxos. Publisher: Beteca Music.

1996 Line and thunder (6'). Orchestra. Commission and premiere: Pittsburgh Symphony Orchestra, Mariss Jansons (con.). Recording: Naxos. Publisher: Beteca Music. Later included in *Folk Dreams*.

1996 The Death of Columbus (105'). Opera in two acts. Commission: National Endowment for the Arts, Washington, D.C. y Caja Madrid. Libretto: L. Balada. Premiere:

concert version Carnegie Mellon Opera, Robert Page (cond.). Publisher: Beteca Music.

1995 Shadows (7'). Orchestra. Commission and premiere: Cincinnati Symphony Orchestra, Jesús López-Cobos (cond.). Recording: Naxos. Publisher: Beteca Music. Later included in *Folk Dreams*.

1995 Diary of Dreams (22'). Violin, cello and piano. Commission: Centre for the Diffusion of Contemporary Music. Premiere: Trío Artis, International Meeting of Composers, Palma Mallorca. Publisher: Beteca Music.

1994 Dawn (11'). Flute and orchestra. Premiere: J. Baker, Carnegie Mellon Philharmonic, Washington, D.C. Publisher: Beteca Music.

1993 Union of Oceans (9'). Band. Premiere: Avilés. Recording: Albany Records. Publisher: Beteca Music.

1993 Musica for Oboe and Orchestra. Lament for the Cradle of the Earth (22'). Commission and premiere: Pittsburgh Symphony Orchestra, Cynthia de Almeida (oboe), Lorin Maazel (cond.). Recording: New World Records. Publisher: Beteca Music.

1992 Symphony no. 4 "Lausanne" (17'). Orchestra. Commission and premiere: The Lausanne Chamber Orchestra. Jesús López-Cobos (cond.). Recording: Albany Records-Troy; Naxos. Publisher: Beteca Music.

1992 Thunderous Scenes (26'). Solo voices, choir and orchestra. Text: L. Balada. Commission and premiere: International Festival, Alicante, National Choir and Orchestra of Spain. Josep Pons (cond.). Recording: New World Records. Publisher: Beteca Music.

1992 Celebració (13'). Ochestra. Commision: "Concert Mil·lenari." Premiere: Prague Symphony Orchestra, Jiri Belohlavek (cond.). Recording: Naxos. Publisher: Beteca Music.

1992 Song and Dance (10'). Band. Premiere: Carnegie Mellon Wind Ensemble. Recording: Albany Records. Publisher: Beteca Music.

1991 Divertimentos (15'). String Orchestra. Commission: The Center for the Diffusion of Contemporary Music del Centro. Premiere: Royal College of Music String Ensemble, London. Recording: Albany Records; Naxos. Publishing: Beteca Music.

1991 Columbus: Images For Orchestra (20'). Symphonic Suite from the opera *Christopher Columbus*. Premiere: Spanish Radio and Television Orchestra. Sergiu Comissiona (cond.). Recording: Albany Records. Publisher: Beteca Music.

1989 En la era (10'). Voice and piano. Text: Vicente Aleixandre. Premiere: Atsuko Kudo (soprano), Antón Cardó (piano), Miraflores de la Sierra (Madrid). Publisher: Beteca Music.

1987 Zapata: Images for Orchestra (19'). Symphonic Suite from the opera *Zapata*. Recording: Albany Records; Naxos. Publisher: Beteca Music.

1987 Reflejos (Music for string orchestra and nonsolo flute) (17'). Premiere: Atlanta Virtuosi (string quartet version). Version for String Orchestra, 1988. Premiered in León by the Iberian Chamber Orchestra, José Luis Temes, conductor. Recording: Albany Records and Naxos. Publisher: Beteca Music.

1987 Fantasías sonoras (14'). Orchestra. Commission:Benedum Center for the Performing Arts. Premiere: Pittsburgh Symphony Orchestra, Sixten Ehrling (cond.). Recording: Naxos. Publisher: Beteca Music.

1987 Alegrías (7'). String orchestra and nonsolo flute. Premiere: Brooklyn Philharmonic, Lukas Foss (cond.). Publisher: Beteca Music.

1986 Christopher Columbus (120'). Opera in two acts. Libretto: Antonio Gala. Commission: Spanish Government and the State Society for the Fifth Centenary. Premiere: Gran Teatre del Liceu, Barcelona, with Josep Carreras (Colombus) and Montserrat Caballé (Isabel the Catholic), 1989. Publisher: Beteca Music.

1984 Zapata (120'). Opera in two acts. Commission: The San Diego Opera. Libretto in English: Gabriela Roepke. Publisher: Beteca Music.

1982 Quasi Adelita (9'). Band. Commission and premiere: Washington and Jefferson College Wind Ensemble.

1982 Concerto for Violin and Orchestra (22'). Commission: Carnegie Mellon University. Premiere: Carnegie Music Hall, New York, F. Siegal (violin), Carnegie Mellon Philharmonic, Werner Torkanowsky (cond.). Recording: Naxos. Publisher: G. Schirmer.

1982 Hangman, Hangman! (50'). Chamber Opera in one act. Libretto: L. Balada in English, Spanish and Catalan. Premiere: Barcelona International Music Festival, Barcelona Chamber Opera, 1982, Josep Mª Espada (cond.). Recording: Naxos. Publisher: G. Schirmer.

1981 Quasi un pasodoble (11'). Orchestra. Commission: National Endowment for the Arts. Premiere: New York Philharmonic, Jesús López-Cobos (cond.). Recording: Albany Records; Naxos. Publisher: G. Schirmer.

1980 Torquemada (25'). Baritone, choir and instrumental ensemble. Text: L. Balada. Commission: Spanish National Radio Radio. Premiere: Pittsburgh. Recording: New World Records. Publisher: G. Schirmer.

1980 Sonata for ten winds (16'). Commision and premiere: the American Brass Quintet and the New York Wind Quintet, Carnegie Hall, New York. Recording: New World Records. Publisher: G. Schirmer.

1979 Sardana (15'). Orchestra. Commission: J. Cendrós. Premiere: Pittsburgh Symphony Orchestra. Michael Lankester (cond.). Recording: Naxos. Publisher: G. Schirmer.

1979 Preludis obstinants (9'). Piano. Commission and premiere: Alicia de Larrocha. Recording: Naxos. Publisher: G. Schirmer.

1979 Persistencies (9'). Piano. Commission for the compulsory test piece for the "Three Rivers Piano Competition," Pittsburgh. Recording: Naxos. Publisher: G. Schirmer.

1978 Four Catalan Melodies (9'). Guitar. Commission: Andrés Segovia. Publisher: Beteca Music.

1977 Three Anecdotes – Concertino for Castanets and Orchestra (10'). Commission and premiere: Lucero Tena, Philharmonia Orchestra of London, Andrew Davies (cond.) Publisher: G.Schirmer.

1977 Transparency of Chopin's First Ballade (10'). Piano. Commission: Dartmouth College. Premiere: Anthony di Bonaventura. Recording: New World Records; Naxos. Publisher: G. Schirmer.

1976 Three transparencies of a Bach Prelude (12'). Cello and piano. Commission: Dirección General de Bellas Artes, Madrid. Premiere: Pedro Corostola. Recording: LP Grenadilla Records. Publisher: G. Schirmer.

1976 Concerto for Four Guitars and Orchestra (19'). Commission and premiere: Tarrago Quartet Barcelona and National Symphony Orchestra of Catalonia, Antoni Ros-Marbà (cond.). Recording: Naxos. Publisher: G. Schirmer.

1975 Minis (15'). Guitar. Publisher: Beteca Music.

1975 Homage to Sarasate (7'). Orchestra. City of Barcelona Prize 1976. Premiere:

Pittsburgh Symphony Orchestra. Recording: Albany Records; Naxos. Publisher: G. Schirmer.

1975 Homage to Casals (9'). Orchestra. City of Barcelona Prize 1976. Premiere: Pittsburgh Symphony Orchestra. Donald Johannos (cond.). Recording: Albany Records; Naxos. Publisher: G. Schirmer.

1974 Ponce de León (24'). Narrator and orchestra. Premiere: Jose Ferrer (narrator), New Orleans Philharmonic, Werner Torkanowsky (cond.). Publisher: Belwin-Mills; represented by G. Schirmer.

1974 No-res (40'). Tragiphony for narrator, mixed choir and orchestra. Commission: Juan March Foundation, Madrid. Premiere: Palau de la Música, Barcelona and National Symphony Orchestra of Catalonia and the Spanish National Choir, Lawrence Foster (cond.), 1997. Recording: Naxos. Publisher: G. Schirmer.

1974 Concerto for Piano, Wind and Percussion (15'). Commission: Carnegie Mellon University. Premiere: Carnegie Hall, New York, Carnegie Mellon Wind Ensemble, Harry Franklyn (piano), Richard Strange (cond.). Recording: New World Records. Publisher: G. Schirmer.

1974 Apuntes (12'). Guitar Quartet. City of Saragossa International Competition Prize. Premiere: Tarragó Quartet. Recording: Quantum Records, Paris. Publisher: G. Schirmer.

1973 Tresis (7'). Flute, guitar and cello. Commission and premiere: "May Festival" New York. Publisher: G. Schirmer.

1973 Auroris (13'). Orchestra. Commission and premiere: Spanish National Orchestra, Rafael Frühbeck de Burgos (cond.). Publisher: Belwin-Mills, represented by G. Schirmer.

1972 Voces no. 1 (9'). A capella choir. Premiere: Choral Chamber Group of Pamplona. Publisher: G. Schirmer.

1972 Steel Symphony (19'). Premiere: Pittsburgh Symphony Orchestra, Donald Johannos (cond.). Recording: Pittsburgh Symphony Orchestra, Lorin Maazel (cond.). Recording: New World Records. Publisher: G. Schirmer.

1972 Persistencies, Symphony Concertante for Guitar and Orchestra (22'). Commission and premiere: Narciso Yepes, National Orchestra of Spain, Jesús López-Cobos (cond.), Tokyo, 1987. Publisher: G. Schirmer.

1972 Elementalis (7'). Organ. Commission: Dirección General Bellas Artes (Madrid). Premiere: Palau de la Música Catalana, Barcelona, Montserrat Torrent. Publisher: G. Schirmer.

1972 Cumbres. Short Symphony for Band. (13'). Premiere: Carnegie Hall, New York, Carnegie Mellon Band. Recording: CD Albany Records-Troy. Publisher: General Music-EMI.

1970 Mosaico (12'). Brass Quintet. Commission and premiere: Aspen Music Festival, Colorado, American Brass Quintet. Recording: Albany Records. Publisher: General Music-EMI.

1970 Las moradas (20'). Choir and instrumental ensemble. Commission: Dirección General de Bellas Artes (Madrid). Premiere: Ávila. Publisher: Unión Musical Española.

1970 Concerto for Bandoneon and Orchestra (18'). Commission: Alejandro Barletta. Publisher: General Music-EMI.

1969 Minis (6'). Bandoneon. Commission and premiere: Alejandro Barletta, New York. Publisher: General Music-EMI.

1969 María Sabina (90' full version - 35' reduced version). Tragiphony for narrators, mixed choir and orchestra. Text: Camilo José Cela. Premiere: Carnegie Hall, New York (1970), L. Balada (cond.). Recording: Naxos; New World Records. Publisher: G. Schirmer.

1969 Cuatris (9'). Wind trio (flute, clarinet, bassoon) and piano. Alternative version for string trio and piano. Premiere: New York. Recording: Albany Records. Publisher: General Music-EMI.

1969 End and Beginning (5'). Instrumental ensemble and Rock Band. Premiere: New York, 1969. Publisher: General Music-EMI.

1968 Sinfonía en Negro (Homage to Martin Luther King) (19'). Orchestra. Commission, premiere and recording: Spanish Radio and Television Orchestra, Enrique García Asensio (dir.). Recording: Albany Records-Troy. Publisher: General Music-EMI- represented by G. Schirmer.

1968 Geometries no. 3 (5'). Bandoneon. Commission and premiere: Alejandro Barletta, New York. Publisher: General Music-EMI.

1967 Tres epitafios de Quevedo (7'). Voice and piano. Premiere: Salvador Novoa, New York. Publisher: General Music-EMI.

1967 Tres cervantinas (9'). Voice and piano. Premiere: Salvador Novoa, New York. Recording: Columna Música. Publisher: General Music-EMI.

1967 Miniatures (9'). String quartet. Premiere: Spanish National Radio Quartet. Publisher: Beteca Music.

1967 Analogías (7'). Guitar. Commission and premiere: Narciso Yepes. Recording: N.Yepes, Deutsche Grammophon. Publisher: Beteca Music.

1966 Guernica (11'). Orchestra. Premiere: New Orleans Philharmonic, Werner Torkanowsky (cond.). Recording: New World Records; Naxos. Publisher: EMI-represented by G. Schirmer.

1966 Geometries no. 1 (9'). Instrumental ensemble. Premiere: Barcelona Festival, José María Franco Gil (cond). Recording: Albany Records. Publisher: General Music-EMI.

1965 Concerto for Guitar and Orchestra no. 1 (18'). Commission and premiere: Narciso Yepes, Philharmonic Orchestra of Madrid, Odón Alonso (cond.). Publisher: General Music-EMI; represented by G. Schirmer.

1964 Concerto For Piano and Orchestra no. 1 (21'). Publisher: General Music-EMI; represented by G. Schirmer.

1963 The Seven Last Words. Organ. Premiere: Montserrat Torrent. Publisher: General Music-EMI.

1962 Tres divagaciones (9'). Guitar. Publisher: G. Schirmer.

1962 Four Songs from the Province of Madrid or Four Spanish Songs (14'). Originally written for Victoria de los Ángeles. Song of Holy Week, Round of Love, Lullaby and Children's Song. Premiere: Teresa Berganza. Publisher: General Music-EMI.

1962 Concerto for Cello and Nine Players (15'). Commission: Gaspar Cassadó. Premiere: Nathaniel Rosen (cello) and Pittsburgh New Music Ensemble. Publisher: General Music-EMI.

1961 Suite no.1 (12'). Guitar. Commission and premiere: Narciso Yepes, New York. Publisher: Columbia Music Co.

1960 Sonata for Violin and Piano (15'). Premiere: Ariana Brone (violin) and Masha Cheransky (piano), New York. Recording: LP Serenus Records.Publisher: General Music-EMI.

1960 Lento with variation (6'). Guitar. Commission and premiere: John Williams, London. Publisher: Columbia Music Co.

1959 Música en cuatro tiempos (8'). Piano. Premiere: Jonathan Sack, New York. Recording: LP Serenus Records and Naxos. Publisher: General Music-EMI.

1959 Música tranquila (5') String Orchestra. Dedicated to Jean and Margarita Redd. Premiere: Santiago de Compostela,1960. Publisher: General Music-EMI- represented by G. Schirmer.

1958 City (12'). Ballet for instrumental ensemble. Three movements: I – On the Street; II – Idyll; III – Party. Estreno: Juilliard Music School, Juilliard Music Ensemble, 1958. Concert premiere: Ensemble Col Legno, Robert Ferrer, conductor, Valencia 2013. Recording: Naxos.

Music for Television

1960 Chaos and Creation (17' total, music 2'). Piano. Aleatory score prompted by a Dalí idea for a picture. Philip Halsman (con.) on a screenplay by Salvador Dalí. Balada appears performing his work.

Happenings

1967 Performance Dalí. Instrumental ensemble. Incidental music for a performance by Salvador Dalí. Aleatory work without a score. Premiere: Fisher Hall, New York, 1967.

Works Outside the Catalogue

1965 La casa (ca.10'). Ballet. Piano. Choreography by Roberto Iglesias. Premiere: New York. Manuscript score.

1965 Triángulo (ca.10'). Ballet. Piano. Choreography by Roberto Iglesias. Premiere: New York. Manuscript score.

1958 Tema i set variacions para piano y orquesta. Dedicated to Amparo Iturbi. Manuscript score.

Undated Estudio. Ballet. Orchestra. End of the Sixties.

Undated Jota. Ballet. Orchestra. Beginning of the Sixties. Sketch written for Roberto Iglesias, director and choreography, a Sol Hurok project, an adaptation of *Blood Wedding* by Federico García Lorca with English texts by Tennessee Williams.

Bibliography

AA. VV., *Sant Just Desvern, un paisatge i una història.* "Abat Oliba" Library, no. 57, Sant Just Desvern Town Hall / Publications of the Abbey of Montserrat, Barcelona, 1987, "Llibre del mil·lenari."

Archive Sant Just Desvern Town Hall (Barcelona)

AA.VV., *El siglo de Dalí,* Exhibition Catalogue. Caja Salamanca and Soria, Gala – Salvador Dalí Foundation, Madrid.

AA.VV., voice: "Balada, Leonardo," international edition of *Who's Who in Music.* Cambridge, Great Britain.

AA.VV., *Hangman, Hangman!* program and *The Town of Greed,* Teatro de la Zarzuela, Madrid, 2007.

AA.VV., *Estreno mundial de Zapata (Imágenes para orquesta), de Leonardo Balada,* interview in "Revista Ritmo" no 588, May 1988, year LIX, 18.

AA.VV., *Dalí & Film;* Gala – Salvador Dalí Foundation, Random Mondadori S.A., Barcelona, 2008 (Original Edition, Tate Gallery and Tate Publishing, London, 2007). Chapter: *Chaos and Creation 1960* by Helen Sainsbury.

Alsina, Miquel, *Cercle de Manuel de Falla de Barcelona: L'obra musical i el seu context.* Institut d'estudis ilerdencs, Lleida, 2007.

Balada, Leonardo, *Carnegie Mellon University,* catalogue and essay, 1982.

Cela, Camilo José, *María Sabina,* Visor Libros SL. 1967.

Cirlot, Juan Eduardo, *Evolución de Alfonso Mier. XXVII, 349* in "Papeles de Son Armadans."

Cirlot, Lourdes, *La pintura informal en Cataluña 1951-1970,* Anthropos Editorial, Barcelona, 1983.

Cureses, Marta, voice: *Balada, Leonardo,* vol. II, 74-79; in (Casares, Emilio, editor): *Diccionario de la Música Española e Hispanoamericana.* 10 vols. Madrid, SGAE, 2002.

Cureses, Marta, *El compositor Leonardo Balada. De Barcelona a Pittsburgh,* in *Cuadernos de música iberoamericana,* ISSN 1136-5536, Vol. 7, 1999, 235-248.

De Dios Hernández, Juan Francisco, *Homenaje a Leonardo Balada,* Aula de (Re)Estrenos, Juan March Foundation, Wednesday, May 28, 2008.

De Dios Hernández, Juan Francisco, *Faust-bal, la rebelión de los símbolos,* in *Intermezzo,* 2008-2009 season, Teatro Real, Madrid.

De Dios Hernández, Juan Francisco, *Ramón Barce, Hacia mañana, hacia hoy,* Author Foundation, Madrid, 2008.

De Dios Hernández, J. F., Martín Quiroga, Elena; (editors and prologue): *Las palabras de la Música. Escritos de Ramón Barce,* Instituto Complutense de Ciencias Musicales (ICCMU).

De Dios Hernández, J. F., *Balada en Alcalá.*

De Dios Hernández, J. F., *Leonardo Balada. La mirada oceánica.* Alpuerto, Madrid, 2012.

Ericson, Raymond, *Concert Brass Quintet, The New York Times,* March 20, 1980.

Fanés, Félix, *Chaos and Creation: un film inédito de Salvador Dalí.* Miguel de Cervantes Virtual Library.

Ferrer Forés, M. A.; de Dios Hernández, J. F., *Leonardo Balada y Camilo José Cela. Crónica de una ópera creada en Palma de Mallorca.* In *Estudis Musicals. XVI Trobada de Documentalistes Musicals.* ACA Foundation, pp. 25-44.

Fontserè, Carles, *Un exiliat de tercera.* Proa memoria, Barcelona, 1999.

Fontserè, Carles, *París, Mèxic, Nova York. Memòries 1945-1951.* Proa Ediciones, Barcelona.

Franco, Enrique, *Escritos musicales*, Marco, Tomás (ed.) Albéniz Foundation, Madrid, 2006. Chapter 137: L. Balada. Ponce de León, pp. 406-408.

Marco, Tomás. *Historia de la música española*. Madrid: Alianza Música, second edition 1988 (first edition 1983), vol. 6.

Marco, Tomás. *Historia General de la Música. Siglo XX*. Vol. 4. Madrid: Editorial Alpuerto, 1981, second edition (first edition 1978).

Miravitlles, Jaume. *Gent que he conegut*, Ediciones Destino, Barcelona, 1980.

Miravitlles, Jaume. *Més gent que he conegut*, Ediciones Destino, Barcelona, 1981.

McIntire, Dennisk, Voice: "Balada, Leonardo," in *Baker's Biographical Dictionary of Musicians*, Slonimsky, Nicholas (emeritus director), Laura Kuhn (ed.) New York: Schirmer Books, 2001, 6 vols.

Pascuet, Rafael; Pujol, Enric, *La revolució del bon gust. Jaume Miravitlles i el Comissariat de Propaganda de la Generalitat de Catalunya (1936 - 1939)*. Viena Edicions, Barcelona, 2007.

Rosenberg, Donald, *Torquemada comes home a winner*, in "The Pittsburgh Press," November 11, 1991.

Stone, P. E., *He writes for the Audience, But on His Own Terms*, in *The New York Times*, November 21, 1982.

Stone, P. E., *Leonardo Balada's First Half Century*, in "Symphony Magazine" no. XXXIV/3, 1983.

Wright, David, Voice: "Balada, Leonardo" in *The New Grove Dictionary of American Music*. (Stanley Sadie, ed.) London and New York, Macmillan Press. Ltd., 1986.

Veiga, Marisella, *Colón: el hombre y la ópera*, in *Aboard, 1989*.

Wright, David, Voice: "Balada, Leonardo," in *The New Grove Dictionary of Opera*.

Articles Written by Leonardo Balada

A selection of articles written by Leonardo Balada for magazines during his stay in New York that are quoted directly or indirectly in the book.

Amigos, July 1961, "Salvador Dalí; mitad magia, mitad arte." The article inside has another title, "Salvador Dalí: Magia y bioquímica."

Bohemia Libre: "John Cran, el millonario abstemio que vive entre borrachos."
- *Graciela Rivera, la cantante y la mujer.*

Hablemos: "Lupe Serrano, belleza alada." "Sobre una bailarina que actuaba en el Metropolitan Opera House."

Revista Temas: "Con Salvador Dalí en Nueva York," (April 1958).
- "Con José de Creeft en Nueva York." Balada title, "el primer escultor norteamericano en español (May 1958).
- "Con María Rosa en Nueva York," (June 1958).
- "Con Joaquín Rodrigo en Nueva York," (August 1958).
- "Con el maestro Federico Moreno Torroba en Nueva York," (July 1959).
- "Con Marta Romero en Nueva York," (December 1959).
- "Con J. J. Tharrats en Nueva York," (May1961).

Gran Vía (published in Barcelona):
Balada has a section called *Carta de Nueva York*.
- "La ópera Americana," (1961).
- "Doris Humphrey y la Danza Moderna," (1961).

Distinción (published monthly in Barcelona from the end of the 1950s and 1960.
- "Alicia Alonso primera bailarina de las Américas."
- "Balance artístico de Nueva York."

Europa:
- "La controvertida obra de Arthur Miller," 21.

Internet:
http://www.andrew.cmu.edu/user/balada/espanol.htm
http://www.filomusica.com/filo20/entrevis.html
http://www.naxos.com/composerinfo/Leonardo_Balada/24784.htm

Index of Names